3/13

# Children of the Greek Civil War

D1599387

# Children of the Greek Civil War

## Refugees and the Politics of Memory

LORING M. DANFORTH
RIKI VAN BOESCHOTEN

The University of Chicago Press
Chicago and London

Loring M. Danforth is the Charles A. Dana Professor of Anthropology at Bates College and the author of several books, including, most recently, *The Macedonian Conflict: Ethnic Nationalism in a Transnational World.* **Riki Van Boeschoten** is associate professor of social anthropology and oral history at the University of Thessaly, Greece, and the author of *From Armatolik to People's Rule: Investigation into the Collective Memory of Rural Greece (1750–1949).*

The University of Chicago Press, Chicago 60637
The University of Chicago Press, Ltd., London
© 2012 by The University of Chicago
All rights reserved. Published 2012.
Printed in the United States of America

21  20  19  18  17  16  15  14  13  12      1  2  3  4  5

ISBN-13: 978-0-226-13598-4 (cloth)
ISBN-10: 0-226-13598-5 (cloth)
ISBN-13: 978-0-226-13599-1 (paper)
ISBN-10: 0-226-13599-3 (paper)

Library of Congress Cataloging-in-Publication Data

Danforth, Loring M., 1949–
    Children of the Greek Civil War : refugees and the politics of memory /
Loring M. Danforth and Riki Van Boeschoten.
        p. cm.
    Includes bibliographical references and index.
    ISBN-13: 978-0-226-13598-4 (cloth : alk. paper)
    ISBN-10: 0-226-13598-5 (cloth : alk. paper)
    ISBN-13: 978-0-226-13599-1 (pbk. : alk. paper)
    ISBN-10: 0-226-13599-3 (pbk. : alk. paper)   1. Greece—History—Civil
War, 1944–1949—Refugees—Europe, Eastern.   2. Greece—History—Civil
War, 1944–1949—Children.   3. Greece—History—Civil War, 1944–1949—
Evacuation of civilians.   4. Greece—History—Civil War, 1944–1949—
Personal narratives.   5. Refugee children—Greece.   6. Refugee children—
Europe, Eastern.   7. Kommounistikon Komma tes Hellados.   I. Boeschoten,
Riki Van.   II. Title.
    DF849.52.D36 2012
    949.507′4—dc23

                                                                    2011020831

♾ This paper meets the requirements of ANSI/NISO Z39.48-1992
(Permanence of Paper).

*For all refugee children*

CONTENTS

# ILLUSTRATIONS

## FIGURES

## MAPS

# NOTE ON TRANSLITERATION

In transliterating Greek words and phrases in the text we have followed the system used by the *Journal of Modern Greek Studies*, which seeks to accomplish two somewhat contradictory goals at the same time: to provide a guide to Modern Greek pronunciation, on the one hand, and to approximate Modern Greek spelling, on the other. For bibliographical entries and some proper names, we have made occasional exceptions to enable readers to find more easily Greek titles and authors' names in other bibliographical sources.

In transliterating Macedonian words and phrases we have adopted standard scholarly practice in which the symbols used are pronounced as follows:

ǵ = gy as in *argue*  
ž = zh as in *pleasure*  
j = y as in *you*  
ḱ = ky as in *cute*  
c = ts as in *bits*  
č = ch as in *chart*  
š = sh as in *show*

ACKNOWLEDGMENTS

Many people have contributed in important ways to the successful completion of this book. We would like to thank Keith Brown, Aigli Brouskou, Victor Friedman, Michael Herzfeld, Anastasia Karakasidou, Effie Voutira, and the anonymous reviewers at the University of Chicago Press, who have all generously shared with us their knowledge and expertise in the anthropological study of refugees and childhood and in the fields of Modern Greek and Macedonian studies.

We would also like to thank Dimitra Stamoyiorgou and Olga Sevastidou for transcribing many of the interviews on which this book is based; Sylvia Hawks, academic administrative assistant at Bates College, for graciously and skillfully preparing the final manuscript; William Ash of the Bates Imaging and Computing Center for help with the photographs; and Erin Gelb and the late Charles Brest for drawing the maps. We are grateful to Risto Chachkirovski and Philip Malkovski in Toronto, Nikos Tolis and Nikos Fasoulis in Greece, and Stoyan Kiselinovski and Mara Kuzman Georgievska in Skopje, who have kindly allowed us to use photographs from their personal collections. Mary Pejoska, director of the Macedonian Museum in Skopje, has generously given us permission to use the museum's unique collection of photographs of the refugee children's journey to Eastern Europe. These pictures have enabled us to add a valuable visual dimension to our account of the experiences of the refugee children of the Greek Civil War.

Finally, we would like to express our thanks to David Brent and Laura Avey at the University of Chicago Press, as well as to Maia Rigas, our copyeditor, for all the careful work that is required to turn a manuscript into a book.

I would like to thank the many people at Bates College who make up the community of students, teachers, and scholars that I have been privileged to be a part of for the past thirty-two years. My faculty and staff colleagues have always been ready to offer the help and advice I sought. I am particularly grateful for the leadership and support of Jill Reich, dean of faculty, for recognizing the central role scholarship plays in the intellectual lives of faculty at a small liberal arts college. A grant from the National Endowment of the Humanities enabled me to devote an entire year to writing an early draft of portions of this book.

I would also like to express my deepest appreciation to my wife, Peggy Rotundo, and my children, Nicholas and Ann Danforth, for lifetimes of love, joy, and inspiration.

*Loring Danforth*

I will never forget the endless evenings spent around a campfire in the village of Perivolaki in northern Greece in the company of former refugee children who had just rebuilt their village, which had been totally destroyed during the Civil War. Their stories about their lives in Eastern Europe and their difficult return to Greece introduced me to the subject matter of this book and helped me understand how personal memories open windows on universal values.

I am very grateful to the Program in Hellenic Studies at Princeton University for granting me a Stanley J. Seeger Visiting Research Fellowship in Hellenic Studies, which enabled me to make use of important resources in the Firestone Library (including the Modern Greek Collection there) and to discuss my work in an extremely inspiring environment. In particular, I would like to thank the program's director, Dimitris Gondicas, for his intellectual guidance and his unconditional commitment to academic freedom and integrity. On a more personal note, I am deeply indebted to my colleagues at Princeton, Peter Mackridge, Alexandros Kazamias, Pantelis Kyprianos, and Anastasia Stouraiti, for their support during a particularly difficult period in my life. My colleagues in the Department of History, Archaeology, and Social Anthropology at the University of Thessaly have been a constant source of inspiration and helped me discover new perspectives in the interpretation of the empirical material of this book.

*Riki Van Boeschoten*

Finally, we would both like to express our profound gratitude to the many refugee children of the Greek Civil War in northern Greece, the Republic of Macedonia, Eastern Europe, Canada, and Australia, who shared with us some of their most personal childhood memories. Their stories were both tragic and inspiring. It is an honor to have been entrusted with them and to have the opportunity to share them with a wider audience. We hope that people who consult this book will be as moved when they read these stories as we were when we heard them. Many of the refugee children we spoke with explicitly stated that they wanted their stories to be told so that other people would learn from the past, so that in the future there would be fewer wars and fewer refugees, and so that children would never again have to grow up without the love of their parents.

# INTRODUCTION

*Princeton University*
*Program in Hellenic Studies*

*Workshop*

*Refugee Children from the Greek Civil War in Eastern Europe:*
*Displacement, Memory, and the National Order of Things*

**Riki Van Boeschoten**
*University of Thessaly*

*and*

**Loring M. Danforth**
*Bates College*

*One of the most controversial issues of the Greek Civil War was the evacuation of about 25,000 children by the partisans from Northern Greece to Eastern Europe. The Greek government characterized the operation as "genocide" and a "crime against humanity" and brought the matter before the United Nations, demanding immediate repatriation of these allegedly "abducted" children. Loring Danforth and Riki Van Boeschoten have been researching this issue since 1998, focusing in particular on the lived experiences of these refugee children. They have visited them in their new homes in Greece, Eastern Europe, or Canada and collected their life stories. These memories of displacement, life in Eastern Europe, and return deconstruct in multiple ways mainstream discourse on Cold War cleavages or the "national order of things." Van Boeschoten's paper will focus on experiences in exile, while Danforth's paper will focus on repatriation.*

*Tuesday, May 10, 2005*
*6:00 p.m.*
**Scheide Caldwell House, Room 103**

When this announcement was distributed electronically on the Modern Greek Studies Association listserv, it provoked a barrage of angry phone calls and email messages. The director of Princeton's Program in Hellenic Studies was accused of "anti-Hellenism" and "treason." He was warned that his program would be "blacklisted" unless he cancelled our presentations. Riki Van Boeschoten was referred to as a "liar and propagandist who calls Slavs 'Macedonians,'" and Loring Danforth was described as someone who "should be banned from Modern Greek Departments." One Greek Macedonian wrote, "We are sick and tired of foreign experts presenting our history to the world."

When the seminar began, over fifty people sat crowded closely together in two rows around a large mahogany table in the main seminar room of the Program in Hellenic Studies. Two reporters and a photographer from the *National Herald*, a Greek American newspaper published in New York, were there, as were officials of the Pan-Macedonian Association USA, Inc., a Greek Macedonian diaspora organization. A member of Princeton's campus security was also present.

Riki Van Boeschoten provided a general overview of our topic and discussed the lives of the refugee children as they grew up in Eastern Europe. Loring Danforth examined the children's experiences when they were repatriated from cities in Eastern Europe to the mountain villages of their birth. At the end of our presentation, a well-dressed man with a gray goatee said that he had lived through the very events we were discussing and wanted to correct some of our misrepresentations. He challenged our use of the words "evacuation" and "refugees." These terms were inaccurate, he said; the children had been kidnapped. When he began to make additional comments, the director of the Program in Hellenic Studies, who was serving as moderator, interrupted him, pointing out that there were other people who wanted to speak. At this point the man said it was clear to him that any dialogue would be impossible, stood up, and left the room. As we later learned, our critic had been none other than Nicholas Gage, the author of the New York Times best seller *Eleni*, a dramatic account of the execution of his mother by the communists during the Greek Civil War. She was killed, Gage wrote, because she had arranged her children's escape from her village so that they would not be kidnapped by the communists.

In what was now a very tense and hostile atmosphere, a Greek Macedonian woman accused us of presenting "too rosy a picture" of what we called the "evacuation program." She said that one of her aunts had been kidnapped by the communists. Why didn't we tell stories like that? We replied that we would be very interested in speaking with her aunt and learning about her experiences. A few days later she emailed us a more detailed account of her aunt's story. In fact, her aunt had not been a refugee or a child in 1948. At the age of twenty she had been forcibly conscripted by the communists to fight in the Democratic Army and had not been evacuated to Eastern Europe at all. A member of the Pan-Macedonian Association objected to our use of the term "Macedonians" for the Slavic-speaking refugee children in Eastern Europe. He insisted that the children were all Greeks and that Macedonians *were* Greeks. After several more academic, and less hostile, questions, the seminar came to an end. The controversy itself, however, did not.

Several days later an article about the seminar in the *National Herald* quoted Nicholas Gage saying "The event was organized so that no one could criticize the conclusions of the speakers; their research was not valid." Then an essay was posted on the Pan-Macedonian Association's website entitled "Provocative Distortion of History and Effort of 'Beautification of Paidomazoma' [gathering of children] in Princeton. Recognition of the FYROM [Former Yugoslav Republic of Macedonia] as 'Macedonia' from Professor who teaches in Greek University!!!"

For several weeks after the seminar Loring Danforth corresponded with Nicholas Gage by email. Gage charged us with "a perverse and dishonest revision of history that dishonored the tens of thousands of children and parents who suffered" under the "brutal policy" of the "communist guerillas." Then he posed what must have been for him an extremely painful question: "If what you said in your presentation were true, why would my mother have sacrificed her life to prevent us from being saved from harm?"

---

As these reactions to our work dramatically suggest, the evacuation of children from northern Greece continues to polarize modern Greek society and its diaspora communities even today. The animosity generated by these events, which took place in 1948, is one of the themes we address in this book. There are, however, two broader conflicts that are directly relevant to understanding the role of this controversy at the beginning of the twenty-first century. One is the Cold War and its legacy; the other is the Macedonian Question, the conflict between Greece and the Republic of Macedonia that has played a central role in Greek foreign policy since the early1990s.

This is a book about the intersection between stories and history. We are interested in the stories told by the refugee children who were evacuated from their homes during the Greek Civil War *and* the history of the Civil

War itself. More importantly, we are interested in the relationships that exist between these stories and this history. We explore the way collective narratives (histories) are constructed from individual narratives (stories) and the way individual narratives deconstruct both the collective narratives of nations and the ideological frameworks in which they exist. In *Anthropology through the Looking Glass*, Michael Herzfeld makes a similar distinction between *"istoria"* ("history in general") as an instrument of state ideology and *"istories"* ("histories" or "stories") as fragments of social experience and intimate social knowledge (1987, 41–46). The latter, he claims, are "the very antithesis of official History" (43).

In this book we show how first-person "histories" (or "stories") may indeed undermine and complicate the certainties of "History," but we also stress that the relationship between the two kinds of history is much more complex than that of a binary opposition. By focusing on the interaction between "history" and "histories," we hope to contribute to new understandings of the history of the Greek Civil War. It is only appropriate, therefore, to begin this book with a "story" about a crucial moment in the process of writing this book—a moment that was at once emotionally charged and intellectually exciting, a moment that challenged us to modify our research program and rethink our analysis of what we had previously learned.

## The Evacuation of Refugee Children from the Greek Civil War

In the early spring of 1948, at the height of the Greek Civil War, the Greek Communist Party began an evacuation program in which 20,000 Greek and Macedonian children between the ages of three and fourteen were taken from their villages in northern Greece (see fig. 1).[1] They were sent to the socialist countries of Eastern Europe, where they would be well cared for and continue their education until they could safely return to their homes at the end of the war. While officials of the Communist Party justified this operation on humanitarian grounds, the removal of children from combat zones served their political and military interests as well. There were fewer civilians to feed, and women, relieved of child-care responsibilities, were more easily mobilized to support the partisan cause. Most troubling of all, however, was the fact that some of the evacuated children were sent back to Greece to fight in the communist-controlled Democratic Army.

At the end of February 1948, the Greek government submitted a formal complaint to the United Nations, claiming that Greek children were

1. A woman and three young children who have stopped to rest beside a rocky path somewhere in the barren mountains along the northern border of Greece. Photograph courtesy of the Macedonian Museum in Skopje.

being forcibly removed from their homes by the communists and that this constituted a crime against humanity and an act of genocide (Baerentzen 1987, 128). The UN General Assembly charged the UN Special Committee on the Balkans with the difficult task of investigating the matter. Three months later the committee submitted a balanced report that was unable to confirm that a mass abduction of children had taken place.

In November 1948 the Greek representative to the UN General Assembly demanded the return to Greece of all Greek children who had been evacuated to Eastern Europe. In response, the general assembly unanimously voted to recommend "the return to Greece of Greek children at present away from their homes when the children, their father or mother, or in his or her absence, their closest relative, express a wish to that effect" (United Nations 1950, 242). The political tensions of the Cold War, however, hampered all efforts to repatriate the refugee children, and by the late 1950s only about five thousand children had returned to Greece. Many more refugee children returned to Greece as adults in the 1970s and 1980s after more liberal Greek governments that were more open to the repatriation of refugees from "communist countries," had come to power.

Children taken to Eastern Europe by the Greek Communist Party were not the only children evacuated from northern Greece during the Civil War. In 1947 the Greek government, in a campaign led personally by the queen of Greece, began the process of settling some 18,000 children from northern Greece in children's homes located in cities and towns throughout Greece. In 1950 most of these homes were closed, and the vast majority of children living in them returned to the villages of their birth.

In one of the first, and still one of the most balanced, accounts of these evacuation programs, Lars Baerentzen makes it clear that "[o]n both sides, the evacuation of children . . . was resented by some parents but accepted or even welcomed by others" (1987, 153). Children in Eastern Europe and children in Greece were housed in institutions that were similar in many ways, even though they were dominated by diametrically opposed political ideologies. While most of the children evacuated to children's homes in Greece returned home fairly quickly, children evacuated to Eastern Europe remained abroad for a much longer period of time. Many of them never returned home again at all. And while refugee children from the Greek Civil War—both those evacuated by the Communist Party and those evacuated by the Greek government—suffered terribly from being separated from their families, many of them benefited significantly from their experiences as well.

## Theoretical Contributions

Our aim in writing this book has been to present a theoretically informed study of one of the most controversial episodes in the history of modern Greece. The analysis of life-history narratives of refugee children of the Greek Civil War that we present here offers new insights into several theoretical issues that are high on the agenda of scholars working in the fields of refugee studies, the anthropology of childhood, and the politics of memory.

We contribute to the anthropological study of refugees by focusing on a specific category of refugee, refugee children from the Greek Civil War, who are of particular interest not only because of their young age, but also because of their positionality—their specific place in history, the political geography of Europe, and the ideological conflict that divided the world during the Cold War. To the best of our knowledge, this is one of the first anthropological studies of refugees hosted in the socialist countries of the Soviet bloc or of refugees cared for in total institutions aimed at transforming them into model citizens.

Following Malkki's critique of the essentialist discourse that until recently has dominated the field of refugee studies, we also question the false universalism inherent in the image of "the refugee," and especially that of "the refugee child," as an image of "bare humanity" stripped of any specific personal or cultural identity (Malkki 1995b, 9–13). We correct this tendency in three ways. First, we embed the experiences of these refugee children in the precise historical and political circumstances that transformed them into refugees in the first place. Second, we analyze the multiple ways in which they responded to these events. And third, we focus on the life-history narratives of individual refugee children themselves. In this way we restore power, agency, and voice to those who all too frequently are regarded as "speechless emissaries" (Malkki 1996, 377).

The distinction between a "sedentarist" and a "cosmopolitan" perspective on refugees, introduced by Bhabha (1992), Breckenridge et al. (2002), and Malkki (1995b), is a useful concept that has guided our work. We question, however, the strict dichotomy generally implied in such analyses and argue that these two perspectives often coexist, complementing one another in complicated ways. Our research also reveals that the "sedentarist" discourse of refugees-in-exile and the heroized identities associated with it are part of a broader *political* discourse used by various organizations for specific purposes. In this discourse refugee organizations often claim they prefer the maintenance of a state of "purity" in exile (Malkki 1995b) to a return polluted by compromise and accommodation.

Whether the Greek evacuation programs were "forced" or "voluntary" is a question that is relevant to contemporary theoretical debates in the field of refugee studies. In the case of refugee children from the Greek Civil War, this dilemma was couched in the ideologically charged terms of the Cold War. In contemporary settings the same question frequently lurks beneath debates about whether asylum seekers are *really* "refugees" or whether they should be seen, instead, as "economic migrants." Although it is important to preserve the definition of refugee status enshrined in the 1951 Geneva Convention in order to offer protection to all those who need it, the Greek case clearly reveals that many factors must be taken into account in order to arrive at a definition that is useful in both academic and applied settings.

The detailed first-person accounts of refugee children presented here reveal that the decision to "leave home" is in some sense always "forced," but that the boundary between "forced" and "voluntary" is easily blurred. It is more productive, therefore, to speak in terms of a "spectrum of coercion" (Richmond 1994) between "forced," at one extreme, and "voluntary," at the other. In addition, our research shows that "refugees" can either become "migrants" when they have settled in their new homes or they can acquire a permanent identity as refugees even when the initial reasons for their flight no longer apply. This may happen, as in the case of Macedonian refugee children who are not allowed to return to Greece, when refugees feel that their present lives are marked by injustices inherited from the past. In this case we suggest, with Edward Said, that refugees are transformed into exiles (Said 2000, 181).

This book also addresses current theoretical concerns in the anthropology of children and childhood. We restore agency to children as active subjects by analyzing their own accounts of their childhood experiences. Instead of treating them as helpless victims completely dependent on the actions of adults, we show how they can be both vulnerable and capable of acting independently at the same time. Our research demonstrates that there is no "universal" child and that ideas of childhood are socially constructed and vary widely across cultures. Finally, this book provides theoretical insights into the impact that war and violence have on children. In spite of the sometimes permanent trauma that has marked their lives, refugee children are remarkably resilient in coping with these painful experiences.

In the field of memory studies, our analysis has been inspired both by the classical work of Maurice Halbwachs (1992) and by more recent work on commemorations, the politics of memory, and the process of individual and collective remembering. This field, marked by the rediscovery of Maurice Halbwachs and the 1997 publication of Pierre Nora's monumental *Les lieux de mémoire* (*Realms of Memory*), has led to significant new insights into the ways in which societies construct public memories of important historical events, such as the Holocaust, World War II, and more recently the period of communist rule in Eastern Europe. Surprisingly, however, this field has largely ignored both the theoretical insights of leading oral historians and the contribution of oral sources to the understanding of memory.

We attempt to bridge this gap in the final chapters of our book by developing the concept of "communities of memory," in which individual memories of experience interact with the master narratives of public memory. Another innovative aspect of our work on the politics of memory is our ability to transcend the narrow national framework characteristic of most such studies by integrating into our analysis the transnational networks and the digital media of diasporic public spheres. In this way we show how local and transnational actors and arenas interact with each other in an increasingly globalized world.

## Historical and Ethnographic Contributions

This book is a truly interdisciplinary project, combining both ethnographic and historical approaches. As a rule, anthropologists are more at home conducting interviews than carrying out archival research. When they attempt to answer important historical questions, however, the advantages of crossing disciplinary boundaries are obvious. By combining new insights from our ethnographic and oral history research, on the one hand, with those from published historical works and archival sources, on the other, we have been able to reconstruct the histories of the evacuation programs carried out by the Communist Party and the Greek government during the Greek Civil War.

As a result of our detailed study of a number of unexplored archival sources, we are able to offer new insights into this controversial episode of modern Greek history. Many aspects of the lives of these refugee children, however, were never written down and cannot be documented by archival sources. We have filled these gaps in the historical record with a wealth of new information gathered from our own ethnographic fieldwork and oral history interviews. The first-person narratives of refugee children of the Greek Civil War clearly demonstrate that the polarized presentation of their evacuation as either forced or voluntary is an oversimplified dichotomy that hides a much more complicated historical reality. Similarly, the excessive focus in the published literature on the moment of departure of the children from their homes has obscured the multiple ways in which they have experienced and interpreted their later lives. The wide range of experiences captured in the life histories of refugee children who were settled in children's homes in Eastern Europe and in Greece illustrates both the impact of totalitarian regimes on their lives and the active role many of them played in the decisions that determined their futures.

Because this is the first scholarly book to examine life-history narratives of refugee children of the Greek Civil War, it stands as an important corrective to previously published popular work on the subject, most of which has been dominated by nationalist, communist, and anticommunist ideologies.[2] This book also breaks new ground because it adopts a broader, more comparative approach than other work on the subject. This is the only book-length study of refugee children of the Greek Civil War that deals with the experiences of both Greek and Macedonian refugee children.

The meaning of the term "Macedonian" is hotly contested. Jane Cowan has rightly noted the many meanings the word "Macedonian" may have for different people and in different contexts (2000, xiii–xvi). Since 1912, when the region known as Greek Macedonia became part of the Greek state, Greek authorities have used a wide range of names to refer to its Slavic-speaking inhabitants: "Bulgarians," "Macedonians," "Macedo-Slavs," "Slavophones," and "bilinguals," to mention just a few. In the 1930s the Greek Communist Party began using the names "Macedonians" and "Slavo-Macedonians" interchangeably. Slavic speakers themselves have also used a variety of terms to refer to members of their ethnic group, from "Bulgarians" and "Macedonians" to more apolitical terms, such as "locals" (*"dopioi"* in Greek and *"tukašni"* in Macedonian) and "ours" (*"dikoi mas"* in Greek and *"naši"* in Macedonian).

The children we refer to in this book as "Macedonians" came from families that spoke a south Slavic dialect they called *Makedonski* (Macedonian). Many of these children did not speak a word of Greek before their evacuation in 1948. In most families, these children learned from their relatives that they were *Makedonci* (Macedonians) and that they were different from their neighbors who spoke Greek, Turkish, or Albanian. During the Civil War, many of these children came to associate the word "Greek" with the Greek Army and Greek-speaking right-wing paramilitary groups who committed devastating acts of violence against their families. During the time they spent in Eastern Europe, they were once again classified as "Macedonian children" (*Makedonopoula*) by the Greek communist authorities who cared for them in children's homes there. Many of these children developed a strong Macedonian national identity and came to see "Macedonian" and "Greek" as mutually exclusive categories referring to people with two different national identities. In this book we use the term "Macedonian" most frequently to refer to people who identify themselves as Macedonians and not as Greeks.[3]

All previous studies of the refugee children of the Greek Civil War have focused exclusively on either Greeks or Macedonians and have completely ignored the other group. This nationalist bias has prevented the complete picture of the Greek Communist Party's evacuation program from being fully understood. We are, therefore, in a unique position to compare and contrast the experiences of Greek and Macedonian refugee children and to explore the complex relationships that developed between them as they grew to adulthood in Eastern Europe.

This book provides a comparative perspective on the experiences of refugee children of the Greek Civil War in another respect as well. Unlike previous work, we examine *both* the experiences of children who were evacuated to Eastern Europe by the Greek Communist Party *and* the experiences of those evacuated by the Greek government to children's homes in Greece. In this way we are again able to present revealing analyses of the similarities and differences that characterize the experiences of these two groups of refugee children.

The life histories we present also reveal important similarities in the ways refugee children of the Greek Civil War, now adults in their sixties and seventies, have structured their memories of these childhood events. In many cases, the meanings they attributed to their experiences as refugee children were quite similar. Whether they identified themselves as Greeks or Macedonians, whether they were raised in Eastern Europe or in Greece, they were all evacuated from their homes, raised in exile, and deprived of their families during a crucial period in their lives. Throughout this book, the gaze of the anthropologist and that of the historian complement one another, contributing to new understandings of the refugee children of the Greek Civil War and shedding new light on the experiences of refugee children around the world.

Our ethnography, however, is not limited to documenting the experiences of the refugee children alone. In the final chapters of this book we shift our attention to the political conflicts generated in public memory over the meanings attributed to the fate of these refugee children. Partly through participant observation during crucial events during which these memories were created and partly through the analysis of texts in which these memories are expressed, we examine how specific communities of memory have constructed master narratives to legitimate their political views. We also consider the various ways they have used both stories and silence in order to deal with their traumatic past.

## Multisited, Collaborative, and Politically Charged Fieldwork

A comfortable living room in the suburbs of Toronto, a shaded front yard in a Greek mountain village, a starkly furnished room in a Budapest hotel, a cramped kitchen in a Skopje apartment, and an elegant conference room at Princeton University. These are some of the many places where we have conducted the fieldwork on which this book is based.

For ten years we have been engaged in a collaborative ethnographic research project that epitomizes what Marcus and Fischer have called "multilocale" ethnography, in which "rather than being situated in one, or perhaps two communities for the entire period of research, the fieldworker must be mobile, covering a network of sites" (1986, 94). This is what Appadurai has referred to as "cosmopolitan ethnographic practice" in which anthropologists attempt to track the "ethnoscapes," the "global cultural flows," of people who no longer inhabit "tightly territorialized, spatially bounded" communities (1996, 33, 48, 50). James Clifford has described this new form of ethnography as "less a matter of localized dwelling and more a series of travel encounters" (1997, 2). More specifically, we have adopted one of several possible techniques of multisited ethnographic research, a strategy that Marcus poignantly calls "follow the life," in which the ethnographer uses autobiographical narratives to follow the life trajectories of people on the move (Marcus 1998, 94).

In the interviews we conducted, refugee children evoked memories of events that have marked their lives; they also reconstructed the social relations and perceptions that have shaped their identities. In addition, they reflected upon how these relations and perceptions changed as they grew older and moved from one place to another. Oral history interviews, in other words, provide a unique opportunity to engage in "retrospective anthropology" (Passerini 1988, 58). In this way, multisited ethnography is able to provide the ethnographic foundation on which anthropologists can produce "thick descriptions" of the past experiences of people who are members of transnational diaspora communities.

In order to situate the narratives of refugee children in the context of their original environments, we carried out research in a number of villages from which children had been evacuated. We spent two weeks in northern Greece, in Epirus and Macedonia, in the summers of 2001 and 2006. Van Boeschoten spent another week in Thrace in 2001. We also did fieldwork in places where refugee children currently live. In 1999, Van Boeschoten conducted research in Budapest with refugee children who remained in Hungary. We returned there together in 2003 and conducted additional interviews. Danforth spent two weeks interviewing refugee children in Toronto in 2000, and we both conducted more interviews there in 2003. During the entire period of our research, Van Boeschoten also maintained regular contact with the community of former refugee children in the city of Volos, Greece, where she lives. Finally, we conducted fieldwork in Skopje at the two international reunions organized by the Association of Refugee Children from Aegean Macedonia to commemorate the fortieth and fiftieth anniversaries of their departure from Greece. Van Boeschoten attended the first reunion in 1988; Danforth attended the second in 1998.

During the research for this book we interviewed 114 refugee children who left their villages as part of the organized evacuation campaigns conducted by the Greek Communist Party and the Greek government. We went to great efforts to interview people with as wide a variety of perspectives and experiences as possible. We interviewed people who were evacuated to children's homes in Eastern Europe and to children's homes in Greece, as well as people who identified themselves as Greeks and people who identified themselves as Macedonians. We interviewed people who were evacuated with their parents' permission and people who were evacuated against their parents' will. In addition, we interviewed people who supported the communists, people who supported the Greek government, and people who tried to remain as neutral as possible. Finally, we interviewed people from different regions of northern Greece, people who had been evacuated to different countries in Eastern Europe, people who had been repatriated to Greece at different times, and people who now make their homes on different continents. Most of these interviews we conducted in Greek; some we conducted in English.

It is significant that our interviews were carried out after the Cold War had ended and after the Republic of Macedonia had become an independent state. These two events had an important effect on the life-history narratives we were privileged to hear. If the Iron Curtain had still been standing or if Macedonia had still been part of the former Yugoslavia, the refugee children's perspectives on the Greek Communist Party and on the relationship between Macedonia and Yugoslavia would have been very different. The wars that accompanied the breakup of Yugoslavia in the 1990s also influenced the content of these narratives, since many of the refugee children we interviewed had recently relived their own traumatic childhood experiences as they watched disturbing scenes of violence and displacement on their televisions.

All our scholarly work on the refugee children of the Greek Civil War has been guided first and foremost by a desire to present accurate information in a balanced manner. When we were criticized for presenting a "procommunist" perspective at Princeton University in May 2005 and again, with more hostility, at a conference on the Greek Civil War in Kastoria, Greece, in June 2006, we committed ourselves to searching even harder for people who had experienced their evacuation to Eastern Europe by the communists as "kidnapping." We followed up leads provided to us by several of our critics, and we placed an advertisement in a Volos newspaper in an effort to contact people who had experienced their evacuation as "kidnapping."

After the Princeton seminar, Nicholas Gage challenged us to come to "his village," the village of Lia in Epirus, where he assured us we would find many people who had been "kidnapped by the communists." In late June 2006 we spent a week conducting fieldwork in Lia and learned a great deal about the history of the village during the Civil War and the impact Gage's book has had on it. During our research in Lia, we heard many stories about left-wing violence. We spoke with people who had been taken by force to Albania when the whole village was evacuated at the end of the war, people who had been mobilized against their will to serve with the communist forces, and people who had been evacuated to Eastern Europe *with* the permission of their parents. We only learned about one person, however, who as a child had been evacuated by force during the organized evacuation program conducted by the Greek Communist Party. What was going on? Why were we unable to find more people who as children had been evacuated from their villages to Eastern Europe against the will of their parents, when our critics claimed that the *paidomazoma* (literally in Greek "the gathering of children") had been an organized campaign of mass kidnapping carried out by the Greek Communist Party?

After much self-reflection, we were finally able to reconcile the gaping discrepancy between the results of our research and the claims of our critics. We realized that for our critics the term *paidomazoma* stood for a wide variety of acts committed by the communists during the Civil War: the organized evacuation program in which children were taken to Eastern Europe, the forced mobilization of people to serve in the communist-led Democratic Army, the forced evacuation of entire villages at the end of the war, and the forced separation of children from their families after the families' evacuation to Albania. For us the term *paidomazoma* had a much more restricted meaning. We were focused more narrowly on the organized evacuation program in which children were taken from their villages and brought to Eastern Europe without their families before the end of the war.

We acknowledge, and have extensively documented, the terror and violence that were involved in the forced mobilizations, the forced evacuations of entire villages, and the forced separation of children from their families in Albania. The Greek Communist Party bears full responsibility for all these actions *and* for sending refugee children back from Eastern Europe to fight in the Democratic Army. From our perspective, though, these acts are part of the larger picture of left-wing violence, which, together with a great deal of right-wing violence, characterized the Greek Civil War. As scholars, however, we are committed in this book to examining a more specific topic—the organized evacuation of children from their homes by both the Greek Communist Party and the Greek government.

## Structure and Organization of This Book

This book is both a "polyphonic" and a "mixed genre" text (Clifford 1988, 46; Marcus 1986, 188). It is divided into three parts, each of which is presented in a different voice. In part 1, *Histories*, we adopt the traditional scholarly voice of social historians making use of archival and oral sources to present a detailed account of the two evacuation programs that constitute the subject of the book. We begin chapter 1 with a brief discussion of the international legal frameworks developed by the United Nations to ensure the humane treatment of refugees and children. This is followed by a short account of other evacuation programs in which children were removed from their homes in wartime Europe in the 1930s and 1940s. We then discuss the historical, cultural, and geographic contexts in which the two Greek evacuation programs took place. Finally, we examine the polarized political discourse that developed during and after the Civil War to describe the two evacuations programs.

In chapter 2 we present an in-depth history of the evacuation program conducted by the Greek Communist Party. We consider in detail the controversial question of whether the children were taken from their villages by force or whether they left voluntarily. Drawing on reports of the UN Special Committee on the Balkans, firsthand accounts of refugee children themselves, and the important theoretical argument that mass movements of people must be understood in terms of a "spectrum of coercion" (Richmond 1994), we refute the two oversimplified, politicized answers usually offered to this question. We then discuss the Greek Communist Party's decision to send some refugee children back from Eastern Europe to northern Greece to fight in the Democratic Army, a decision that seriously undermined the claim that the evacuation program was motivated exclusively by humanitarian concerns. After describing the prevailing conditions in postwar Eastern Europe, we offer an account of daily life in the children's homes, the relationships between Greek and Macedonian children in the homes, and the children's educational and professional lives. Finally, we consider their repatriation to Greece and their reunification with other members of their families.

Chapter 3 presents a parallel account of the evacuation program conducted by Queen Frederica and the Greek government. After describing the establishment of the Royal Welfare Fund, the organization responsible for the evacuations, we show that this program, initially presented as a humanitarian effort to improve the lives of children living in refugee camps throughout Greece, was later recast in explicitly ideological terms as an effort to save the children of northern Greece from being "kidnapped by the communists." We then examine the evacuation process itself, living conditions in the children's homes, and the children's repatriation to their villages in the early 1950s. After examining the ideological content of the education program offered in the homes, we conclude with a comparison of the evacuation program of the Greek Communist Party and that of the Greek government.

Part 2, *Stories*, contains seven life-history narratives in which refugee children recount their own experiences in their own words. These narratives are an integral part of this book; they constitute a powerful refutation of the oversimplified, politicized master narratives that have dominated virtually all public discussion of this most controversial episode of the Greek Civil War. These individual life-history narratives demonstrate forcefully that refugee children are not passive, silent victims, as they are so often portrayed. The narratives presented here restore both agency and voice to the refugee children of the Greek Civil War.

Reading their stories—hearing their voices—we also come face to face with the complexity and uniqueness of their individual accounts. Each one of these life-history narratives must be acknowledged as equally valuable. Nicholas Gage and anticommunist Greek nationalists, on the one hand, and procommunists and Macedonian nationalists, on the other, insist that their own individual *story* of their own personal experiences in the Civil War constitutes the one true collective *history* of the Greek Civil War as a whole. This is obviously not the case. The *history* of the Greek Civil War must be carefully constructed from a synthesis of all these individual *stories*.

We selected for inclusion in part 2 the accounts of seven of the 114 refugee children we interviewed according to several criteria. Above all, we chose narratives that are emotionally powerful and are of historical, ethnographic, and psychological interest. We chose vivid accounts of specific lived experiences rather than impersonal or ideologically motivated accounts. We also attempted to select narratives that present a balanced sample of the wide range of experiences contained in the life-history narratives we elicited during our ten years of research. Chapter 4 contains life-history narratives of two Greek and two Macedonian children who went to Eastern Europe; chapter 5 contains the narratives of two Greek children and one Macedonian child who went to children's homes in Greece.

All the accounts included in part 2 were tape-recorded. In selecting, editing, and translating these life stories, our primary goal has been to create written texts that were engaging to read. The process of transforming oral narratives into written texts involves the exercise of a significant degree of editorial judgment. Unedited, literally translated oral narratives usually do not produce effective written texts. We have, therefore, eliminated many features of oral language and nonstandard English (on one occasion, at the explicit request of the narrator) in order to create more powerful written accounts. At the same time, however, we have attempted to capture the uniqueness and individuality of the people we interviewed. With one exception, as noted, we have used the real names of the seven people whose life histories we present in part 2. The names of people referred to elsewhere in the text are pseudonyms.

In part 3, *Ethnographies*, we assume again a more traditional scholarly voice. This time, however, it is the voice of interpretive anthropologists. In chapter 6 we analyze the experiences of refugee children from the Greek Civil War in light of recent anthropological work on refugees, displacement, and the meaning of home. By integrating a sedentarist and a more cosmopolitan perspective, we are able to achieve a nuanced understanding of the paradoxes and contradictions that characterize the lives of refugees scattered in transnational diaspora communities around the world. We explore experiences of childhood separation from parents that are perceived as both tragic and liberating, narratives of long years in exile that undermine some identities and create others, and stories of family reunions that show how painful it is when strangers become "mothers" and mothers become strangers. Then we contrast the relationship between identities, on the one hand, and concepts of "place" and "home," on the other, as they are experienced in different ways by three groups of refugee children: Macedonians who cannot return to the villages of their birth, Greeks and Macedonians who were repatriated to northern Greece in the 1950s, and Greeks who made the difficult decision to return to Greece in the 1980s after living most of their lives in Eastern Europe.

In chapters 7 and 8 we shift our attention to what we have called "ethnographies of memory." Our goal here is to analyze the different forms that the controversy over the evacuation of children during the Greek Civil War has taken in the present post–Cold War world order. To do this we distinguish between two different types of community of memory, "experiential" and "political," both of which constitute diasporic imagined communities. The members of "experiential" communities of memory are linked together by shared experiences in the past, and the narratives they produce serve primarily to make sense of the narrators' own lives. The members of "political" communities of memory, on the other hand, are linked by shared political views of the past, and their narratives are directed toward political action in the present.

In chapter 7 we identify common patterns of memory in the narratives of two experiential communities of memory, one made up of refugee children evacuated to Eastern Europe and the other of those raised in children's homes in Greece. We focus on four themes that recur in the life histories of both groups: departure, material objects, powerlessness, and empowerment. In the case of each of these themes, we identify similarities and differences between the accounts of the two groups of refugee children and demonstrate the many ways in which they undermine the polarized dichotomies of the Cold War master narratives that have dominated public discourse on the two evacuation programs.

Chapter 8 explores the "memory wars" that continue to be fought in transnational public arenas around the world over the political meanings that can be attributed to the evacuation of refugee children from their homes to Eastern Europe during the Civil War. We consider the "politics of memory" associated with this event by analyzing four ethnographic examples. The first two involve mutually exclusive political communities of memory: the Association of Refugee Children from Aegean Macedonia, a transnational organization of refugee children who identify themselves as Macedonians (and not Greeks), and the Pan-Macedonian Association USA, Inc., a transnational organization of Greek Macedonians, people who have a Greek national identity and a Macedonian regional identity. We examine the crucial role the evacuation of refugee children has played in the construction of a master narrative of the nation in both organizations. Members of each community of memory consider the refugee children to be innocent victims of an evil plot conceived by outsiders and aimed at destroying their own national community.

In the third example, we analyze the presentation of the evacuation program of the Greek Communist Party in Nicholas Gage's book *Eleni*, a key text in the construction of a political narrative of the Greek Civil War by the anticommunist right that describes the mass abduction of innocent children by evil communists. In this way Gage attempts to legitimate the dominant master narrative of the Cold War in order to justify the global war against communism. In our last example, we analyze how Gage's village of Lia in Epirus has been transformed into a "memorial village" as a result of the success of *Eleni*. We describe local memories of the evacuation of children from the village in 1948 and the ambivalent feelings residents continue to nurture about Gage and his book *Eleni*. Then we examine the process of memorialization through an analysis of the newly built guesthouse, a memorial to Gage's mother, Eleni, that has deeply divided the community of Lia and transformed the village into a site of contested memories. We conclude by considering the interaction of the global and the local by analyzing the comments left by visitors in the guest book of the guesthouse and the efforts villagers make in their everyday lives to mend their social relations and heal the traumas of the past.

In the epilogue we reflect on the dialectical relationship between remembering and forgetting in the "memory wars" that continue to be fought over these tragic events. We attempt to answer the crucial question that has preoccupied us throughout our research: why is the memory of the evacuation of refugee children of the Greek Civil War still relevant in contemporary Greek political discourse? Drawing on recent anthropological literature on globalization, conflict resolution, and the post–Cold War order, we argue that this phenomenon is not simply a mechanical reproduction of Cold War political discourse, but a new response to a new situation that links the open wounds of the Civil War with one of the major issues in Greek foreign policy, the Macedonian Question. Research on similar conflicts has shown that reconciliation with the past is only possible through public recognition of the suffering experienced by both sides. We conclude by joining our voices with the voices of refugee children themselves in a call for peace and reconciliation. This is the message we would like to offer the children of future generations.

# PART ONE

# Histories

# ONE

# Framing the Subject

Exile . . . is the unhealable rift forced between a human being and a native place, between the self and its true home.

—Edward Said 2000, 173

In 1948, when tens of thousands of children were forced to leave their homes during the Greek Civil War, the vast humanitarian enterprise known as the "international refugee regime" (Zolberg, Suhrke, and Aguayo 1989, 258) had only recently come into being, and no binding legal framework was available to guarantee their protection. Today this international refugee regime consists of a worldwide network of organizations and laws for managing refugees as a global humanitarian "problem" and for protecting their fundamental human rights. According to *The State of the World's Refugees 2006: Human Displacement in the New Millennium*, in 2006 the office of the UN High Commissioner for Refugees (UNHCR) provided assistance to over nineteen million "people of concern" in 115 countries throughout the world. Over nine million of these "people of concern" were refugees; the others were internally displaced people, stateless people, and asylum seekers. Nearly half of the refugees were children under eighteen. The refugees under the care of the UNHCR had been driven from their homes in Vietnam, Somalia, Bosnia, Rwanda, Afghanistan, Iraq, and Sudan as a result of wars, campaigns of ethnic cleansing, and acts of genocide (UNHCR 2006).

The beginnings of the international refugee regime are to be found in the efforts to address the humanitarian crisis caused by the forced migration of millions of Europeans during World War II. In her valuable review article on the anthropology of refugees, Liisa Malkki situates "the birth of the modern, internationally recognizable figure of 'the refugee'" in Europe during the period after World War II (1995a, 497). In 1943 the UN Relief and Rehabilitation Administration (UNRRA) was founded to repatriate seven million refugees who had been displaced from their homes in Central Europe. More importantly, in 1951 the UNHCR was established, and the Geneva Convention relating to the Status of Refugees was adopted. This convention, as modified by the 1967 Protocol, which expanded its scope beyond the postwar European context, has become "the universal instrument of refugee law" (Nobel 1988, 21).

According to Article 1 of the 1951 Geneva Convention relating to the Status of Refugees,

> the term "refugee" shall apply to any person who . . . owing to well-founded fear of being persecuted for reasons of race, religion, nationality, membership of a particular social group or political opinion, is outside the country of his nationality and is unable or, owing to such fear, is unwilling to avail himself of the protection of that country; or who, not having a nationality and being outside the country of his former habitual residence as a result of such events, is unable or, owing to such fear, is unwilling to return to it.[1]

In *The Unwanted: European Refugees in the Twentieth Century*, Michael Marrus provides a more general definition of the term "refugee," according to which all "people obliged by war or persecution to leave their dwellings and seek refuge abroad" are considered refugees (1985, 3). We propose to extend this definition even further to include people who leave their homes in search of refuge from war or persecution, but who remain within the borders of their own countries. In the context of the "international refugee regime" these people are officially referred to as "internally displaced people" or "IDPs." While there are important differences between people who cross international borders during their flight and those who do not, in many cases the similarities that characterize their experiences warrant the use of the term "refugee" to encompass them all.

According to Malkki, the discourse of the "international refugee regime" generally treats refugees as a political and humanitarian "problem" whose solution involves their voluntary repatriation to their country of origin, their voluntary resettlement in a third country, or their integration and assimilation into their host country. This discourse has had significant influence on the interdisciplinary field of "refugee studies" that emerged in the 1970s and 1980s. In the process of constructing "the refugee" as an object of scholarly knowledge, much of the early work in this field exhibited a tendency toward essentialism. In an effort to define "the refugee experience," this work posited "a single, essential, transhistorical refugee condition" and made the assumption that all refugees "shared a common condition or nature" (Malkki 1995a, 507–11). An unfortunate consequence of this essentialism has been the creation of a single universal image of refugees as anonymous victims, powerless to say or do anything to influence the future course of their lives.

The image of refugees as innocent victims is even more compelling when the refugees are children. The vast international legal system for the protection of children that exists in the early twenty-first century was still in its infancy in the early 1940s. Many of the basic ideas concerning the rights of children that would later be enshrined in humanitarian law played a significant role in public debates about the fate of the refugee children of the Greek Civil War. In 1959 the United Nations first expressed public concern for the protection of children in its "Declaration on the Rights of the Child." Three decades later this concern took legally binding form with the adoption of the Convention on the Rights of the Child by the UN General Assembly in November 1989.[2] This convention is based on the principle that children are "entitled to special care and assistance" and "should grow up in a family environment," since the family is "the fundamental group of society and the natural environment for the growth and well-being of all its members and particularly children." For this reason, the family "should be afforded the necessary protection and assistance so that it can fully assume its responsibilities within the community" (preamble). More specifically, according to Article 9 of the convention, "state parties shall ensure that a child shall not be separated from his or her parents against their will, except when competent authorities subject to judicial review determine in accordance with applicable law and procedures, that such separation is necessary for the best interests of the child."

There can be no doubt that the 1989 Convention on the Rights of the Child, as well as the specific focus of humanitarian organizations on the children affected by war, has had very positive effects. International human rights discourse on children, however, like that on refugees, has been marked by a tendency toward essentialism. It has adopted a universal, cross-cultural model of the "generic child" (Mann 2004) based on a specific form of childhood that developed in Europe and North America during the industrial age. Social scientists involved in the study of childhood have argued that by relying on this mistakenly universalist model of childhood, human rights discourse on children inaccurately presents them as helpless victims rather than as independent actors (Boyden 1997, 254).[3]

It is certainly true that infants and young children *are* extremely vulnerable; they *are* in need of care and protection. The same is significantly less true, however, in the case of older children in their mid- to late teens. In many cultures—and this includes rural Greek culture in the 1940s—even young children play an important role in family life and have to make independent decisions in looking after the family's survival or in caring for their younger siblings (Mann 2004). Recent research with children affected by war has also shown that, even when severely traumatized, children frequently exhibit remarkable resilience and are able to play an active role in determining their own fate (Boyden and de Berry 2004, xvii; Panter-Brick 2000, 11). To regard such children as powerless, without voice, and unable to act independently as agents in their own right is clearly inappropriate. This insight has led to an important paradigm shift that emphasizes the need to counterbalance an exclusive focus on children's vulnerability with a new interest in their competence and agency. It is necessary, in other words, to listen to children's own voices.

Since the work of Philippe Ariès (1962), sociologists and anthropologists have rejected the notion that childhood is a natural or universal stage in the human life cycle and have embraced the idea that childhood is a social construction that varies widely from culture to culture. In order to avoid accusations of ethnocentrism or worse, cultural imperialism, it is essential that international human rights discourse on children reject a monolithic view of childhood and remain sensitive to the cross-cultural variation in conceptions of "the child." It is equally important, however, to reject a totally relativistic perspective that makes concern for human rights impossible (Cowan, Dembour, and Wilson 2001). Only by striking a careful balance between these two extremes is it possible to understand both the many ways children can participate actively in shaping their own lives and the many ways in which they genuinely need the care and protection of their parents, other adults, and in extreme circumstances, the state.

International human rights discourse treats refugee children who have been separated from their parents as powerless victims for two reasons: because they are refugees and because they are children. They are treated as "matter out of place" (Douglas 1966, 48) for the same reasons. As refugees, they should be returned to their homeland; and as children separated from their parents, they should be returned to their families. Just as repatriation is the solution to the "refugee problem," family reunification is the solution to the problem of "unaccompanied children." While in many cases repatriation and family reunification *may* actually represent the best solution to the difficulties facing refugee children separated from their parents, this is not always the case. The proper goal of international organizations committed to the welfare of the world's children is "to devise policies of protection that do not so much rescue and save children as involve and empower them" (Panter-Brick 2000, 12).

In this study of refugee children from the Greek Civil War, we attempt to reverse this tendency toward dehistoricization and depersonalization by focusing on the specific historical moment and the unique personal and family circumstances in which these children were separated from their homes and became refugees. We seek to empower refugee children of the Greek Civil War by restoring to them their own voice and listening carefully to their own stories. Only in this way is it possible to understand how refugees are able to construct meaningful lives for themselves in the aftermath of these tragic events.

## The Evacuation of Children during War in Europe in the 1930s and 1940s

In the twentieth century alone, from the Armenian massacre to the disintegration of Yugoslavia, unaccompanied children have been among the most tragic victims of war. In many such conflicts refugee children have been removed from their homes and families in organized evacuation programs. Some of these programs have been noble humanitarian efforts to rescue children from genocide; others have been genuinely evil attempts to kidnap children in order to create a "master race." The aims of still other evacuation programs have been more mixed: to serve the goals of particular military strategies, to facilitate specific plans for social change, or to prevent children from having to live under repressive political regimes.

The scope of the suffering of refugees, displaced people, and unaccompanied children in Europe during World War II and the Spanish Civil War that preceded it is difficult to imagine. According to estimates, by the end of the war in 1945 there were six and a half million refugees and displaced people living in Europe. This included over a million children who were living in institutions because they had been "orphaned," "abandoned," or separated from their families in some other way (Ressler, Boothby, and Steinboch 1988, 18, 22).

After the first year of the Spanish Civil War (1936–39), 90,000 children had been orphaned or abandoned. Accompanied by school teachers and Roman Catholic priests, many of them were taken to France, England, Mexico, and the Soviet Union. As often happens, what was originally expected to be a short period of separation became a much longer one for several reasons: Franco's victory, the outbreak of World War II, and political conflicts between the host countries and the Franco regime. Two-thirds to three-quarters of the children from France and England had returned to Spain by 1940. As a result of the Cold War, the repatriation of children from the Soviet Union did not begin until 1956. In Spain, France, and other countries where they now live, refugee children from the Spanish Civil War have formed social organizations that sponsor reunions and pilgrimages where they commemorate and share their past experiences.[4]

With the incorporation of Austria into the Third Reich in 1938 and the spread of anti-Semitic laws and pogroms into other countries in Central Europe, a variety of plans were developed to evacuate unaccompanied Jewish children to safety in other parts of Europe. In a program known as the *Kindertransport,* 10,000 Jewish children were evacuated with the consent of their parents from countries under Nazi control and settled in England prior to 1940. During the war and the immediate postwar period, 10,000 more Jewish children were given temporary asylum in Switzerland before being resettled in other countries, and through the Youth Aliyah program over 20,000 more were evacuated to Palestine (Ressler, Boothby, and Steinboch 1988, 20–21). For the great majority of these children, the end of the war brought tragic news of their parents' deaths in Nazi concentration camps.[5]

Within days of the British declaration of war against Germany in September 1939, 750,000 unaccompanied children were evacuated from urban areas to the countryside throughout England to avoid the anticipated German bombing campaign. British children were also evacuated overseas, primarily to Canada and the United States. The Children's Overseas Reception Board made plans to evacuate tens of thousands of children, but the program was ended after only 2,700 children had been evacuated when a transport ship was sunk by a German torpedo boat, killing 73 children (Ressler, Boothby, and Steinboch 1988, 29). At the end of the war, the majority of these children were safely repatriated to Great Britain (Bailey 1980).

When Finland was invaded by both the Soviet Union and Nazi Germany in 1939, approximately 67,000 children between the ages of one and fourteen were evacuated to Sweden—over 7 percent of all the children in Finland. There is evidence that many parents with large families to support may have agreed to the evacuation of one or more of their children in order to save them from poverty and provide them with better opportunities in Sweden. Contrary to the general understanding that the children would return to their families in Finland after the war, 15,000 of them remained in Sweden (Ressler, Boothby, and Steinboch 1988, 28–29).

While the Kindertransport program stands at one end of the moral continuum between good and evil, the program carried out by the Nazis, in which children with "desirable racial characteristics" were abducted from German occupied territories and subjected to a process of forced "Germanization," stands at the other. In 1941, Nazi officials established a program in which a large number of children were kidnapped from Eastern Europe, mainly from Poland and the Ukraine.[6] "Worthless" children were sent to concentration camps, while "racially valuable" children of suitably "Nordic appearance" were either placed in state boarding schools run by the Lebensborn Society or given to German families for adoption, where they were raised as Germans with no knowledge of their origins. In 1946, 40,000 of the 200,000 Polish children reported to have been abducted were returned to their homes (Sereny 2001, 45–52). At the Nuremberg Trials of 1948, Schutzstaffel (SS) officers responsible for this program were convicted of war crimes, genocide, and crimes against humanity.[7]

Programs of evacuation and repatriation of refugee children, such as those of the Greek Civil War that are the subject of this book, raise many important questions. In time of war, when, if ever, is the separation of children from their parents justified? When children's lives are in danger, what does it mean to ask whether this separation is voluntary or involuntary? What course of action most effectively serves the children's best interests? To what extent should children's own views be taken into account? What role should be played by their parents and the government of their country of origin in these decisions? To whom, in other words, do refugee children belong? To their parents, to the state, or to themselves?

## The Greek Civil War

Hitler's army invaded Greece on April 6, 1941, and in a few weeks completely overwhelmed the Greek and British troops defending the country. The king of Greece and his government immediately fled to Egypt and soon established a government-in-exile in Cairo. German, Italian, and Bulgarian forces quickly took control of the entire country and installed a quisling government in Athens. The Axis occupation of Greece was a period of great deprivation and hardship. In Athens nearly 300,000 Greeks starved to death (Mazower 1993, 41), while in the countryside German and Italian troops burned hundreds of villages to the ground and massacred thousands of villagers.

The social and political divisions that developed in Greece during the Occupation contributed directly to the outbreak of the Civil War in 1946.

Leading roles in the resistance were played by the National Liberation Front (EAM) and its armed wing, the Greek Popular Liberation Army (ELAS), both of which, although controlled by the Greek Communist Party, enjoyed broad popular support among Greeks with a wide range of political views. The initial success of these resistance organizations, as well as the introduction of increased local autonomy, participatory democracy, and gender equality to village life in communist-controlled territory, generated significant support among large sectors of the population (Mazower 1993, 265–290; Van Boeschoten 1997, 95–126).

As liberation from Axis occupation approached, political control of postwar Greece became an increasingly urgent issue. In March 1944, the National Liberation Front established a provisional government in the "Free Greece" and began to make plans to assume power after the war. By doing so it presented a serious challenge to the Greek government-in-exile and its British allies. The National Liberation Front finally agreed in September 1944 to take part in a government of national unity led by George Papandreou. Efforts to ensure a peaceful transition to a democratically elected government lasted only a few months, as the tensions that had emerged during the Occupation gradually led to the development of a full-blown civil war (Close 1993, 1–31).

The power vacuum that remained after the German withdrawal from Greece in October 1944 was filled by a government of national unity that lacked both the legitimacy and the military power to rule effectively. Both right-wing and left-wing paramilitary units roamed the countryside seriously undermining the government's efforts to regain control of the country. In December fighting broke out in Athens between ELAS, on the one hand, and the Greek police, British troops, and irregular right-wing bands, on the other. With the Varkiza Agreement of February 1945, ELAS agreed to disarm. In exchange, the government agreed to hold national elections and conduct a referendum on the return of the king. There followed a period known as "the White Terror," in which right-wing groups took vengeance against leftist supporters of EAM and ELAS. During this period the balance of power swung decisively in favor of the right. In March 1946, the communist leadership decided to abstain from elections because of the violent conditions that prevailed throughout the country. The royalist right won the elections, and King George II returned to Greece later that year after a referendum whose legitimacy has been widely questioned.

The new government was unable to control the countryside, where violence continued and local power was now largely in the hands of right-wing bands. As the government gradually regained control over the state apparatus, the persecution of the left took on a more institutionalized form. By the end of the Civil War, the government held 18,000 political prisoners and 31,000 detainees in concentration camps, while an estimated 8,000 leftists had been sentenced to death and executed (Panourgiá 2009, 98–103; Voglis 2002, 59–63). Gradually leftists began to rearm, and in October 1946 leaders of the Communist Party established the Democratic Army of Greece. Shortly thereafter, full-fledged civil war broke out.

The greatest strength of the Democratic Army lay in the mountainous regions near Greece's northern border with Albania, Yugoslavia, and Bulgaria. While the Soviet Union provided no assistance to the Greek Communist Party, the United States assumed the role of the British as the primary patron of the Greek government. Under the Truman Doctrine it began to provide substantial economic and military aid to Greece in March 1947. At the end of the year, the Communist Party announced the formation of the Provisional Democratic Government of Greece. The Democratic Army enjoyed some success on the battlefield in 1948, but was never able to gain control of a town of sufficient size to serve as the capital of the provisional government.

The tide of the Civil War soon began to turn in favor of the Greek government, and the partisans waged their final and ultimately futile battles in the mountain strongholds of Grammos and Vitsi along the Albanian border in northwest Greece. At the end of August 1949, the defeated partisans and their Communist Party leaders retreated across the border into Albania, and on October 16 the Democratic Army Radio announced what it called a "temporary end" to hostilities. Over 140,000 refugees left Greece and went into exile in Eastern Europe, many of them never to return (Close 1995, 219). With that the Greek Civil War came to a bitter end.

Although the military conflict itself was over, the traumatic impact of the Civil War continued to polarize Greek society for decades. Until 1963, Greece was ruled by a succession of right-wing governments whose anticommunist policies led to the persecution of a whole generation of leftists. People needed to obtain "certificates of loyalty" in order to enter universities, obtain civil service jobs, or be issued passports (Voglis 2002, 62). New laws deprived political refugees living in Eastern Europe of their Greek citizenship and authorized the confiscation of the property they had left behind. The Greek government used this legislation to justify its continued refusal to allow the repatriation of political refugees who had left Greece after the Civil War.

On April 21, 1967, a small group of army colonels seized control of the Greek government in a military coup. They immediately suspended articles of the constitution protecting human rights, dissolved political parties, and imprisoned, exiled, and tortured many of their left-wing opponents. After the disastrous Turkish invasion of Cyprus in July 1974, the junta collapsed, and Greece returned to civilian rule. The new moderate-right government of Constantine Karamanlis held a referendum abolishing the monarchy and legalized the Communist Party. This process of liberalization and political reconciliation continued when the Panhellenic Socialist Movement (PASOK) came to power in 1981. The new government officially recognized the communist-led resistance to the Axis occupation during World War II and passed legislation facilitating the return of many of the political refugees who had left Greece after the Civil War. With their return, the damaging legacy of the Civil War, which had polarized Greek society for almost half a century, was at least partially overcome. Nevertheless, memories of the Greek Civil War remain a powerful divisive force in Greece today.[8]

## The Human Geography of Northern Greece

The northern border of Greece stretches over 650 kilometers from the Ionian Sea in the west to Turkey in the east (see map 1). The mountainous region of Epirus in northwestern Greece is separated from Greek Macedonia by the massive Pindus mountain range. Greek Macedonia stretches from the Prespa Lakes (where the borders of Greece, Albania, and the former

Map 1. Northern Greece

Yugoslavia meet) and the high peaks of Mounts Grammos and Vitsi, across the wide plain of the Axios (Vardar) River and the city of Thessaloniki, to the Nestos River valley. From there, Greek Thrace extends to the east in a narrow coastal strip backed by the Rhodope Mountains to the Evros River and the Greek-Turkish border.

The geography of northern Greece had an important influence on the events of the Greek Civil War. The Democratic Army controlled the more isolated and inaccessible mountainous regions along Greece's northern border, which were well suited to the guerrilla tactics it adopted for most of the war. Because of its tremendous superiority in motorized transport, armored vehicles, and airpower, the Greek Army controlled the plains and valleys that were well served by transportation and communication networks. The Democratic Army mounted occasional attacks on cities and towns in government-controlled territory, while the Greek Army regularly attempted to push up into the mountains to drive out the partisan forces.

Villages in the foothills of the mountains of northern Greece, which were occupied by the partisans at night and the Greek Army during the day, endured some of the most suffering of the war. In villages under their control, the partisans requisitioned food, animals, and supplies; forcibly recruited both men and women to join the Democratic Army; summarily executed villagers accused of collaboration with the enemy; and at the end of the war, with their defeat imminent, forcibly evacuated entire villages across the border to the north. The Greek Army, together with right-wing paramilitary groups, burned villages and evacuated their inhabitants in order to eliminate the base of support on which the Democratic Army had come to depend. The Greek Air Force conducted bombing raids on many villages, dropping napalm late in the war in order to maximize the terror and destruction it inflicted on its targets (see fig. 2). In addition, the Greek government executed prisoners accused of supporting the partisans and imprisoned or sent into exile their wives, children, and parents.

After the war, thousands of people evacuated by the Greek Army returned to their villages in northern Greece. Thousands, however, remained in the cities where they had been housed or joined the massive postwar population movements to the major urban centers of Athens and Thessaloniki. Thousands more emigrated to Western Europe, North America, and Australia in search of better lives for themselves and their children. High in the wooded mountains along the northern borders of Greece, the foundations of houses and abandoned churches stand in silent witness to the tragic events of the Civil War.

The south central Balkans has long been an area of extraordinary lin-

2. Eight children and an adult woman standing in front of a bunker built to
protect the residents of their village from the bombing raids of the Greek Air Force.
Photograph courtesy of Mara Kuzman Georgievska.

guistic, religious, and cultural diversity. In the nineteenth century the in-
habitants of the geographical region known as Macedonia included Al-
banian-speaking Muslims and Christians, Slavic-speaking Muslims and
Christians, Greek-speaking Christians, Turkish-speaking Muslims, Aromani
(Vlahs), Jews, and Roma (Gypsies). Western Thrace, with its population of
Turkish- and Slavic-speaking Muslims, and Epirus, with its population of
Albanian-speaking Muslims and Christians, were also inhabited by very di-
verse populations.

The relationship between ethnicity and nationality in the southern
Balkans has always been complex. Before the pioneering work of Fredrik
Barth, ethnic groups were generally defined as social groups that shared a
common origin, history, language, religion, or culture. Barth rejected this
reifying and essentializing approach and defined ethnic groups as "categories of ascription and identification" that people use to classify themselves
and others (1969, 10). The anthropological understanding of the nation
has similarly shifted from a group of people bound together by a set of
shared traits or qualities (blood, race, language, religion, or culture) to
what Benedict Anderson (1991, 15) has called "an imagined political community," a definition that emphasizes the fact that nations are socially and
culturally constructed through complex historical and political processes.

The difference between ethnic groups and nations is generally considered to involve size, degree of politicization, state power, and relationship to a particular territory. Nations, in other words, are large, politicized ethnic groups that exercise, or hope to exercise, state sovereignty over a specific territory.

The area that is now northern Greece was part of the Ottoman Empire until it was incorporated into the Greek state in the early twentieth century. Epirus and Macedonia became part of Greece after the Balkan Wars in 1913, while western Thrace was incorporated into Greece in 1920, shortly after World War I. Under Ottoman rule, the inhabitants of this area were organized into communities known as *millets* based on religion, rather than language or ethnicity. As nationalist ideologies began to develop in the Balkans in the late eighteenth and early nineteenth centuries, people who had previously identified themselves as members of the Orthodox, or *rum*, millet began to develop national identities and gradually came to define themselves as Serbs, Bulgarians, or Greeks. Crucial agents in this nation-building process of assimilation and homogenization were the church, the military, the educational system, and the civil service (Vermeulen 1984).

The Hellenization of the population of northern Greece was greatly facilitated by the exchange of populations between Greece and Turkey that took place in 1923. At this time, the Muslim population of Greece (with the exception of western Thrace) was resettled in Turkey, and over one and a half million Christian refugees from Asia Minor were resettled in Greece. Many of these mostly Greek-speaking refugees were settled in rural areas of Greek Macedonia and Thrace.[9] The Greek state continued its process of nation building throughout northern Greece during the 1920s and 1930s. The Slavic-speaking Christians of Greek Macedonia, many of whom defined themselves as "Bulgarians," "Slav-Macedonians," "Macedonians," or simply "Orthodox," were of particular concern to the Greek government, which referred to them as "Slavophone" or "bilingual" Greeks. During this time Slavic personal and place names were Hellenized, and the speaking of what the Greek government called a "Slavic idiom" was discouraged. During the Metaxas dictatorship that preceded World War II, these policies were applied in a particularly harsh and repressive manner.[10]

The memory of this period of repression affected attitudes of the Slavic-speaking population of Greek Macedonia during the 1940s in different ways. During the first years of the Occupation, some Slavic speakers greeted the German and Italian forces as "liberators" from Greek rule and collaborated with them in fighting against the Greek resistance. Others, however, joined the left-wing resistance because they were attracted by the policies of the Greek Communist Party, which acknowledged the existence of a Macedonian minority in Greece and promised to grant them equal rights after the war. In October 1943, the Greek National Liberation Front reluctantly agreed to the creation of the Slav-Macedonian National Liberation Front (SNOF), which would operate under its command.

Relations between Greek and Macedonian members of the resistance were characterized by intense mutual distrust, which erupted several times into open conflict. Toward the end of the Civil War, when most of the fighting was taking place in border areas inhabited by Slavic speakers, the latter constituted approximately 30 percent of the Democratic Army (Clogg 1979, 163). While the support of the Macedonians of northern Greece was invaluable to the partisans, it also made the partisans vulnerable to charges of treason on the grounds that they supported ceding Greek Macedonia to the Slavs (Close 1995, 95). In the villages of western Macedonia, the majority of Asia Minor refugees, as well as many Slavic speakers who had developed a Greek national identity, supported the Greek government. The divisions between these different ethnic groups had become politicized, and the Civil War took on overtones of a conflict between loyal Greeks on the right and "Slavocommunists" on the left.

This "ethnic dimension" of the Greek Civil War remains a sensitive issue in Greece today. The legislation passed by the socialist government in 1982, which restored the citizenship of political refugees who had left the country at the end of the Civil War and allowed them to return to Greece, applied only to refugees who were "Greeks by birth" (*Ellines to yenos*), specifically excluding people who identified themselves as Macedonians and not Greeks.[11] Since then, many Macedonian refugee children from northern Greece have been refused permission to enter Greece even for short visits. The recent controversies surrounding the name of the newly independent Republic of Macedonia and the recognition of the Macedonian minority in northern Greece also demonstrate that the wounds of the Greek Civil War have still not fully healed.[12]

## Refugee Children in the Discourse of the Greek State and the Greek Communist Party

The position of the Greek government on the evacuation of children from northern Greece by the Communist Party is dramatically evoked by the image on the cover of a booklet entitled *Iron Curtain Holds Greek Children Captive*, published by the Royal Greek Embassy in Washington, DC, in March 1950, as part of the Greek government's campaign to enlist international support for their repatriation. A group of young children silhouetted in black struggle frantically to escape from a barbed wire enclosure. In front of them Greece—personified as Athena with her white tunic, helmet, and shield—kneels, weeping. The caption below reads: "Greece mourns for her 28,000 children abducted by the Communists."

Official Greek discourse on the refugee children has been resolutely nationalist: the young refugees were first and foremost *Greek* children. Regardless of the fact that approximately half of them spoke Macedonian as their first language and that many of their families identified themselves as Macedonians and not Greeks, in official Greek discourse these young refugees were "children of Greece" (Royal Greek Embassy 1950, 25). According to the powerful metaphor of the nation as family, Greece is a mother lamenting her lost children.

In Greek nationalist discourse, the Communist Party's evacuation of the refugee children is generally referred to as the *paidomazoma*, a powerful metaphor referring to *devshirme*, the Ottoman practice of removing Christian children from their families, converting them to Islam, and training them to serve as Janissaries, the elite guards of the Ottoman sultan. Many Greeks consider these children traitors to the Greek nation. BBC correspondent Kenneth Matthews, who worked in Greece during the Civil War, described the emotions associated with the word *paidomazoma* at that time:

> Merely to pronounce the word sent a shiver down the spine, so fraught it seemed with perversion and diabolism. In literal translation it meant no more than "collection of the children" but after its passage through countless horrified lips, "rape of the children" might be a fairer rendering. (Matthews 1972, 177)

A booklet published in 1949 appealing to an international audience for assistance in the Greek government's campaign to bring these children back to Greece employed this metaphor to full effect:

> Greece survived the abduction . . . of many of her male children and their forced conversion to Islamism to form the corps of Janissaries or praetorian guards of the Sultans. Greece will survive the loss of a few thousands of her children of this generation and their forced conversion to totalitarian communism to swell the praetorian guards of the Kremlin and of its satellite states.[13]

In the nationalist discourse of the Greek government, Greek Communists had engaged in a "monstrous . . . plot to strike at Greece through her children." They had "snatched" these children from the arms of their mothers, "abducted" or "kidnapped" them, and taken them on a "death march" across Greece's northern border (Royal Greek Embassy 1950, 5, 6). Then the partisans placed them in "concentration camps," held them as "hostages" or "prisoners," raised them as "Slavs," and trained them to return to Greece to fight as enemies of the Greek state (Royal Greek Embassy 1950, 21). Their goal was to "denationalize" or "dehellenize" a whole generation of Greek children.

With the full support of the Greek government, the queen of Greece led an international public relations campaign calling for the repatriation of the Greek children who had been evacuated to Eastern Europe. Queen Frederica described her own evacuation program, which brought children from northern Greece to children's homes in government-controlled areas of Greece, as an act of "protecting" or "saving" children (*paidofilagma*), in contrast to the Communist Party's program of "kidnapping" or "abducting" children (*paidomazoma*). On December 29, 1949, the day the Greek Orthodox Church commemorates Herod's slaughter of the innocents, the Greek government declared a national day of mourning for the 28,000 Greek children who had been "abducted by Communist bands and forcibly taken into countries that lie behind the Iron Curtain" (Royal Greek Embassy 1950, 21).

On the eve of the commemoration, the queen held a press conference at the Royal Palace in Athens, which was broadcast by radio to Great Britain and the United States. Dressed in black—a mother mourning her lost children—Frederica appealed in the name of the entire Greek nation for international help in bringing about the repatriation of "her" children. After contrasting her own family's joyful celebration of Christmas with the "tortured souls" and "empty arms" of the mothers of the "abducted children," she quoted the words of Jesus Christ: "Suffer the little children to come unto me . . . for of such is the Kingdom of God" (Royal Greek Embassy 1950, 21). The following day, "a two-gun salute from Mount Lykabettus woke Athenians at dawn," newspapers appeared with "black framed front pages," flags were flown at half-mast, church bells tolled all day, and theaters and nightclubs remained closed. The event was also marked by special church services, demonstrations, parades, and a half hour of silence, during which "all traffic stopped, streets emptied, doors were closed and blinds drawn."[14]

The Greek government's discourse on the children evacuated to Eastern Europe was dominated by two sets of powerful imagery: religious and nationalist. The first set of imagery contrasts the atheism of communist ideology with the Orthodox Christianity of the Greek nation. It compares the evacuation program of the Greek Communist Party with Herod's program of infanticide, whose purpose was to kill Christ, the king of the Jews. In her appeal for the return of "her" children, Queen Frederica identifies herself with Mary, the mother of Christ, as the epitome of the loving mother. She also identifies Greece with the kingdom of God, the ideal place for raising Christian children.

In the second set of imagery, the Greek nation, personified as Athena or Queen Frederica herself, is portrayed as a mother mourning her children. These children are symbolically "dead" to the Greek nation because they were "converted" to communism and raised as Slavs, just as the Janissaries were converted to Islam and raised as Turks. The ultimate goal of the Greek government in its international public relations campaign on behalf of the evacuated children was to restore "the national order of things" (Malkki 1992, 25) by returning "the children of Greece" from Eastern Europe to their "homeland" (Royal Greek Embassy 1950, 24, 25). Only in this way could they be restored to full membership in the Greek "national family" (Queen Frederica of the Hellenes 1971, 10).

The positions of the Greek Communist Party and the Greek government were exact opposites and at the same time, paradoxically, exact parallels. According to the Communist Party, the evacuation of children in March 1948 was a response to requests by families in "Free Greece" to send their children to the "democratic" countries of Eastern Europe that had agreed to provide "hospitality" for the "victims of the American conquerors" (Baerentzen 1987, 130). In 1951, the League for Democracy in Greece, a leftist organization founded in London in 1945 to inform British public opinion about the situation in Greece, published a booklet in order to counter the Greek government's international public relations campaign concerning the refugee children. This booklet describes "a vast humanitarian enterprise which rescued . . . helpless children from starvation and misery in their devastated homeland by evacuating them from a battle area . . . with the full consent of their parents," so that they could be "lovingly cared for in a new world of peace and prosperity" (League for Democracy in Greece 1951, 2).

In his 1979 book significantly entitled *Meiname Ellines* (*We Remained Greeks*), Thanasis Mitsopoulos, a former administrator of the Communist Party's educational program in Eastern Europe, writes that the children were evacuated by the partisans to protect them from "the danger they were exposed to by the military operations, the hunger, the diseases, and the generally difficult conditions that prevailed in the isolated mountain regions where military operations were constantly being conducted" (15). According to Mitsopoulos, the majority of children who were evacuated to Eastern Europe were children or close relatives of partisans and were sent with their parents' full consent (17). The goal of the educational program the Communist Party offered the children in Eastern Europe was "the preservation and cultivation of the national consciousness, the Greekness, of so many thousands of Greeks" (193). The homes where the children lived were "little Greek oases," "cradles of patriotic education," whose classrooms were decorated "with our national colors and with pictures of our beautiful fatherland, the heroic accomplishments and cultural achievements of our ancestors, and where Greek songs are taught, Greek holidays celebrated" (64). The ideology of the Greek Communist Party, like that of the Greek government, was strongly nationalist. Unlike the nationalism of the government, however, the nationalism of the Communist Party had no place for the Greek Orthodox Church.

From the communist perspective, the Greek government and Queen Frederica, who was referred to as "a former German princess and one-time member of the Hitler Youth" (League for Democracy in Greece 1951, 4), were the ones guilty of conducting a *paidomazoma* by seizing children against their parents' will and locking them up in "reform schools" and "indoctrination camps," where they were raised as Janissaries and taught to hate their parents, whom Greek officials called "Slavs," "communists," and "traitors to the Greek nation." Queen Frederica, on the other hand, defended and promoted her own campaign to evacuate children from northern Greek villages as absolutely necessary in order to save "her children" from "being carried across the border and being educated as enemies of their country" (Queen Frederica of the Hellenes 1971, 134).

In the discourse of the Greek Communist Party and the Greek government, the refugee children of the Greek Civil War have been portrayed as universal symbols of suffering and misery, as anonymous, powerless victims of forces beyond their control. This is a specific instance of the more general essentializing and universalizing discourse of the "international refugee regime" and the field of refugee studies that was being developed by humanitarian and scholarly organizations of the time. Whether victims of "Slavocommunism" from the perspective of the Greek right, or victims of "monarchofascism" from the perspective of the Greek left, refugee children of the Greek Civil War were victims. From both these perspectives, then, refugee children were denied the agency to participate in, let alone make, the decision to leave their homes. They were also deprived of the ability to determine their own identities and their own futures by accepting or rejecting the ideological content of the education they received. The politically motivated discourse of the Greek Communist Party and the Greek government has focused primarily on the interests of the party and the state rather than on the interests of the children as articulated, whenever possible, by the children themselves.

In the analysis that follows, we demonstrate that both the Greek government and the Greek Communist Party have constructed oversimplified, one-sided accounts of these complex events in which refugee children of the Greek Civil War are portrayed as passive victims of the policies and programs of one side or the other. We show that, on the contrary, these children were active participants in the tragic events they experienced and that, although they were both refugees and children, they were able to construct meaningful lives from the turmoil and chaos of these traumatic experiences. We hope to empower these refugee children by listening carefully to their voices so that we can hear what they have to say for themselves as they narrate the stories of their lives.

# TWO

# The Evacuation of Children to Eastern Europe

I am a child of war. That feeling never left me; it still haunts me today.

—A refugee child from Thrace evacuated to Bulgaria

In the cold spring of 1948, when columns of ragged children were walking through the mountains toward the northern borders of Greece, morale among supporters of the Greek government in Athens was low. During the previous year the Democratic Army had won several important victories, and the Greek press was reporting alarming rumors about an imminent invasion of foreign communist troops from the north and a communist plan to abduct over 80,000 Greek children, take them to Eastern Europe, turn them into Janissaries, and send them back to fight against the Greek state. Many Greeks feared that their country would soon be taken over by "Slavic hordes" and lost forever to the "Western world."

The year 1948, however, marked a major turning point in the Civil War that would eventually lead to the defeat of the Democratic Army. Its inability to capture Konitsa in December 1947 and its defeat on Mount Grammos the next summer meant that it had failed to fulfill the most important goal set by the communist leadership in September 1947: taking control of a large area in northern Greece and establishing a "free Greece" as the locus of an alternative power structure. Nor was the Democratic Army able to realize its second most important goal for 1948, unrealistic as it was: tripling its forces to 60,000 men in just a few months' time (Kondis and Sfetas 1999, 90–91; Margaritis 2000, 341). In a desperate attempt to enlarge its much-needed reserve forces, the leaders of the Democratic Army increasingly resorted to the forced recruitment of men, women, and teenage children.

In the mountain villages of northern Greece, increased fighting, the presence of many partisan troops, and mopping-up operations carried out by the Greek Army had completely disrupted normal village life. Most adult men were absent; they were serving in one of the two opposing armies, they had been imprisoned, or they had escaped to cities under government control or across the border to the north. In areas controlled by the Democratic Army, women and children were being requisitioned to carry the wounded, prepare food, build fortifications, deliver messages, and transport supplies. In areas under the control of the Greek Army, women and the elderly were also used to clear mines.

Schools had been closed since the outbreak of hostilities in 1946, and hunger and disease were rapidly spreading. Daily bombing and heavy shelling had caused many civilian casualties and killed whatever livestock remained. Many people whose villages had been burned down were living in temporary shelters in caves or in forests. These were the circumstances under which officials of the Greek Communist Party decided to evacuate children from the war zone to Eastern Europe.

## Initial Planning for the Evacuation Program

In a pamphlet that was widely publicized in the English-speaking world, the Greek government claimed that the communist leaders had already decided to remove children to Eastern Europe in early 1947 (Royal Greek Embassy 1950, 5). Archival evidence, however, suggests that this decision was reached no earlier than January or February 1948. The first indication that the leaders of the Democratic Army had become alarmed about the humanitarian situation in the area under its control was conveyed in a radio message sent to representatives of the Provisional Democratic Government on January 29, 1948, concerning the outbreak of a typhus epidemic in the Konitsa area. It instructed the representative of the Greek Communist Party in Yugoslavia to ask officials of the Yugoslav Communist Party if they could provide "care for young children from the free zone who suffer from famine and other privations."[1] A week later Yugoslav officials replied that Yugoslavia was ready to host a certain number of children, especially orphans of partisans, and that the other communist countries would help in the effort.[2]

On March 3, 1948, the Democratic Army announced that parents had agreed to move children aged three to thirteen to Poland, Czechoslovakia, Romania, and Yugoslavia and that 4,784 children from fifty-nine villages in the border area had already been enrolled for evacuation. Each group of twenty-five children would be accompanied by a female schoolteacher chosen by the parents. The announcement invoked both humanitarian and military reasons for the operation: children would be saved from the hardships of war, and parents would be able to concentrate all their energy on the war effort. The following day, during the Conference of Balkan Youth in Belgrade, the Balkan countries agreed to accept 12,000 children from "free Greece" and care for them until the end of the Civil War.[3]

The Greek government had been informed of these plans one week earlier through an intercepted radio broadcast from Radio Sofia on February 27, 1948, announcing the imminent arrival of six hundred children in Budapest, Hungary.[4] On the same day, the Greek government lodged an official complaint with the United Nations about the children allegedly abducted by the partisans and taken to Eastern Europe. Although this was a full month before the first children actually crossed the border, the government's public statement about the partisans' "abduction" campaign created widespread panic among the Greek public and eventually led to the escalation of the Greek government's own evacuation program, headed by Queen Frederica, which had already been initiated in July 1947. On March 6, 1948, the government in Athens announced it would move 14,000 children from the "bandit-controlled areas" of the north to southern Greece (Baerentzen 1987, 138).

From this point on, public statements on both sides justifying the two evacuation programs were increasingly influenced by the unfolding propaganda war. As the Greek government's evacuation program expanded, the Democratic Army broadened the scope of its own evacuation program to include children from areas under the control of the National Army. This decision was presented as a response to parents' demands to save their children not only from war and famine, but also from Queen Frederica's evacuation program.[5] Fear among supporters of the partisans was intensified by rumors that the Greek Army was removing children against their parents' will.

Actual preparations for the Democratic Army's evacuation program began in the second half of February 1948. On February 20, Markos Vafiadis, commander general of the Democratic Army, cabled a party official in Belgrade that the preparation for the first phase of the evacuation was proceeding well, that about six thousand children from Slavic-speaking villages would be sent first, and that the total number of children would probably amount to ten thousand.[6] On March 22, the first five hundred children were ready to cross the border into Yugoslavia, but they did not reach Belgrade until March 30 (Ristović 2000, 22).[7]

While the Provisional Democratic Government justified this operation on humanitarian grounds, the removal of children from combat zones also served the Democratic Army's strategic interests. As the Democratic Army prepared for what it thought would be its victorious battle on the high peaks of Mount Grammos near the Albanian border, everyone able to carry a rifle had to be recruited voluntarily or by force. On February 20, the Provisional Democratic Government announced the forced mobilization of women in areas under its control (Vervenioti 2005, 108). The removal of children from the war zone facilitated the mobilization of women by relieving them of their child-care responsibilities, while it also reduced the Democratic Army's burden of feeding the civilian population. Older children could be called back from Eastern Europe to serve as a reserve force for the quickly dwindling partisan forces. Finally, the evacuation of children by both the Democratic Army and the Greek Army effectively served to hold the local population "hostage" to whichever side had custody of their children (Margaritis 2001, 610).

## Counting the Refugee Children

More than fifty years after the fact, there still is considerable confusion as to the exact number of children involved in the evacuation program of the Greek Communist Party (Vervenioti 2005, 108–10). Official figures have varied from 25,000 (cited by sources close to the Greek Communist Party) to 28,000 (cited by the Greek government). Yet these sources ignore the fact that many of these children had crossed the border with their families long before the evacuation program was planned. By the end of 1947, there were 25,000 refugees from Greece living in Albania and 18,000 in Yugoslavia, nearly 14,000 of whom had settled in the People's Republic of Macedonia (Kondis and Sfetas 1999, 110–11). Among these refugees there were many children—more than 6,000 in Yugoslavia alone—most of whom were living with relatives. Although a small percentage of these children eventually became residents of children's homes in Yugoslavia or elsewhere in Eastern Europe, most of them remained with their families.

In most sources these children are included in the total number of children evacuated by the partisans. Although both groups left for similar reasons, from the children's perspective there was a tremendous difference between living in exile with their families and living apart from their families with other children in children's homes. The focus of this chapter is on the experiences of the latter group of children, in other words, children who, during the first years of their exile, lived *apart* from their parents in the institutional environment of the children's homes operated by the Greek Communist Party in Eastern Europe.

Statistics on the movements of refugee children were kept by the Yugoslav Red Cross, the Greek Communist Party, and the Greek Committee for Child Support (EVOP), an organization specifically established by the Greek Communist Party in 1948 to oversee the education and welfare of the refugee children. Table 1 offers a comparative overview of these data. The second column presents the data of the Yugoslav Red Cross on the numbers of children sent from Yugoslavia to other Eastern European countries in 1948. The third column presents the numbers of children settled in children's homes in Eastern Europe as they were registered by EVOP in June 1949. The fourth column gives the total number of refugee children settled in Eastern Europe (excluding Yugoslavia) in October 1950, as they were presented at the Third Plenum of the Central Committee of the Greek Communist Party.

The October 1950 report of the Greek Communist Party "ignored" the children who remained in Yugoslavia for political reasons. Since July 1949, when General Tito broke with Stalin and closed Yugoslavia's borders with Greece, the Greek Communist Party officially regarded Yugoslavia as an "enemy state." According to the Yugoslav Red Cross, in early 1950 there were 9,119 refugee children left in Yugoslavia, 7,274 of whom were living with their parents or other relatives, while the remaining 1,845 were living

Table 1. Refugee children in Eastern Europe

| Country | Yusoglav Red Cross estimate (1948)[1] | Children registered by EVOP (1949)[2] | Children resettled according to Greek Communist Party (1950)[3] |
|---|---|---|---|
| Romania | 3,300 (April 1948) 3,105 (Dec. 1948) | 5,000 | 5,132 |
| Czechoslovakia | 2,492 (April 1948) 561 (Jan. 1949) | 3,000 | 4,148 |
| Poland | 150 (April 1948) | 2,500 | 3,590 |
| Hungary | 2,254 (April 1948) 797 (Dec. 1948) | 2,500 | 2,859 |
| Bulgaria | n.a. | 2,500 | 672 |
| East Germany | n.a. | 700 | 1,268 |
| Yugoslavia | n.a. | 11,000 | n.d. |
| TOTAL | 12,659 | 27,200 | 17,669 |

[1]From Ristović (2000, 28).
[2]From Martinova-Buckova (1998, 33).
[3]From Kirijazovski (1989, 37).

in children's homes run by the Yugoslav Red Cross (Ristović 2000, 96). Adding this number to the 17, 669 total cited by the Greek Communist Party produces approximately the same number—26,788—as the EVOP report of 1949. Consequently, it is safe to conclude that the total number of refugee children in Eastern Europe, including Yugoslavia, was about 27,000. This does not mean, however, that all 27,000 had been part of the *formal evacuation program* of the Democratic Army. Since most of the 7,000 children living with their families in Yugoslavia had arrived there with their relatives long before the evacuation started, the number of children formally evacuated by the Democratic Army can be estimated at approximately 20,000.[8]

All evacuated children were first given temporary shelter in Albania, Yugoslavia, or Bulgaria. Since they were the poorest countries in the communist bloc, these three countries were unable to cope with this sudden stream of hungry and often sick children. The situation reached crisis proportions in Albania. By the first week of April 1948, four thousand children had gathered in southern Albania, near Korçe; a few days later their number had reached six thousand.[9] Children were forced to beg for food or to fend for themselves by eating orange peels or the leaves of leeks. Some older boys tried to walk back to their villages in Greece; a few actually managed to do so (Manoukas 1961, 20; Raptis 1999, 58–67). Under these circumstances there was an urgent need to transport the children further north where they could receive better care. Although this was actually part of the initial evacuation plan, most of the children and their parents believed that they would remain in Albania, Yugoslavia, or Bulgaria for a short time and then return to their homes. It was only when the children left Belgrade by train heading north for other countries in Eastern Europe that they realized they were setting off on a long journey that would take them further away from home than they could ever possibly have imagined.

Children in Albania were loaded onto trucks and taken to Bitola in Yugoslavia. From there they were transported by train to Romania, Czechoslovakia, and Hungary in April and December 1948 (Martinova-Buckova 1998, 40–41). Poland was initially reluctant to receive refugee children from Greece, and for a long time denied it was hosting any refugee children at all. According to oral accounts, many refugee children were moved from Romania and Albania to Poland in the autumn of 1948, while others arrived there in the spring of 1949 from Yugoslavia and Romania. Additional refugee children (together with adult refugees) reached Poland directly from Albania by boat after the defeat of the Democratic Army in the fall of 1949.

From Bulgaria most children were moved to Hungary and East Germany in the summer of 1950. Only about 1,200 refugee children, nearly all of them Greek-speaking, were settled in East Germany. The first group of children arrived in the Dresden area in August 1949 from Albania by way of Czechoslovakia (Troebst 2004). A year later they were joined by children from the Evros region in Greek Thrace, who were sent there from Bulgaria. These children were terrified when they learned they were being sent to Germany. They had no idea that Nazi Germany, whose soldiers had caused so much suffering in their villages, had ceased to exist and that the Iron Curtain now divided Germany and all of Europe into two opposing worlds.

## Departures

In the discourse of both the Greek government and the Greek Communist Party, the evacuation of children from northern Greece in 1948 and 1949 was presented in drastically oversimplified terms: the children were either "kidnapped" against the will of their parents or "saved" from the horror of war with the full consent of their parents. In fact, the movement of adults and children across the border was considerably more complex. Oral accounts identify three different sets of circumstances that led to the departure of children from their homes: first, organized evacuations of children from border areas in the spring of 1948; second, unorganized, often chaotic departures throughout 1948 and 1949; and third, organized compulsory evacuations of entire villages carried out forcefully by the Democratic Army near the end of the Civil War. In the politicized master narratives of the left and right, these three different cases are often conflated and, depending on the political views of the narrator, presented as either completely "voluntary" or completely "forced."

Between March and July of 1948, 14,827 children were evacuated from northern Greece to Eastern Europe by the Greek Communist Party (Kirijazovski 1989, 37; Mitsopoulos 1979, 16). Most of these children left their villages between the end of March and mid-April and came from the Slavic-speaking areas of Kastoria, Florina, and Aridea (see map 2). As the radio messages exchanged between the Democratic Army and communist officials in Eastern Europe indicate, in most cases the children's departures were planned and carried out in a relatively orderly manner. In villages under partisan control, local leaders announced the evacuation program, explained the reasons why the children were being removed, and asked parents to volunteer their children for participation in the program. Then they compiled a list of all the children who were to be evacuated.

Map 2. Epirus and Greek Macedonia

During what were sometimes angry and hostile meetings, parents, or in their absence grandparents, aunts and uncles, and even older siblings, were initially reluctant to let the children go. In the end, many parents agreed, sometimes under duress, to enroll their children in the program. Many others, however, simply refused. Some parents agreed to send only one or two of their children and insisted on keeping the others at home. In some villages, all the children left for Eastern Europe, especially in Slavic-speaking areas or in villages where children had already been killed by bombing, shelling, or land mines. In other villages, however, only a few children departed at this stage of the war, and they were generally members of left-wing families or children who had no one in the village to take care of them.

Children between the ages of three and fourteen were eligible for evacuation, but often younger or older children were included as well. In some cases, parents lied about their children's ages so that they would be included in the evacuation program and not left behind in the village to be injured in the fighting or conscripted by the partisans. The village council or the local communist organization chose the women who would accompany the children to their final destinations. Each of these women was responsible for a group of twenty to twenty-five children and had to sign a form with the names of all the children in the group she was responsible for.

The criteria on which these women were chosen varied from village to village, but moral reputation, political reliability, degree of education, and family situation were all taken into account. Teachers, widows of partisans, young women whose brothers were fighting in the Democratic Army, women who would have been recruited themselves had they stayed behind, and young mothers whose own children were enrolled in the evacuation program were preferred. These "group leaders" or "mothers" would play a crucial role in the lives of the children they were responsible for.

After saying good-bye to their parents and grandparents, the children set off from their villages on foot. Their journey across the border was dominated by cold, hunger, and fear. Partisan soldiers led long columns of children and "mothers" over snow-covered mountain paths. They often traveled at night and hid in the forest during the day to avoid the bombing runs of the Greek Air Force. Older children carried their younger brothers and sisters on their backs. Some parents accompanied their children for part of the journey (see fig. 3).

Refugee children took four main routes to the border. Children from the Florina area spent the night after their departure in the village of Andartiko. The next day they walked along the shores of the Prespa Lakes,

3. A column of refugee children being evacuated from their villages by the Greek Communist Party. They are walking along a dirt road through the mountains of northern Greece on their way to a reception center in Albania or the former Yugoslavia. Photograph courtesy of the Macedonian Museum in Skopje.

crossed the border into Yugoslavia, and spent the next night in Dupeni or Ljubojno, the first villages they reached in Yugoslav territory. There they joined hundreds of other children with very little to eat, sleeping in stables or schools, and covered with fleas and lice. Children from the Konitsa and Kastoria areas walked to the Albanian border; from there they were taken to Korçe or Elbasan, where they were given temporary shelter. Children from the Greek-speaking villages of the Pindus range (around Grevena and Kozani) followed the same route, but had to walk for several days, while children from the region of Aridea further east crossed the Yugoslav border near Gevgelija. These three routes converged at the railway station in Bitola, from where the children were taken to Eastern Europe by train (see fig. 4.). Children from the district of Evros in Greek Thrace crossed the Rhodope Mountains into Bulgaria, where they were settled in temporary shelters, holiday resorts, or children's homes until their departure for other countries two years later.

Not all departures were part of the organized evacuation program carried out by the Communist Party. Some children crossed the border in panic, sometimes, but not always, accompanied by adults. When government soldiers forcibly removed about two hundred children from the

4. Young refugee children and their "mothers" getting off a train at a station in Skopje on their way to their final destinations elsewhere in Eastern Europe. Photograph courtesy of the Macedonian Museum in Skopje.

be repatriated to their villages. Although the Minister of Welfare advocated their immediate repatriation, the process did not begin until the summer of 1950. In this way children were able to complete the school year they had begun in the paidopoleis. But this was not the only reason. Once again, the repatriation process revealed the close association of humanitarian and ideological concerns. The committee stated that "the appropriate prerequisite" for the children's repatriation was "the healthy national beliefs of their parents and the safety of their place of residence" (Vervenioti 1999, 6). Children would remain in the paidopoleis if both their parents had died, had not yet been repatriated to their villages from government-controlled territory, had supported the communist cause, were in prison, or were in exile in Eastern Europe. The Executive Committee of the Queen's Fund explicitly stated that children whose parents were partisans should be treated as "orphans" and required to remain under the protection of the Queen's Fund in order to be saved from "anti-national" propaganda (Mela n.d., 87; Vervenioti 2001, 18). The Queen's Fund, in other words, considered these parents "dead." By betraying the nation, they had forfeited their rights as parents to care for their children. It became the responsibility of the Greek state, therefore, to intervene and take care of these "orphan" children.

On June 3, 1950, the first group of children to be repatriated were taken by army truck from paidopoleis in Thessaloniki to their villages in the Florina region (Mela n.d., 88). In some cases, both the children and their parents realized there was no future for them there, so the children returned to the paidopoleis in Thessaloniki to continue their education. Several weeks later, on June 24, 1950, over three thousand children from paidopoleis throughout Greece celebrated the repatriation of children from the paidopoleis to their villages at the Tomb of the Unknown Soldier in Syntagma Square in the center of Athens. This ceremony provided children of the paidopoleis an opportunity to express their gratitude to "the armed forces whose heroism had saved them" from the communists and "to send a message of protest to the countries of the Free World concerning the continued detention of the kidnapped Greek children" (Vervenioti 2005, 119).

Over the following decade a small but steady stream of refugee children returned from Eastern Europe to their villages in Greece where they had been born. Many of them found it difficult to adapt to the poverty and isolation of village life, and some of them were sent away again, this time to paidopoleis or to the Royal Technical School of Leros. According to minutes of the Executive Committee of the Queen's Fund, in most cases parents of children who had returned from Eastern Europe applied for their children's admission to a paidopoli (Vervenioti 2001, 21); in other cases children were encouraged by a teacher, a police officer, or the village president to apply.

For these children, leaving their families again was a desperate step taken in the hope of escaping the restrictions of village life and obtaining an education or finding a job in the city. From the perspective of the Greek government, however, this was also a chance to "reeducate" children who had been exposed for years to the "indoctrination" of "Slavocommunists" in Eastern Europe. As the Greek minister of foreign affairs put it in a confidential report, the Queen's Fund had an obligation "to take care of the national education of the repatriated Greek children in order to rid them of the virus of anti-national propaganda" (Vervenioti 2001, 21). A 1957 account of the first ten years of the Queen's Fund claims that the "family atmosphere" of the paidopoleis, with the help of the "Greek blood that flowed in their veins," would allow these young repatriates to "become model Greek children" (Vasiliki Pronoia 1957, 50).

Some of these repatriated refugees describe this offer as a genuine effort to help them readjust to life in Greece by obtaining an education or learning a trade. One young man who had recently returned from Hungary to his village north of Konitsa described joining a group of thirty or forty repatriated refugee children from nearby villages in a convoy of army trucks on their way to Ziro. He recalled a good friend of his who wanted to come with them but who was not allowed to because his grandparents needed him to stay in the village to take care of them when they grew old. A young woman from a village near Florina who had just returned from Yugoslavia had the opportunity to go to a paidopoli, but she refused because she was afraid she would be forced to forget her mother tongue, Macedonian.

Many of the repatriated refugee children who were sent to the Royal Technical School of Leros found it to be a very unpleasant experience. A Macedonian refugee child said Leros was nothing more than a "reformatory" (anamorfotirio) whose only purpose was to convince him that he was Greek. Several Macedonian refugee children who had been repatriated from Eastern Europe said that while they were on Leros they were treated like "black sheep." They were called "Bulgarians," and they were forced to stand up in public and tell lies about how terrible their lives in Eastern Europe had been.

Some of these repatriated refugee children, however, described their time on Leros less harshly, calling it simply "a waste of time," since the education and training they received there were vastly inferior to what they had received in Eastern Europe. The Greek government just wanted to help them forget the anger and the hatred they felt as a result of the treatment they had received during the Civil War. "They put us in quarantine" one said, "so they could calm us down a little bit." Another said, somewhat ambivalently, "They were *royal* technical schools. They tried to make you a royalist, but at least they made you a human being."

In 1950, after the Civil War had ended, 16,000 of the 18,000 children who had been housed in the paidopoleis were repatriated to their villages. The 2,000 children unable to return to their homes because their parents had died, were missing, or had been imprisoned or sentenced to death as communists, continued to live in the nine paidopoleis and the three royal technical schools that remained open after the war (Brouskou 1989, 78). After the program to repatriate children from the paidopoleis to their homes was well underway, Queen Frederica grew concerned about the children's ability to adjust to life in villages that had suffered such terrible destruction during the Civil War. In March 1950, therefore, the queen decided to establish a system of youth centers, known as *"spitia tou paidiou"* (children's homes), in small villages along Greece's northern border. By 1957 over 27,000 children were attending programs at one of these village youth centers (Vasiliki Pronoia 1957, 43).

The young women who staffed these village youth centers, many of whom had either taught at, or "graduated" from, paidopoleis themselves, were responsible for cultivating the children's "patriotic and religious sentiments" (Mela n.d., 121). Because she was particularly concerned with the future of children from Macedonian-speaking villages in the districts of Florina and Kastoria, Queen Frederica decided to establish nursery schools in the youth centers there. The administrators of the Queen's Fund believed that if children from "Slavic-speaking" villages were taught to speak Greek at a very early age, then "that barbarous mixture of dialects" would certainly disappear (Mela n.d., 204–5, Vasiliki Pronoia 1957, 45).

These youth centers provided village children with entertainment in the form of organized games, sports, and movies shown by traveling teams of projectionists. They also offered a variety of educational and vocational programs presented in a manner that served to reinforce the traditional gender roles and the division of labor characteristic of rural Greek society at the time. Boys were trained in construction, ironworking, furniture making, shoe repair, and beekeeping. Girls were given lessons in child care, first aid, embroidery, sewing, weaving, and cooking. Finally, the centers offered programs in public health, animal husbandry, and agriculture to the entire village.[19] In the 1960s the Queen's Fund was responsible for the operation of some 250 youth centers serving over 50,000 children in villages throughout northern Greece.

## Ideology and Goals of the Paidopoleis

The political ideology that pervaded the paidopoleis and all the programs of the Queen's Fund was resolutely nationalist. In what Voutira and Brouskou (2000, 98) have called a system of "education as indoctrination," children in paidopoleis were taught to become loyal citizens of the Greek state and full members of the Greek nation. According to the basic tenets of traditional Greek nationalism, Greece was a nation-state, a state whose citizens were all members of the same culturally homogeneous community, the Greek nation.

The defining characteristics of the Greek nation, according to the particular version of Greek nationalist ideology that dominated Greek society in the decades after the Civil War, were first and foremost Orthodox Christianity and the Greek language. That is why communism, associated as it was with atheism and Slavic-speaking peoples to the north, has been perceived by Greek nationalists as such a serious threat to both the sovereignty of the Greek state and the purity of the Greek nation. Other important values in traditional Greek national ideology include xenophobia, a commitment to the nuclear family, and support for the military and the monarchy.[20]

For these reasons absolute dedication to the values of "Greek-Christian civilization" and implacable opposition to the evils of "Slavocommunism" played a central role in the life of the paidopoleis (Hasiotis 2009, 287–89). The link between good citizenship, Greek national culture, and Christianity is emphasized in a report on the activities of the Queen's Fund published in 1949: "The spirit of citizenship constitutes the basic component of the educational program [of the paidopoleis]. Every effort is made to . . . [keep] alive the ideals of their country's religion and national traditions."[21] The function of the paidopoleis was not only to provide room and board for Greek children displaced by the Civil War. It was "to cultivate the national convictions of the children," which had been "dulled" or "blunted," and to destroy the "bad habits" they had acquired as a result of the communist teachings to which they had been exposed (Vasiliki Pronoia 1957, 39).

The nationalism that dominated life in the paidopoleis was expressed by the director of the entire system of paidopoleis, a general in the Greek Army, during a visit he made to the Paidopoli of Saint Christopher on the island of Syros. He told the children there: "You all understand the reason why you are here: the danger our fatherland is facing from an enemy who wants to destroy our country and change our language and our religion. They want to make you Slavs, so that you will hate your own fatherland" (Voutira and Brouskou 2000, 102).

Children evacuated to paidopoleis whose mother tongue was not Greek became obvious targets of the program of eradication of "barbarous dialects," which was one of the goals of the educational system of the Queen's Fund. When John Tolios, a Macedonian from a village near Florina who lives now in Toronto, arrived at a paidopoli in Thessaloniki, he spoke no Greek at all. Since children there were not allowed to speak Macedonian, John learned Greek very quickly. After seven years, he said, he had completely forgotten "his own language." Many years later at his home in suburban Toronto, John observed matter-of-factly: "They had these schools so they could Greekonize you."

Anticommunism also permeated every aspect of the children's lives. In the paidopoleis the partisans were generally referred to as "bandits," "criminals," or "traitors." The following passage from an essay written by a child living in a paidopoli demonstrates the virulent anticommunism that held sway there:

> [The partisans] burned villages, destroyed homes, annihilated whole families, murdered innocent victims, and worst of all, kidnapped Greek children from the arms of their mothers and sent them to enemy countries. But the Greek soul resisted with all its might, and armed young Greeks freed our land from the Slavic hordes. Fortunately for us our Great Queen, our loving mother, saved us from the claws of the enemies of our fatherland by gathering us together in the paidopoleis. (Gritzonas 1998, 124–25)

The children of the paidopoleis encountered this ideological message in songs, classes, speeches, and lectures. As adults, however, many former residents of paidopoleis downplay its significance; they say it had minimal impact on them both at the time and later on in their lives. As one man who spent much of his childhood in a paidopoli put it, the attempt to "inoculate" them with right-wing propaganda "didn't take." Other children, however, were deeply affected by the ideological component of the education they received. One boy from a Macedonian-speaking family who lived in a paidopoli for several years insisted on speaking Greek with his parents after his return to his village, even though they did not understand a word he said.

Many children whose parents supported the partisans found it very difficult to deal with this aspect of their "education as indoctrination." They knew it was *their parents* that officials of the paidopoleis were portraying as evil villains, and they knew that this was not true. The dissonance generated by this anticommunist message presented a challenge that many children struggled with for the rest of their lives. It was as if they were living in two different worlds, an official, public world in which the "Slavocommunists" were the enemy, on the one hand, and a private world of home and family in which the Greek government was the enemy, on the other (Dalianis-Karambatzakis 1994, 187).

The royalist character of the ideology promoted in the paidopoleis is self-evident. Queen Frederica was the benefactor and savior of all Greek children. She was praised in songs and poems recited by the children on official occasions, and her photograph hung on classroom walls next to religious icons and portraits of Greek national heroes. The central feature of the queen's position in the ideological world of the paidopoleis was her identification as the "mother" of all the children who inhabited it. While the wife of the head of state is often designated the "First Lady," Queen Frederica was the "First Mother of Greece." She was also the "Mother of all Greek children" and the "Mother of the Orphans" (Papanicolaou 1994, 164, 381).

The metaphor of Queen Frederica as mother is part of a larger system of nationalist imagery in which members of the nation, like members of a family, are bound together in a single entity through "primordial attachments, . . . the assumed 'givens' of social existence," which include religion, language, kinship, and blood (Geertz 1973, 259). This metaphor has particular force when it is employed by representatives of the state while they are engaged in the process of removing children from their parents and placing them in the care of state institutions. The metaphor of queen as mother serves to legitimate the classification of leftist parents in wartorn villages as unable or unfit to care for their children, or even worse, as "dead." It also justifies the Greek government's decision to classify the children as "orphans" and assume responsibility for them by taking the place of their biological parents. As Karen Dubinsky points out, "when the nation becomes the parent, birth parents disappear," and from that point on, the children belong to the nation (2007, 146).[22]

The staff of the paidopoleis exploited this metaphor to the fullest by portraying Queen Frederica and King Paul as good parents who cared lovingly for "their children," in contrast to the children's own parents, who were portrayed as more devoted to their political ideals than they were to the welfare of their children. The director of the Paidopoli of the Holy Trinity described the biological mothers of the children living there as having "ceded their place" to the young Greek women working at the paidopoli, who were serving there as representatives of the queen (Georgitsa-Papadimitrakopoulou 1997, 486–87).

The conflict between these two maternal figures—Queen Frederica, the good mother, and the children's biological mother, the bad mother—generated a great deal of conflict for many children from leftist families. Niki was born in 1948 while her mother was being held in Averof Prison. Niki's mother had been arrested, tortured, and sentenced to twelve years in prison for serving as a messenger in the Democratic Army. Niki lived in three paidopoleis between 1951 and 1962 and often participated in ceremonies held to welcome the queen during her official visits. Once Niki sent a photograph of herself sitting on the queen's lap to her mother. Her mother just tore it up and threw it away (Dalianis-Karambatzakis 1994, 153).

In addition to raising the children entrusted to their care as full members of the Greek nation, the staff of the paidopoleis also made a determined effort to assimilate them into middle-class Greek society, to "civilize" them by transforming them from "backward" and "ignorant" peasants into model citizens of the new Greek state. After she visited the Royal Technical School of Leros, Queen Frederica wrote, "The impression they made on me was that they were subhuman. They looked like animals" (1971, 102). When the first children arrived at the Paidopoli of the Holy Trinity, the director described them as "wild men who could never be educated" (Georgitsa-Papadimitrakopoulou 1997, 133). They had to learn how to walk in shoes, take showers, brush their teeth, and use toilets. They also had to learn how to sing the national anthem and say their prayers. They even had to learn how to celebrate Christmas (Brouskou 1989, 77, Gritzonas 1998, 92; Queen Frederica of the Hellenes 1971, 103). A former resident of the Paidopoli of Saint Iakovos on the island of Mytilini said that when he returned home he began to look down on his fellow villagers, as if they were "people from the Third World, from Asia or Africa." He wondered if he had really been a human being before coming to the paidopoli (Keskini 2003, 36).

The system of imagery used by the "queen's ladies" and administrators of the paidopoleis to describe the upward social mobility of the children under their care is an expression of the strong class bias and the fear of the "uncivilized peasant" that is often found among the middle class and the elite of Greek society. This imagery is often associated with civilizing missions of various kinds. It involves the transformation of the natural into the cultural, the primitive into the civilized, and the nonhuman into the human. This imagery often engenders a powerful sense of alienation and inferiority in the people who are its targets.

The ultimate goal of the programs administered by the Queen's Fund was not simply to encourage the children of the paidopoleis to embrace the values of the urban middle class for their own benefit; it was to raise the standard of living in the villages of rural Greece through an ambitious project of reconstruction and modernization. The primary agents of this transformation were to be the young "graduates" of the paidopoleis, who would return to their homes and share with their fellow villagers the new knowledge, skills, and values they had acquired. In this way the inhabitants of the poorest and most ethnically diverse regions of Greece would enjoy an improved standard of living and become full members of Greek society. On the second anniversary of the founding of the Paidopoli of the Holy Trinity, the director urged her charges to be "ready and fully armed for the glorious struggle, for the rebuilding (*anoikodomisi*) of their villages" (Georgitsa-Papadimitrakopoulou 1997, 486).

The children of the paidopoleis would be assisted in this task by the establishment of youth centers and rural self-help programs in the isolated mountain villages where they lived. The periodical *Paidopolis*, which first appeared in 1950 and continued publication under the new name *Spiti tou Paidiou* (Children's Home) until 1969, was an important component of the campaign conducted by the Queen's Fund to promote Greek nationalism to the young people of rural Greece. According to the American embassy, this periodical also made an important contribution to the "dissemination of American ideals to the children of Greece" (Hasiotis 2009, 284). The first issue presented a message from Queen Frederica to the children of the paidopoleis encouraging them to "return [to their villages] and help their parents and friends rebuild their destroyed houses" (2009, 291). It also contained a "fairy tale" about a hideous firebreathing dragon that had descended from the north to seize the young children of Greece from the arms of their mothers. The terrified children were saved when Queen Frederica welcomed them to her castle and the dragon, mortally wounded, fled north to die.

The administrators of the Queen's Fund hoped to slow the rate at which rural areas of northern Greece were being depopulated as a result of migration to the urban centers of Thessaloniki and Athens, as well as to Western Europe, Canada, and Australia. According to members of the Executive Committee of the Queen's Fund, children in the paidopoleis should be taught to "love their villages" by developing a "rural consciousness," because if the process of urbanization occurred too quickly it would undermine the social and economic order of the entire country (Vervenioti 2001, 18). Executive Committee members were concerned that a rapid increase in the population of Greece's few large cities would run the risk of contributing to the creation of a restless urban proletariat or an educated elite that would cause political problems for the ruling right-wing political establishment.

This danger is specifically cited in a 1949 booklet promoting the activities of the Queen's Fund, which stressed that nothing was being done at the paidopoleis "to alienate the children from their native rural surroundings . . . or to direct their thoughts and aims toward the large towns, with their already too great number of intellectuals and overcrowded liberal professions."[23] Officials of the Queen's Fund were not committed to giving the children of the paidopoleis a strong secondary education, since their goal was to ensure that each child "returned to and remained in his village" (Vasiliki Pronoia 1957, 41). A Macedonian refugee child who spent a year at the Royal Technical School of Leros after his return from Romania understood this clearly. "The main purpose," he said, "was not to make you rich, not to open your eyes too much, but to teach you very basic skills so you could settle in your village." He was able to avoid this fate himself by emigrating first to Athens and then to Canada.

The ideology that dominated life in the paidopoleis was marked by a fundamental contradiction. On the one hand, the educational program there was designed to assimilate children into Greek national society and culture by instilling in them urban middle-class values. This goal inevitably involved the denigration of rural Greek villagers as backward peasants. On the other hand, the educational program of the paidopoleis attempted simultaneously to present a positive and highly romanticized image of traditional rural Greek society and culture in order to encourage the children to return to their villages and play a leading role in their reconstruction.

This conflict was never resolved. Most children in the paidopoleis did not receive a secondary education or the kind of vocational training that would enable them to participate successfully in an urban economy. Instead, they were given a primary education and trained as cobblers or carpenters, seamstresses or housewives, and sent back to the villages of their birth. The fact that after their repatriation many of these children left their villages again in search of better lives elsewhere suggests that this effort to fight the depopulation of the northern Greek countryside was largely unsuccessful. Census data for the area during the postwar period confirm this view (Laiou 1987), as do the ruins that stand as silent monuments to the many villages in the mountains of northern Greece that were abandoned after the Civil War. The pace of development and modernization in these villages could not match the new expectations for a higher standard of living that the paidopoleis had raised. Although it may have "saved the children," the evacuation program of the queen could not "save" their villages.

## The Evacuation Programs of the Greek Communist Party and the Queen's Fund: A Comparison

The evacuation of children from the war-torn villages of northern Greece to children's homes in Eastern Europe by the Greek Communist Party and the evacuation of children from the same areas to paidopoleis in Greece by the Queen's Fund have generally been approached from one of two partisan political perspectives. Supporters of the Greek government have characterized the evacuation program of the Communist Party as an act of "kidnapping," and that of the Queen's Fund as an act of "saving," the children of northern Greece. Supporters of the Communist Party use the same terms, but in reverse.

An analysis of the two evacuation programs together, however, reveals striking similarities. Each program was motivated by a combination of humanitarian, strategic, and ideological concerns. Each side was genuinely concerned with providing a safe haven for children whose lives were endangered by military activity in their villages. The partisans depended on the civilian population under their control to meet their logistical needs, and the Greek government sought to deprive them of this base of support. The partisans conscripted some of the children they evacuated and forced them to return to the front lines to fight. The Greek government drafted all men over the age of eighteen to serve in the national army.

In addition, each side attempted to instill in the children it evacuated an ideology that would prepare them to rebuild Greek society according to the specific political model that it envisioned for the future of Greece. The Greek Communist Party sought to produce a generation of skilled factory workers, managers, and engineers who were loyal party members and who would contribute to the creation of the new socialist states of Eastern Europe and build a new, "democratic" and socialist Greece. The goal of the Greek government, on the other hand, was to produce a generation of young people who were loyal to a royalist and capitalist Greek state and who would return to their villages to improve the standard of living there without threatening the class hierarchy, gender roles, and family values of traditional Greek culture. Finally, each side fully exploited the two evacuation programs for propaganda purposes in both the domestic and the international public relations campaigns that marked the early years of the Cold War.

Both the Greek Communist Party and the Greek government evacuated children from their villages under a variety of circumstances that ranged widely along a "spectrum of coercion" from "voluntary" to "forced." Families were often willing to enroll their children in the evacuation program carried out by the side they supported, while they often hid their children to prevent them from being taken away by the side they considered their enemy. Some families sent their children away with "their" side to prevent them from being taken by the "other" side. There were families in which one child was evacuated to Eastern Europe and another to a paidopoli. There were also children who were taken first to Eastern Europe and then to a paidopoli after their return to Greece.

The programs established by the Greek Communist Party and the Queen's Fund to house the evacuated children under their care were similar in many ways as well. The Greek Communist Party was responsible for 20,000 children living in eighty homes throughout Eastern Europe, while the Queen's Fund cared for 18,000 children living in fifty-four paidopoleis in Greece. As institutions, the children's homes in Eastern Europe and the paidopoleis were very similar. They were all "total institutions" in which children were raised in a strictly regimented and highly politicized environment.

Although material conditions varied among the children's homes in Eastern Europe and the paidopoleis, children were generally well cared for, given the economic limitations and the child rearing conventions of the societies in which they were raised. In each program the children encountered devoted caregivers and teachers, on the one hand, and those who were harsh and incompetent, on the other. They were also given a range of educational and vocational opportunities, although the nature of these opportunities was very different and their quality seems to have been better in Eastern Europe.

Children in each program were subjected to a strong campaign of ideological indoctrination. In Eastern Europe they were "the children of Stalin," who would grow up to become model workers and party members in a new socialist Greece, while in the paidopoleis they were "the children of Frederica," who would grow up to become full members of the Greek nation and loyal citizens of the Greek state, contributing their new skills to the modernization of life in rural Greece. Charges by the Greek government to the contrary, Greek children evacuated to Eastern Europe did not lose their identity as Greeks; they retained it, just as many Macedonian children who were evacuated to Eastern Europe retained their identity as Macedonians. As they became assimilated into the Eastern European societies where they lived, however, these children also acquired identities as Romanians, Hungarians, Czechs, and Poles. Later still, many of them became Canadians and Australians.

There was, however, one fundamental difference that distinguished the experiences of children evacuated to paidopoleis in Greece from those of children evacuated to Eastern Europe: the amount of time they were separated from their families. By 1950, 16,000 of the 18,000 children living in paidopoleis had returned to their villages and been reunited with their parents. The vast majority of children evacuated by the Queen's Fund, in other words, lived apart from their families for less than two years. The experiences of children taken to Eastern Europe could not have been more different. By the end of 1951, less than three hundred of the 20,000 children living in children's homes in Eastern Europe had been repatriated to Greece, all of them from Yugoslavia (Ristović 2000, 84). By 1958, ten years after their departure, only 5,000 had returned to Greece, although many children had been reunited with their parents inside Eastern Europe. While many Greek political refugees returned to Greece in the early 1980s, those who had been evacuated as children in 1948 were by then adults. The vast majority of children evacuated to Eastern Europe by the Greek Communist Party, therefore, spent their entire childhood away from their families without the love and care of their parents. As children, they never saw their parents again.

The reasons for this fundamental difference between the two evacuation programs are many. The Greek Communist Party lost the Civil War, and its leaders were evacuated to Eastern Europe. Unlike children evacuated to paidopoleis, children evacuated to Eastern Europe were taken across international boundaries and across what was to become the Iron Curtain. Meaningful cooperation between Greece and the countries of Eastern Europe was precluded by Cold War tensions, the same tensions that led the Greek government to abandon its early support for the repatriation of refugee children and block the return of political refugees it considered "undesirable." The two evacuation programs, while similar in many ways, had a dramatically different impact on the lives of the children who participated in them.

# PART TWO

# Stories

FOUR

# Refugee Children in Eastern Europe

## Kostas Tsimoudis[1]

*Kostas Tsimoudis, a Greek refugee child, was born on July 15, 1937, in the village of Mavroklisi in Thrace about twenty kilometers from the Turkish border. When he retired from his job in Germany in 2000, he returned to Greece and bought a spacious apartment in Alexandroupolis, where he and his wife now live surrounded by modern furniture, old photographs, and shelves of books. In 1998, Kostas wrote a book in German about his experiences during and after the Civil War. He called it* A Modern Greek Odyssey. *Kostas' continued ties with Germany, where he lived most of his life, seem to have kept him young, active, and engaged with the wider world.*

### Civil War

My mother died in 1943 and left my father with six young children. The youngest was three, I was six, and my oldest sister was fifteen. I was seven years old when the Germans left. What I remember most is the terror and the injustice that existed when they were gone. I don't even think my father knew what "right wing" and "left wing" meant. He was never a member of any party; he was practically illiterate. We thought that Greece would see better days, but instead we felt even more fear than before.

In '46 or '47, I was out with my older brother herding our sheep; we were up in the mountains outside the village. As we walked along, we saw someone hanging from a tree. I was terrified. The dead man had a piece of paper tied around his neck. My brother had finished elementary school, so he could read. It said: "This is what will happen to all the partisans." That was the first time in my life I'd seen a dead body. Another time we found a dead body in a clearing in the woods. The dead man was dressed in civilian clothes; they'd cut off his head and put it beside his body. Dogs were barking all around. I was scared out of my mind. Everyone in the village saw it and was talking about it. That's how the fear spread.

A group of *bourandades* [right-wing irregulars] came to the village. They weren't from our village, but they knew who they were looking for. They had a list of names; they knew where to go and who to arrest. They came to our village looking for a man we knew, but they couldn't find him. He'd already fled to the mountains, but his wife was at home with their three children. They set the house on fire with a mortar. His wife escaped with two of their children, but their baby girl was left inside. She burned to death; we couldn't save her. A wall collapsed. All the villagers were outraged, not just the leftists. Everyone saw what happened: they couldn't find the father, so they killed the baby.

Gradually villagers began to divide themselves up into the good, on one side, and the bad—the bandits and the Bulgarians—on the other. Automatically, without understanding how it happened, people just started asking, "Which side are you on?" They pushed you to one side just because you had a relative on that side.

In '47, they arrested my father to keep him from joining the partisans. They put him in jail in Didimotiho. So now my brothers and sisters and I were left alone in the village with my grandmother. I don't know how we survived a whole year without our parents; we were starving. My older brother—he was fifteen or sixteen—wanted to leave home and join the partisans. I didn't know anything about it. One day we were watching the sheep, and the partisans came to get him.

"Yes, I'll come with you," he said, and went home to get his things.

My grandmother and my brothers and sisters were there. My brother burst into tears; he didn't want to go after all.

"I changed my mind," he said. "How can I leave the children here?"

"It's too late," the partisans said. "You have to come with us. We have orders to take you; we can't leave you here."

So they took him away. We survived for a year all by ourselves. Sort of. We were barefoot; we had lice and mange. My older sister, Sofia, was afraid the right-wing irregulars would rape her. She wanted to leave too, but she couldn't abandon us.

### Departure

I don't know how it happened or who arranged it. All I remember is that one evening one of the partisans came and talked to my grandmother. She was eighty or eighty-five years old then, and she was blind, poor thing. My older sister said, "Listen to me, children! This man will take you with him. You're leaving." It was as if we were going to celebrate a holiday with a relative somewhere. What did we have to lose? We didn't say "yes" or "no"; we didn't cry. Nothing. We were leaving. That's it. My sister said, "Don't be afraid! You won't be hungry anymore. They'll give you food to eat." We were starving. We just started walking.

I remember when we said good-bye to my grandmother and my sister. I didn't know I was leaving for a lifetime; I thought I'd be coming back. That's why it wasn't tragic. It wasn't as if they were taking me away by force and I was crying and hugging my grandmother and sister. It was as if we were just going somewhere and coming right back. I never thought we'd be gone for a whole lifetime; I could never have imagined that. It was just the three of us who left together—my sister, my brother, and me. Our dog followed us for a few kilometers; then he went home. There was no crying, no screaming.

We walked to the next village. Then someone took us to the Bulgarian border. We walked and walked and walked—barefoot. Our feet were sore, and we began to get hungry. At the border there were some caves; we stayed there for a week or ten days. That's where we met other children for the first time. Some women there took care of us—our feet and our clothes. There weren't any houses, just caves. One evening they told us to get our things ready and not to make any noise. Some trucks were coming to take us away. There were about thirty or forty of us from all the villages in the area. That's when I rode in a truck for the first time. We thought they were big monsters made of iron that stopped and started all by themselves.

### Life in Bulgaria

They took us to Bulgaria; I don't know exactly where. We didn't stay there long. Then they took us to Sofia. There were doctors in white coats; they treated us as if we were on an assembly line. They burned our clothes, gave us showers, and cut our hair. They cleaned us up from top to bottom.

Many years later I thought, "That's the way they treated the Jews." They were examined by doctors; they were told to go here and there; they were told to take a shower. We didn't know what would come down on us. Water? Zyklon? We had no idea. The analogy came to me later in Germany when I saw movies about the Holocaust. I said, "That's just what they did to us."

If you had mange, they put yellow ointment on you, sulfur, I think. It burned, but what could we do? We couldn't cry; we couldn't ask for help. They were all foreigners. After the medical examination, they separated the children who were healthy from those who were sick. They gave us new shoes, new pants, and new shirts. We left the room looking like totally different people. We'd escaped the fear and the poverty we'd known in the village. That's why I never had the impression that they were doing anything bad to us, that they were kidnapping us or anything like that, as many people claim. When they took us to Bulgaria, they gave us jam and candy. It was wonderful; it was like Christmas and New Year's all in one.

We didn't stay in Sofia long though. After a month or two they called us together and read out our names. About fifty of us were going to Burgas, on the Black Sea. We went to a beautiful children's home there with bedrooms, a nice dining room, and bathrooms. We began a new life. They woke us at seven or eight o'clock, we washed and ate, and then we went to school until twelve or one o'clock. We didn't know anything; we were totally illiterate. In the beginning they taught us Greek and Bulgarian, just the languages. They taught us a little about Greece; they explained the Civil War to us. In the evening we listened to news about the war on a Greek radio station. Naturally they talked to us about the politics of the struggle of our brothers and fathers and mothers, but we were only seven or eight years old. What did we understand?

They took us from Greece like little lambs. We'd seen horrible things in Greece, and we were programmed to accept the leftist ideas they were feeding us. We didn't know what leftists were, but because we'd seen the burning houses and the dead bodies we were ready to believe that the other side had done these evil things to us. And now the teacher said, "They killed your brother; they killed your father; they burned your village." As young children, we believed it; we thought, "We have to fight those people." Slowly hatred grew inside us because we learned that *they* were the bad guys. In Greece *we* had been the bad guys. Now our teachers were telling us that *we* were the *good* guys and *they* were the *bad* guys. We didn't understand anything about ideology; we were illiterate. But slowly we began to realize that the partisans were fighting for our freedom, that they were fighting for the good of Greece. So in Bulgaria and later in Germany it was easy for the party to orient us toward a certain ideological position. We didn't know anything else.

The change from the village to the children's home in Bulgaria—food, sleep, toys, joy—was the difference between night and day. When they say that they shut us in with barbed wire and turned us into Janissaries, that's not true. But they did make us leftists; they couldn't have done anything else. That was the party line.

In Bulgaria we practiced self-criticism at our morning assemblies. If someone committed a serious infraction, he'd have to stand up and admit what he'd done. That terrified me—to stand up in front of a hundred children and teachers and say, "I did this, and I ask for forgiveness." In Bulgaria I don't remember children ever being beaten. We were all well disciplined and easily frightened.

The children who were there are still like a family today. We lived together in Bulgaria and Germany for fifty years in the children's home, at school, at work. The reunion we have every year at Dadia is something that someone on the outside can't understand. They ask, "Why the joy, the hugs and kisses, the dancing?" One year I took my sister to Dadia—the one who stayed in Greece.

"Kosta," she said to me, "what's going on? Who are these people?"

"They aren't brothers and sisters," I said. "They're closer than brothers and sisters."

Of course there were times when children cried for their mothers. A children's home is a children's home. Children who were used to having their mother hug and kiss them goodnight found the separation difficult; but children like me, who never experienced that, didn't miss it. In Bulgaria we went swimming in the sea; we ate good meals; we went to school. It was a comfortable life. We weren't beaten; we weren't hungry; we weren't terrified by airplanes and bombs. Our lives changed like a rose that blossoms overnight.

### From Bulgaria to Germany

We spent two years in Burgas. Then we heard they were going to divide us up and send us to other countries in Eastern Europe. A committee came to Burgas and announced that they were sending us to Poland, Romania, Czechoslovakia, and Germany. When we heard "Germany," we were frightened because in Bulgaria they'd told us what the Germans had done in Greece from '41 to '44. We thought the Germans were bad people. A Greek man read the names of the ten or twenty children who were being sent to Germany. My sister and I were on the list, but not my brother. He was only nine, and the Germans were just taking children between the ages of ten and fifteen. My sister begged them to let my brother come too, and that's what happened. They sent him too, so all three of us stayed together. Otherwise he would have been left behind in Bulgaria.

A day or two later they took us away. We said our good-byes. It was hard to leave Burgas, to tell you the truth; it was hard to leave our friends, our classes, the children's home, and go somewhere totally new again. In Bulgaria they told us we weren't far from Greece, but when we heard "Germany," we realized we were going far away from our village and our family. That's when we were frightened; that's when we cried. Not when we left the village.

The trip was terrifying. They told us it would take many days to reach Germany. We didn't know where Germany was. It was far away, yes, but where? We were on the train for a week or ten days; there were a thousand children on it. Romania, Hungary, Czechoslovakia. We couldn't get off the train at all. The Red Cross brought us something to eat and drink, but it was a long trip. We couldn't ask where we were, and they wouldn't tell us when we'd get there. They didn't know themselves. It amazes me. A thousand children on a train all that time! We had to eat and drink and sleep and go to the bathroom. I don't remember any problems. Somehow we all survived.

We went to Bischofswerda near Dresden. That was our first stop. The Germans welcomed us with music and flowers and speeches in German and Greek. We stayed there about a week; then they divided us up again—girls and boys, different ages. They sent most of us to Dresden. The destruction of Dresden in the war made a big impression on me. Everything had been burned; the city had been totally destroyed by the American bombs. In 1950, Dresden was a city of ghosts; the roads were full of rubble and fire.

Then they took us to Radebeul, where there was a children's home with beautiful villas and houses. They put fifty or a hundred of us in each building depending on its size. I was with my brother and sister. We had a soccer field in the back, a dining room, and bedrooms—the boys on one side, the girls on the other. That's when the third phase of our lives began. The first phase was in the village, the second in Bulgaria, and the third in Germany.

### *Education in East Germany*

We studied Greek and German for a year or two depending on our age. Some of us knew a little Greek, but some of us didn't know any at all. With German we all began from scratch. Then they sent us to learn a trade. You couldn't say, "I want to be an electrician," or "I want to be a machinist." First of all, we didn't know what trades there were. Second, we didn't know the language, so we couldn't go to the university and become doctors. After two or three years of school, they sent us to learn a trade. Some people came and said, "You will become an electrician. You will become a machinist." They decided that ten or fifteen of us would be sent to the state phone company to study telecommunications. I think the Committee for a Free Greece was involved; it was part of the Greek Communist Party. They wanted children in every trade so that in the future Greece would have workers trained in all fields. In 1952, I began two years of classes to become a telecommunications specialist in the East German telephone company.

For the first few years, discipline was very strict. In the evening some of us snuck out of the *internat*, the student dormitory. That caused problems with the Germans. We were Greeks; we were foreigners. We had real problems after the coup in '51–'52. The Russians came with their tanks and guarded the children's homes so that the Germans wouldn't kill us. There were still lots of Nazis around who were *not* our friends. But most Germans treated us very well. There were some wild boys who wanted to go out with girls and dance the boogie-woogie or the samba. Our teachers said, "That isn't the right thing for us to do as Greeks," and gave them a good beating. Today that seems ridiculous.

We were completely in the dark about sex. Years later my sister told me, "Kosta, once I woke up, and my bed was red. I was scared. What was the matter with me? Was I sick?" She didn't know she was having her period. We Greeks were very conservative. They didn't teach us certain things that they should have. We weren't ten years old; we were seventeen and eighteen. But for us sex was a taboo topic. Girls and boys went out, but they couldn't hold hands. It was primitive. During our first two years at the children's homes, romantic relationships weren't allowed, but after that they began to occur. When the teachers realized they couldn't stop them, they said, "Take whichever girl you want and leave us in peace."

As the children grew older, the teachers began to let boys and girls get married, but there were no apartments. They gave each couple a room in an *internat*. They made a kitchen for the three or four couples on each floor. We thought it was a wonderful arrangement. We had our room; we had our little kitchen. We were a couple. Then we had children. Each mother took a turn watching all the children. We were all one big family.

When we left the children's homes to continue our education, our lives really changed. We gained more personal freedom; we lived in our own apartments and went to German schools. That's when the Greek Communist Party lost control over our lives.

*While Kostas was living in Dresden, he met his wife; she was working in a tele-graph office there. They spent time together at meetings, dances, and parades spon-sored by the Free German Youth. Their "socialist wedding" was held at the factory where Kostas worked in 1960, the year his wife turned eighteen. The company paid for the entire ceremony. Kostas' union helped him find an apartment a year later just before their first child was born. Life was difficult in East Germany after the Berlin Wall was built. It was hard to find things like milk and eggs, bananas and apples. People had to wait years to buy a car, and even then they couldn't buy spare parts for it.*

### The Politics of Repatriation

In the '70s, when we couldn't return to Greece, many Greek political refu-gees left East Germany for West Germany. We had jobs and money and peace of mind, but we weren't Germans. We didn't have passports; we only had red identity cards. We were *Ausländer*, foreigners. If you really wanted to leave, they made life difficult for you. But you could leave. Many people went to West Germany between '71 and '78 because from there they could go back to Greece. Germans couldn't go to West Germany, but Greeks could. Because my wife and children were Germans, I couldn't go to West Berlin. Not a chance. But many Greeks did. The police gave them a hard time, but they let them go. When I asked them why they'd left, they said, "Listen, Kosta. First of all, every day on television we saw how wealthy people in West Berlin were. On top of that, we wanted to return to Greece someday, but our East German marks were worthless in Greece. We went to West Germany so we could save some money and be in a position to return to Greece one day, so we could buy a house and raise our families there."

The Greek Communist Party said it wasn't a good thing to do, but they couldn't stop people from leaving. They said, "Don't betray the system! Don't betray our ideals!" But they couldn't say, "No, you can't go!" When you were an adult, the Committee for a Free Greece lost control over you. You were on your own; you dealt with the police, the factory, or the union on your own. You were responsible for yourself, but still there were prob-lems. Even from West Germany we couldn't go to Greece for a visit because Greece labeled us "undesirables." We didn't have passports. The Greek em-bassy wouldn't *give* us passports. My brother tried twice to go to Greece, but both times they turned him back at the border. That was during the dictatorship. So even if you were in West Germany, you couldn't solve the problem of repatriation.

When PASOK came to power in 1981, it was easier to return to Greece for a visit to see if you wanted to return for good. That's when the Germans said, "Are you Greeks or Germans? There are no refugees anymore! What will you do?" That's when they told us to become German citizens. But I said, "No!" I have relatives in Greece. Someday I might want to leave, and if I'm a citizen of East Germany, I won't be able to. They said we either had to leave or become German citizens. But they didn't deport us. There are still many people in East Germany who weren't expelled and who never became German citizens. The Greek government gave amnesty to some of the people whose citizenship had been taken away, but not to everyone.

I was so involved with my job and my family that personally I felt like a German. It never occurred to me to leave for the West because I had a German wife and children, because I had a good job, and because I was so close to my friends and colleagues. My wife and I earned enough money, but not enough to move back to Greece. We had another problem. When I got my apartment in 1961, I paid 48 marks a month, and when I left in 1981—I swear—I was paying 48 and a half. At a time when I was earning 1,700 marks a month. That's why we never developed the mentality of building something or buying something of our own, that sense of shrewdness that exists in Greece and other countries in the West. When I paid 48 marks for rent from a salary of 1,700 marks, it never occurred to me to buy a house. Why should I buy something when the government was giving it to me for free?

### Return to Greece

The first time I thought about returning to Greece was in 1978, when three men from the Greek Telephone Organization came to the telecommunications ministry in East Berlin where I worked. They wanted to buy telecommunications equipment for the big transmission lines in Greece. The German government asked me to serve as interpreter for them and to show them around for three months.

"Kosta, come back to Greece!" they said. "We need you; you're a good technician. We'll hire you."

"If I don't go now," I thought, "when will I ever go?"

That's when people were saying, "What should we do? Should we become Germans?" I realized I had to decide.

"Will I really find work in Greece?" I asked.

"We'll hire you," they said. "We'll give you a job wherever you want."

I thought about it; I talked to my wife. "What should we do?" we said.

"Let's leave!" When we decided to leave, we lost all our rights. The Germans removed us from our positions of responsibility and gave us other jobs. A year later all our papers were in order, and in August 1981 we put all our possessions on the train, bought a car, and moved to Greece.

When we arrived in Thessaloniki, I went to see one of the men I'd met in Germany. "Here I am," I said. "When do I start work? Athens? Thessaloniki? It doesn't matter to me." And then the drama began. One month went by, two months. . . . I asked; I asked again. Then I started to get nervous. Maybe they weren't telling me the truth; maybe they wouldn't give me a job.

"Come outside," I said. "We need to talk. Tell me the truth. What's going on?"

"Listen, Kosta," he said. "We want to hire you, but we don't make the decisions. They're using the excuse that you're forty-three years old, and the age limit is thirty-five. Then there's the fact that you're a political refugee. I don't think they're going to offer you a job, Kosta."

When I heard that, it was as if I'd been struck by lightning.

"Why did you do this to me?" I said. "You knew what I was leaving behind. I quit my job; I took my children out of school. My wife is German. What can I do now?"

"I don't know," he said, "but I don't think they'll ever give you a job here."

I went home. My wife was in tears; my children were all upset.


### Return to Germany

"Listen," I told my wife. "Go to the German embassy! Take the kids, and get out of here!" I didn't have anything. I came with a temporary passport that was only valid to enter Greece. I couldn't leave. "You're German," I said to my wife. "Go to the embassy and tell them you want to go back to Germany. Go to Frankfurt, to the reception center and say that you want to live there." We went to the embassy; I bought her a ticket; she took the children and left on the train for Frankfurt.

I stayed here and started the paperwork necessary to get a passport. I moved heaven and earth in the process. When I finally received my passport, I called my wife and told her I was coming.

After a month, the German officials asked my wife, "Where do you want to go?"

"To West Berlin," she said, "because I have a brother there."

So they sent her to West Berlin by plane; she wasn't allowed to go by train.

I took my Greek passport, got in my car—a Lada with East German license plates—and set off through Yugoslavia and Austria on my way to Berlin. I entered West Germany without any problems. When I crossed from West Germany into East Germany, they saw my license plates and asked for my papers.

"Pull over to the side of the road, please," the officer said.

I sat there and waited and waited and waited. I thought, "They'll send me back now."

"Where are you coming from?" he asked.

"I left East Germany," I said. "I'm Greek; I have a Greek passport. I went to Greece, and I've come to visit my brother in West Berlin."

He took all my papers and walked away. Finally he came back and said, "Have a good trip!"

What a relief! I was home free. But before I entered West Berlin, I had to cross one more border. Now I was afraid of what the police in West Berlin would do. I went slowly, slowly, slowly. No one was there; no one stopped me to check my papers. I crossed the border. Then I pulled over to look at a map to see where my brother lived. I was totally exhausted. That's my story.

I found a job in West Berlin. My children finished school and found jobs there. Last January, I retired. I took my pension, and we moved back to Greece. It's a new beginning for us. It hasn't been easy. We'll see. . . . If we stay healthy, we may live a few more years and get used to the way things are here. We don't know Greece that well. It's a different life here.

---

## Evropi Marinova[2]

*Evropi Marinova, a Macedonian refugee child, was born in 1943 in the village of Prekopana, which in Greek is called Perikopi. The village sits high on the shoulder of Mount Vitsi between Florina and Kastoria. In 1940, Prekopana had over five hundred Macedonian-speaking inhabitants. During the Civil War the village was destroyed by the Greek Army. Many villagers were killed; many more fled across the border into Yugoslavia. By 1951, Prekopana had been totally abandoned. The efforts of the Greek government to rebuild it were unsuccessful. According to the 1991 census, Perikopi had just six inhabitants.*

*Evropi has worked for years as a chemist in a patent office in Budapest. Several years ago she purchased a small piece of land on Lake Balaton, near Balatonalmadi, the children's home where she lived as a child. Evropi helps her daughter by taking care of her only grandchild as often as she can. Heavy-set with blue eyes and blond hair, Evropi is a strong, successful woman. Yet in some ways she is still a refugee child haunted by the horrors of war. She is still a little girl searching desperately to find her lost mother.*

## Civil War

Just before we left the village, some Greek soldiers arrested my father and beat him really badly. They brought him to our house, and two or three days later he died. The army came through and drove everyone out. We couldn't leave because we were taking care of my father, but we had to get out of the house. So we took my father out into the yard and put him down under a tree. The whole village was going up in flames. Two soldiers came up to us—four young children, their mother, and their grandmother—and told us that they weren't going to burn our house down and that we could go back inside.

My oldest brother, who was twelve years old at the time, together with my mother and grandmother lifted my father up. As they were carrying him into the house—right there on the stairs—he said to my mother, "Just look after the children." He said it in Macedonian: "*Samo gi gleda decata.*" Those were his last words.

My mother kept saying, "He died. Thodoros died." The soldiers came again and told us that we had to leave because they *were* going to burn our house down after all. My brother dragged my father down the stairs; he and my mother couldn't lift him. My sister, Hariklia, and I tried to help them carry him out. I didn't realize that he was dead; I thought he was just sleeping. I didn't know yet what it meant for someone to die.

We took my father outside, and we stayed with him under the tree all night. The next day my brother made a coffin out of wood. They put him inside and buried him in the cemetery—it wasn't far away. My grandmother, my mother, and my brother buried him; then they came back. We had a mule. My mother put a few things in some old sacks, and we left the village.

There was no one else there. Before my father died, the church bell rang, and everyone went to the village square. They said that everyone had to leave in an hour or two because the Greek army was going to burn the village down. People took whatever they could, but they didn't have much. There were no animals left. The army and the partisans, who were up in the mountains, up on Vitsi, had taken everything.

### Departure

After we buried my father—we just put a little dirt over him—we left the village. We spent a week or two living under a huge rock. One night while we were asleep, I woke up because I heard some voices. My mother was talking with someone. Years later I learned that it was my uncle, my father's youngest brother. He came to look for us because he knew my father was badly injured. After the war he went to Russia. He lived in Tashkent for a long time with his wife and child.

The next day we went down to the village of Melisotopi—Olišta in Macedonian. We didn't have a house to live in, so we stayed in a stable. After a few days my mother gave birth; she'd been pregnant with my younger brother. From there we left Greece—seventeen or eighteen children from our village, including lots of my cousins. We set out from Melisotopi, for somewhere, but no one knew where.

When we left the village, my mother began to cry. She said to my brother, "Don't leave! Don't leave me alone with the baby!" But my brother, my twelve-year-old brother, left anyway. We walked for a while, and then he turned back. He felt sorry for my mother and went back. That's why he stayed home. My mother let me and my sister go because she couldn't feed us, but she kept my brother to help her cut wood for the fire. She had the baby to take care of.

We left without shoes, without clothes, without food, without anything. We walked, and we walked, and we walked. We were little children. We traveled at night. We heard the airplanes coming and the bombs falling; we heard explosions. Finally we arrived somewhere; we were in Bitola, in Yugoslavia. All the children were in a big park. We were covered with fleas and lice. The children from each village were holding hands to stay together, but they separated us anyway. They put us on trains—not in passenger cars, but in boxcars, the ones they use for animals. We boarded the trains, but many children were left behind. Some cars came to Hungary; others went to Czechoslovakia.

### A Hungarian Family

My sister and I were holding hands. They brought us to Hungary together with my cousins, to an army base. They gave us a bath and new clothes and put us in beds, iron beds. There were twenty or thirty of us in each room. We were there for quite a while; they divided us up by village. The first few months the children cried a lot; they missed their parents. The adults who were with us did everything they could for us. They played games with us; they let us sing songs and recite poems—to help us forget. In a few years people do forget. After living with other children for a few years, a four-year-old stops missing his mother.

In 1950, they decided that children like me who didn't have parents would be placed with Hungarian families so that we could understand what it meant to have parents. There were announcements in the newspapers and on the radio. Many Hungarian families came to the homes and took children. They didn't adopt them permanently; they just took them temporarily. There was one child who went to live with a Hungarian family. Years later he found his mother and father, and he said, "Now I have a Hungarian mother *and* a Greek mother."

The children who stayed with these families lived very well. They were part of a family; they had beautiful clothes. The couples who came to take them didn't have any children of their own. For about three months I was with a family like that, but I couldn't stay with them. I didn't know Hungarian, so I couldn't communicate with them at all. When a Greek teacher came to see how I was doing, I began to cry. I told her to take me back to the children's home. I missed my sister and my cousins; I was happier there with all the other Greek children.

I was six or seven years old then. Later, when I was in high school studying to become a chemist, I was the only Greek in the dormitory. That was hard. Everyone had a visitor, a mother or father, but no one came to visit me. Those were the most difficult times for me, I think. At the children's homes no one had a mother or father; we were all in the same situation. But when I was in high school, I began to think about how nice it would have been if I had stayed with the family that wanted to adopt me. But what can you do? I didn't know any better then, and I lost them. I only knew that they were named Erzi and Karoli. I stayed with them for just three months.

I regret it now. Because if I'd known then that my whole life would be spent in Hungary. . . . But we always thought we were living here temporarily. That's what our teachers always told us. "You should study hard so that you can return to build a new Greece." And that's what we believed. Until 1980 we didn't think about buying houses or property. Then we had to decide whether to live here or in Greece. For thirty-two years we lived temporarily. Imagine what kind of life that was!

## *Education in Hungary*

Then they took us to Balatonalmadi, where we started school. They didn't ask what grade we'd completed; they just lined us up according to height and said, "She's in first grade. She's in second grade. She's in third grade." I went to first grade with my sister because I was a little tall for my age, but I wasn't really old enough to go to school.

That's when we began to learn Greek and Macedonian. We studied Greek geography, Greek history, and Greek grammar. We didn't know a word of Greek then, not even "Hello." The person who taught us Greek had been a teacher in Greece. Whatever Greek we learned, we learned from him. He was excellent; we really loved him.

We didn't know how to write Greek very well, but he had us write a letter to our parents. We all wrote the same letter: "Dear Mom and Dad, How are you? We are well. We are in Hungary, and we are going to school," and so on. He told us what to write. We gave him the letters, and he sent them to Greece. He knew what village each of us was from. So in 1953 my mother received a letter from me for the first time, and she wrote back. That's how our correspondence started. My mother knew how to write Greek well; she'd gone to school. That's when she first learned where we were. From '48 until '53 we didn't know what happened to our parents, and they didn't know what happened to us.

Later we studied Macedonian grammar, literature, geography, and history. We learned about Ilinden and about how Macedonia was divided. We also learned how to speak and write Macedonian. We learned more Macedonian than Greek. Greek we learned like a foreign language; Macedonian we learned as our mother tongue.

From first grade through fourth grade I was at Balatonalmadi, and from fifth grade through eighth grade I was at Balatonkenese. Everything was organized; everything had its place. The teacher was the teacher; he was like God. They say we were raised like Janissaries, but that's not true. We learned how to live properly; we learned respect. The children who were at Balatonalmadi and Balatonkenese all became human beings. I don't know any one of them who doesn't have a job or who's been in jail. Hungarians respected the Greeks and the Macedonians who worked in the factories with them.

When we finished eighth grade, whoever was a good student went to secondary school. Whoever wasn't became an electrician or a machinist. I was a very good student, so I went to high school to study chemistry. I had to take exams just like the Hungarian children. I did well in chemistry and math, but not in Hungarian. I didn't know Hungarian very well yet, because we Greeks—we Greeks and Macedonians. . . . If you were Greek, I'd speak Greek to you, if you were Macedonian we'd speak Macedonian. We never spoke Hungarian. So when we went to high school, we didn't know Hungarian very well. Those four years were really difficult.

### Greeks and Macedonians

When they took us to the children's homes, the Greek children and the Macedonian children lived separately. The Macedonian children were at Balatonalmadi, and the Greek children were at another home, Fehérvárc-sóurgo. Sometime later they decided to put the older children—Greeks and Macedonians together—in Balatonkenese and the younger children in Balatonalmadi. At that time it didn't matter whether you were Greek or Macedonian; we loved each other like brothers and sisters. The only difference was that when we had Macedonian classes, the Greeks played outside. We were jealous of them. If they didn't study Macedonian, why did we have to study Greek? We also studied Hungarian. It was our third language. Later we studied Russian too. We learned four languages.

There weren't any problems between Greeks and Macedonians then. That problem is recent. Then the Greek children respected us as Macedonian children, and we respected them. Until now we haven't had problems with the Greeks in Hungary. We lived together happily. But now that we want some Macedonian things—a school, a place to gather. . . . We celebrate Greek Independence Day on March 25th. Why shouldn't the Greeks celebrate a Macedonian holiday too? We want to celebrate Ilinden together with the Greeks. Now somehow Macedonian songs and holidays have been lost, and we ask why. In spite of all the years we've lived here, our fatherland has always been Greece—Macedonia and the villages where we were born. It's a shame that Greece doesn't feel the way we do, because even though we lived here, we always said, "Our fatherland is there." But Greeks called us "foreigners."

We were just children. If the war hadn't broken out, we would still have our homes and our property there. We left everything we owned in Greece, and all these years we haven't been allowed to go back. I don't understand how the Greek government could have refused to let me enter Greece all these years. Just because I was born a Macedonian? My mother and father were Macedonians, but my husband was Greek. When we fell in love in Hungary, it didn't matter that he was Greek and I was Macedonian. When you're in love, it's all the same. We didn't pay attention to what we were. I didn't understand the problem until I wanted to go to Greece.

*In 1956, Evropi moved to Budapest to study chemistry at a technical high school and to be near her sister. After her graduation in 1960, she found work in Budapest as a chemist.*

### Dohan-gyar

Dohan-gyar was a huge building; it had been a cigarette factory. When the Greek political refugees came, they emptied it out and moved the workers somewhere else. There was a big hallway from one end of the building to the other with rooms on both sides. At the end of the hall there was one kitchen and one bathroom for everyone on the hallway. People took turns cooking. When one person finished, the next person came in. That's the way people lived. During those years life was difficult for everyone; not just for us, but for the Hungarians too. The government had to rebuild all of Budapest after the war. The tram system hadn't been constructed yet, so we went everywhere on foot. We walked for hours. Given the difficulties it faced at that time, Hungary helped us a great deal.

When I moved to Budapest, I knew the Greeks lived at Dohan-gyar, so I went and asked if I could live there because I didn't have a house. They gave me a bed there. That's where I met my husband. We went everywhere together. There was a big yard between the dormitories; it was closed off from the outside. The Greeks spent evenings together there. Men played soccer or sat on benches discussing politics. The yard was always full of people. We went out to eat at an inexpensive restaurant nearby. There was music—Greek and Macedonian music—and the young people danced.

My husband and I got married in 1961. We went to city hall and signed the papers. No priest or anything; that was it. Then I went back to the girl's dormitory, and my husband went back to the men's dormitory. We waited our turn to get a house. Seven or eight months later they gave us a house, and we began our life together.

*One day in 1988, Evropi was waiting for the bus on her way to work, when Ilonka, an eighty-six-year-old widow whose apartment had no heat or electricity, asked her for help.*

### An Amazing Coincidence

We went back to her apartment; it was filthy. I sat there, and we began to talk.

"My name is Evropi," I said. "I'm Greek. I don't know how much you know about the Greek children. . . . "

"My brother," she said, "may he rest in peace, had a little Greek girl in his house for a short time, a beautiful little girl with blond hair and blue eyes."

After a few questions I realized I was that little girl. After 40 years! I started to cry.

"Yes! Yes! Yes!" I said, "I'm that little girl!"

"Come over to my house!" I told her. "It's warm and clean; you can stay there until your furnace is fixed."

She stayed a few days, and I kept telling her, "Your house isn't warm yet." The poor woman told me her whole life story. Then after a month I wouldn't let her leave.

She'd come and knock on my door at two o'clock in the morning.

"Are you asleep, dear?" she'd say. Then she'd come in and cover me up so I wouldn't be cold.

"Go back to sleep," I'd say. "I'm an adult, I'm not a little girl. I can pull up my own blankets."

"But, my dear," she'd say, "If you get sick, what will happen to me?"

When my husband died, it didn't upset me half as much as it did when Ilonka died. When *he* died, I still had *her* at home. I'd go home, and she would talk to me better than a mother would. But when I lost her and I was left alone in the house, I was afraid. She didn't just give me love; she also gave me this ring—I never take it off. It was her wedding ring. She gave it to me the day she died. I was all dressed up when I went to visit her in the hospital. She looked at me with her big eyes full of tears and said, "You're so beautiful." As long as I live, I'll see those eyes. I sat next to her and held her big hand. It was all bones.

*During the eight years they lived together, Ilonka often talked to Evropi about her brother and his wife. They had searched for Evropi for years after she returned to the children's home, but they had never been able to find her. "That family wanted to adopt me permanently," Evropi said. "I could never pay them back, so I had to pay Ilonka back."*

### Reunion of Mother and Daughter

My mother and I corresponded for years. In 1965, right before she left for Australia, she came to Skopje. The year before, my sister had moved from Hungary to Skopje because her husband's parents were there. My mother could travel to Skopje then because Greece was on good terms with Yugo-slavia. But Greece was not on good terms with Hungary, so she couldn't come to visit us here, and we couldn't visit her in Greece.

My mother and I met at my sister's house in Skopje. My mother was very thin, nothing but skin and bones. She was exhausted from rebuilding the family house in Prekopana after the Civil War and from working in the fields by herself all those years. She was dressed in black from head to toe, with her kerchief. The poor woman! She looked at us, and we looked at her . . . like strangers, not like mother and daughter. It was sad. After two weeks she went back to Greece.

### *Return to Prekopana*

When I started working, I began saving money because I wanted to go to Greece. We needed visas, so we filled out all the forms. When we went to the Greek embassy in Budapest in 1975, one of the employees called me into his office.

"What village are you from?" he asked.

"Prekopana," I said.

"What's your father's name?"

"Todor Marinov," I said without thinking.

"You're village is called Prekopana?" he asked again.

"Yes," I said. "Prekopana."

"Fine," he said. "Thank you."

My daughter and my husband received their visas right away, but not me.

I can get a little short-tempered when things don't work out the way I want them to. So I went back to the embassy.

"Why can't I get a visa?" I asked.

"Don't ask why," he said. "Now step outside please."

"Why should I step outside?" I asked. "Wasn't I born in Greece? Aren't I from Prekopana? My husband is Greek. What's the matter? Why can't I go to Greece?"

"Please step outside," he said.

As I left the room, I turned to him and I said, "I shit on your coun-try and on all the Greeks who live there, because you don't recognize that we're from there." The least he could do was say, "You can't go because you're Macedonian and because you said 'Prekopana' and not 'Perikopi.'" I applied for a visa many times, but they never gave me one. Finally, in 1988, with the help of a personal acquaintance in the embassy—I can't say who—I succeeded in getting a visa for the first time.

I went to Greece with my daughter and her husband. When we arrived in Prekopana, when I saw the village again for the first time, there were only five houses. They were all in ruins. The village was just as I'd left it in '48, when it was burned to the ground. Two women dressed in black were sitting on a blanket in the village square. I was looking for my aunt, my father's sister. I went up to them.

"Good morning," I said in Greek. "I'm looking for Eleni Toli."

One of the women turned to the other and said in Macedonian "She's looking for Lena Toleva."

So I said to her in Macedonian, "Yes, I'm looking for Lena Toleva. I'm from Hungary. My father was Lena's brother. I'm Evropi, Todor's youngest daughter."

"Lenaaa!" She began shouting in a wild voice, full of grief and sorrow. "Lenaaa! Lenaaa! Come here! It's Evropi! Todor's daughter! Lenaaa!" Her voice echoed through the empty village. When my aunt heard her calling, she began running toward us, in her black clothes—both her husband and her son had died. My poor aunt! When she reached the square, she stopped about a meter in front of me.

"Are you Todor's?" she asked. "Are you Todor's daughter?"

And she began to cry. What tears! You only see tears like that in the movies. She cried and cried and cried. She grabbed me and hugged me. I was crying, too. The other two women . . . we were all crying. My daughter was standing behind me crying. My son-in-law couldn't speak because of what he saw.

Afterward my poor aunt took us back to her house. It looked just the way it had fifty years earlier. There was no bed, the same fireplace—nothing had changed. There we were. Later we went to see my other aunt. We sat in front of her house on a big chest. She called my other aunt, Kalliopi, the one who lives in Athens. They're building a house in the village now. Kalliopi came over with her husband, my father's brother, the one who was in Tashkent. Tears, tears, tears! We sat there for two days. Then we went to Athens. I returned to Hungary from Athens by train. I had to get back to work. My daughter and her husband stayed in Athens. They spent a week visiting some of the islands and then drove back to Hungary.

## Mothers and Daughters

The most important thing in my life is my daughter, Aphrodite. I would do anything for her. I used to tell myself that whatever happened I would never let my child be separated from me. If I'm killed, my child will be killed too. I wouldn't let my child grow up without parents the way we did.

When I was in high school, I didn't have nice shoes or nice clothes. When I worked in the summer and earned some money, that's what I bought. I wanted to be beautiful, to be nicely dressed. High-heeled shoes and nylon socks were in style then. I really wanted to dress like that, because that's how the children who had parents dressed. I envied them. But I envied them even more when we had dances at school and their mothers came. Their mothers sat and watched them dance. I danced beautifully too—rock-and-roll and the twist; all the boys wanted to dance with me. But I envied the other girls when I saw them come with their mothers. No one ever came with me.

---

## Stefanos Gikas[3]

*Stefanos Gikas, a Greek refugee child, was born in the early 1940s in a village in Epirus near the Albanian border. After he returned to Greece in 1958, he worked his whole life in the construction industry. Stefanos retired recently and now lives in a northern suburb of Athens in a large, elegantly furnished house that he built himself. Stefanos is a short, stocky man. While generally quiet and reserved, he becomes very animated when a subject really engages him.*

### Civil War

Before the war, the village wasn't divided up into right wing and left wing. Everyone there was poor; they were all shepherds. They didn't care about politics, but the Civil War made them care. The partisans kidnapped people, anyone who was the right age. If they saw a boy out with his sheep or goats, they just took him to fight. People in the village didn't know what communism meant; they didn't have electricity or running water. What did they know about politics? But the partisans took them and taught them. Lots of young people from our village were lost.

### Departure

It was chaos. The partisans took us at night so the planes couldn't bomb us. My mother had an old horse; she loaded it with the few things she owned.

She had four small children. She put the youngest one on the horse, but the horse was old and couldn't walk fast enough, so we were always falling behind. One night I got lost. I fell into a ravine; a branch stopped my fall. I was crying. Two older boys ran away because they wanted to go back to the village. When they heard my voice, they came and found me and brought me back to my mother. The partisans scolded her. The poor woman! She was crying, "I lost my child! I lost my child!"

They took us to Albania. There were a lot of refugees there; all of them were Greek. We stayed there a few months. My mother would send us to get water from a spring about five hundred meters away. One day we went to get water, and some army trucks came. They gave us each a loaf of bread and loaded us on the trucks. They put my older brother and me on one truck and my mother on another. We traveled for two or three days. On the way, we saw lights from villages and towns. We'd never seen lights before; we didn't have electricity in our village until 1980.

### Arrival in Hungary

We ended up in Budapest. They took us to a beautiful old building. Some women came and gave us new clothes. They took our old clothes, lit a big fire, and burned them all, because we had lice. Then they gave us a bath. They also gave us each a box of toys; at the bottom there was a big chocolate bar. We'd never eaten chocolate before; we loved it. They took good care of us. They asked us our names. Some children didn't even know their names. It was total confusion.

After a few days they lined us up by height. They asked us how old we were, but we didn't know. If we had an older relative with us, she would tell them. If not, they decided whether to send us to first or second grade by our height. They kept my brother and me together; they put us in the same class, but my brother got sick, and they sent him to a hospital. When he recovered, they brought him back again. By then he'd learned Hungarian really well. The rest of us were slow to learn Hungarian because in first and second grades we only studied Greek. In third grade we started studying Hungarian.

### Life in Hungary

We were at Balatonkenese for three or four years. There were lots of Slav-Macedonian children. At first we didn't know what they were; but then we learned they were Slav-Macedonians. They were fanatics. They were always saying "We're Slav-Macedonians"; they wanted Macedonia to be independent. We didn't get along with them very well. When we were older, we played soccer. It was their team against ours. If I got in a fight with one of them, the Greeks supported me, and the Slav-Macedonians supported him.

We lived well at Balatonkenese. The building was huge; it was like a palace. There were statues, everything you could possibly want. It belonged to a wealthy landowner; then the state took it over. There were fields and orchards. The whole district must have belonged to him. That's what Hungary was like before the war; a few people owned everything.

After a few years at Balatonkenese, they took us to Balatonalmadi. We were young. We caused some trouble—stealing fruit, things like that. If they caught us, they punished us: "You can't go to the movies." But we learned a lot there. We learned how to play chess, how to swim. Some children had a talent for gymnastics, some for painting; some were interested in airplanes. I was a good soccer player; I was on our school team. I was a good chess player too. We played chess all day.

We had Greek and Hungarian teachers there; some of them were good. We had an excellent math teacher. He explained things to us so well that no matter how stupid you were you learned something. But there were other teachers who didn't know much, who were just there to supervise us. If we caused them any trouble, they just slapped us in the face. They weren't real teachers; they were just partisans who'd been given positions there. Some of them had been wounded. One was missing a leg; another an arm. There were also women who took care of us. We called them "mothers." They took good care of us. A few of them had their own children there. Those children lived with us, but their mothers took a little better care of them than they did the rest of us.

If we had a problem—"So-and-so hit me," "So-and-so took my ball"— we went to the teacher. We didn't have a mother or father to tell our problems to, but we were used to living without parents. I only got emotional once. My mother sent me a shirt from Romania. It was a beautiful shirt; I was really proud of it. I said, "It's from my mother." I couldn't even remember who she was, but do you know how much that shirt meant to me? More than my eyes! It was from my mother.

When we were a little older, they started talking to us about politics. We weren't interested; we just wanted to go out and play soccer. But the director of the home wouldn't let us; he kept us inside and lectured us about the Communist Party. It was really boring. Most of the children didn't want to have anything to do with it, but the few who showed an interest enjoyed privileges later in their careers.

There were photographs of Lenin, Stalin, Marx, and Engels. But we didn't pay any attention to them. When Stalin died, they told us, "Your father is dead." Some people cried, but we didn't care. That was in '53; I was nine or ten years old then. What did I know about Stalin? It had an impact on the older children; it was as if they were in mourning. But the younger children just wanted to go out and play soccer.

### Technical School in Budapest

I didn't stay as long at Balatonalmadi. I had one grade left in elementary school when they sent us to Budapest. Our school was in an old four-story apartment building; we slept there too. It wasn't like the palaces at Kenese or Almadi. It was in Old Budapest. That's when we began to appreciate what a beautiful city it was. They took us on walks; they took us to museums, to the theater, to the opera. The first time we went to the opera it was as if we were watching a fairy tale. We'd never seen anything like it before.

When we finished elementary school, they sent us to a technical high school in New Budapest. There were only five Greek students; all the rest were Hungarian. At first they didn't know we were Greeks because we spoke Hungarian so well. Later when they learned who we were, they began to call us "the Greeks." But they were good kids; we all became friends. One boy took me home to his village for Christmas to meet his mother and father. What kindness! That's when I understood what a family was. I said, "He has a mother and a father! How wonderful!" I was jealous; I wanted to live like that too. I don't remember his name or the name of his village. If I did, I'd go find him and bring him a gift to repay him for his kindness.

At the technical school they gave us a little money each month. They also gave us tickets for the tram, so we could ride all over Budapest for free. That's when we learned about money. They taught us that if you had this amount of money and put it in a bank at a certain interest rate, then at the end of the year you would have this amount of money. I said, "Wow! I'll make some money; that's what I'll do."

### The Hungarian Revolution

When the revolution took place in Budapest, we were a little older and we understood what was going on. In 1956, we were in the eighth grade. Russian soldiers and tanks entered the city. We ran away from school and went looking for abandoned cars. We stole wires to make little radios, just for fun. We searched through abandoned houses and ruined apartment buildings and stores. Everyone was doing it, but it was dangerous. We took whatever we could find—canned food, jam, things like that. We found a few old tanks and stole some parts. Hungarian soldiers caught us a few times, but they just yelled at us and let us go.

Our Hungarian friends really hated the Russians, but we liked them because they were stronger. We were just kids; we didn't get involved in politics. What did we know? We supported whichever side was winning. A few Greeks joined the resistance, but they were older. The Hungarian security forces caught them and beat them. I remember one boy. . . . If he hadn't been Greek, they would have killed him. But he said he was Greek, and they spared his life. It's funny, but we weren't scared. We didn't understand how serious it was. We were playing soccer in the schoolyard while they were firing machine guns next door—Boom! Boom! Boom! Can you imagine? We were furious because they made us stop playing. Dumb kids. We didn't know any better.

### Return to Greece

I was studying to become a draftsman; I was learning how to design ships. I chose that career myself; I was seventeen. I had good friends in Budapest— Hungarians—and they treated us well. We were starting to feel part of Hungarian society, just a little. Of course we didn't feel like Hungarians, because we knew we'd return to Greece. We wanted to come back because of all the good things they'd told us about Greece. We felt superior. They taught us about ancient Greece, about Homer. We listened with open mouths. We said, "We have all that! You Hungarians don't!" We'd get in fights once in a while. We even said, "You Hungarians don't even have oranges!" Can you believe it?

But right in the middle of our good life there, they brought us back to Greece. My brother did the paperwork; he knew where the other members of our family were. I had no idea; I didn't ask, and I didn't care. I was used to being on my own. My brother wanted to come to Greece, so he went to the Greek embassy and made all the arrangements. One day he came and took me to the embassy to sign something. I saw the Greek letters outside and the huge seal; it made a big impression on me. My brother made me come back; I didn't want to.

In the meantime my teachers were trying to convince me not to leave. "Finish two more years of school," they said, "and then go back! So you'll have a trade, so you can earn a living." They were right, but that's not what happened. We left. All the children who stayed in Hungary received a good education. They attended university; the state supported them. If I'd stayed longer, I would have gotten an education too.

I wanted to go back to Greece, and yet at the same time I didn't. I had no idea what I was doing; I was seventeen years old. I said good-bye to a few Hungarian teachers who really liked me. I had one teacher. . . . I said good-bye to her. She was sad; she said, "Stay here, Stefanos!" I was really upset that I was leaving my friends, Greeks and Hungarians. I was upset because we'd reached an age where we went to dances. Our school was all boys; the girls' schools were separate. On Saturday and Sunday evenings we went to dances together, to get to know each other. I had a Hungarian girl-friend. It was sad to leave all that behind. But what did I know? If I'd stayed a year or two longer. . . . It was wonderful there.

### A Fly in Milk

We left for Greece in 1958, on July 20; we went by train. It was just my brother and me. When we arrived in Greece, I felt like a fly in milk. We stood out. Our clothes were different; our manners were different. We were very polite; people here were like barbarians. They didn't have the good manners that we'd been taught—respect for your elders, giving up your seat on the bus. We never saw things like that here.

They took us to Thessaloniki. None of our relatives were there, just two men from the government. They took us to a hotel. "What's going on?" we asked. "Is everybody here rich?" We'd never seen cars like that in Hungary. Monster cars! Stores! A totally different category of consumer goods from what we'd known in Hungary. They had stores in Hungary, but not like the stores in Thessaloniki. Everything here looked more expensive.

People could pick us out by our shoes, our clothes, our accent. We didn't speak Greek very well. If someone saw us on the street or in a store, they'd say, "Where are you kids from? You're not from around here, are you?" We'd say, "We came from abroad." We didn't know any better. As soon as they heard we were from Eastern Europe, they'd say, "Oh!" They assumed we weren't good people.

We spent two nights in the hotel; we ate at a restaurant. What good food! We didn't have any money, of course, but they paid for everything. Then they gave us money to go home. I had no idea where our village was, none at all, but my brother did. They put us on a bus; it was an all-day trip. We arrived in Pirsoyianni and found an old man, some relative of ours, who was there doing some shopping. "Where's the village?" we asked. It was four hours away by foot, so we walked. Along the riverbed. Back then there wasn't a road. The old man showed us where to cross the river, but we were kids. We just jumped from rock to rock. It was fun.

### Eighteen Days in the Village

"Where's the village? Where's the village? Ah! There it is!" The village was at the edge of a steep ravine—old stone houses. My first disappointment; I couldn't believe it. I didn't recognize anyone. The old man showed us our father's house. We went there and met our parents. "This is your father. This is your mother. This is your sister. This is your brother." One person said, "I'm your uncle"; another said, "I'm your cousin." We had no idea what was going on. Everything was so unfamiliar, so strange.

They welcomed us the best they could, but they were poor, really poor. All they had were a few sheep and goats. My mother was very emotional. She'd returned in 1954 with my two other brothers; my father had stayed in the village. Four years later my brother and I came back. We didn't know anyone. That's when I met my relatives for the first time.

I didn't stay in the village for long; I couldn't stand it. They were all strangers. They had nothing to offer us; they had nothing themselves. All they had was milk, all the milk you could drink. Nothing else. Just milk and bread.

I only stayed in the village for eighteen days. I had an argument with my father.

"I don't like it here," I said. "I'm leaving."

"Where will you go?" he asked.

"I don't know, but I'm not staying here. I'd rather become a beggar than stay here."

### The Royal Technical School of Leros

When my father realized I wasn't going to stay, he went to the government and filled out some forms to send me to one of Frederica's schools in Athens. To get in, you needed to have connections. If you went to one of the royal technical schools, they made you a royalist, but they also made you a human being. Unfortunately the school in Athens didn't accept any children who had been in Eastern Europe.

My brother and I came to Athens and went to the office listed on the forms. It was in the Plaka, right under the Acropolis. That was the first time I saw the Acropolis; it was beautiful. "Take these tickets," they said, "get on the trolley, and go to Piraeus. Someone will meet you there." When we reached Piraeus, some other government officials were waiting for us. Before I realized what was happening, they put us on a boat and sent us to Leros, to the Royal Technical School. There were thousands of children there—poor children, children whose parents had been killed in the Civil War, street children, juvenile delinquents. They were just rounded up and sent to Leros for a year. We didn't learn much there. For most of the kids it was a complete waste of time.

My first impression was negative. We didn't know where we were or why we were there. It was a huge building that the Italians had used as a military base. We adapted quickly because we knew all about that kind of life. We'd lived that way for years, and we didn't mind. We ate well; they gave us a lot of food. The quality might not have been very good, but we never went hungry. We adjusted.

In the morning we lined up, and they took attendance to see if anyone was missing. In the morning we all ate together. Then some kids went off to learn plumbing, others carpentry, others construction. Until noon; then we ate. After that we slept. We weren't used to that. People in Eastern Europe don't sleep in the afternoon, but here in Greece you have to because it's really hot. That seemed strange to us. In the beginning we didn't like it, but we gradually got used to it.

When we said our prayers, we were totally lost. We didn't know anything about religion. If we swore or if we cursed Christ or the Virgin Mary, they reported us to a teacher. They brought us a priest once to teach us religion. We began asking him questions, this and that, backward and forward, until he got up and left. They made us go to church on Sundays and holidays. It was deadly; we had to stand for hours. The other children were all lighting candles and chanting. The only thing they knew was religion. They thought we were strange because we didn't believe in God. We weren't believers, but we weren't nonbelievers, either. We'd just never learned anything, that's all.

Obviously life there wasn't as nice as it had been in Hungary, but it was fine. We played soccer and volleyball. They had ping-pong tables too, but the Greek kids—the ones who had grown up in Greece—never used them. They didn't know how to play ping-pong or chess, and it seemed strange to them that we did. The teachers and the supervisors there liked us because we knew lots of things the other kids didn't. Eventually they saw that we didn't have bad intentions; they realized we weren't interested in politics. They said, "They're just innocent kids."

There was a big difference between Greece and Eastern Europe. We didn't learn as much here as we did abroad. They realized that we'd learned something there, but they didn't help us make any progress back here. People in Greece didn't want us to get ahead; it wasn't in their interest. I realized that many years later. I didn't understand it then, but that's the way it was.

Life in Eastern Europe was better. We were freer then; on Leros we weren't free. A boat came once a month, and they guarded it so that no one could escape. We were forced to stay there for a whole year. Lots of kids wanted to leave. I didn't, because I had nowhere else to go. I didn't want to go to my village; there was nothing there. How could I live there? What could I do? I didn't have a trade.

On Leros they let us out every Sunday. If you had some money, you could go buy a cup of coffee or something to eat, but we didn't have any money. We stole figs and oranges, just the way we did in Hungary; we were troublemakers. We went swimming; we got to know the local kids. They taught us how to catch octopus and squid. We learned a lot from them.

On Leros they tried to teach us things they thought we didn't know. They thought we were uneducated, so they put us in special classes to teach us writing and arithmetic. But as soon as they realized we knew all that, they left us alone. They didn't give us any political lessons, that's true, but most of the kids there were uneducated. Life on Leros was all right, but the only reason I can say that is because when we left, things got even worse.

### Life in the Real World

When my brother and I left Leros, we came to Athens and found a man from our village who worked in construction. He took us in and gave us jobs. We worked from dawn to dusk carrying dirt and bricks, cleaning wood and nails, things like that.

They gave us twenty drachmas a day, but we didn't work every day. The person who hired us had a house for us to live in. We had to pay him rent. We didn't have any money, so he gave us loans. We earned some money, but not enough to eat. Those were the worst years of my life, 1959 and 1960. We were miserable. We didn't know anyone. Those were difficult years in Greece. There weren't any jobs; people went hungry; life was hard.

When I was discharged from the army, I came back to Athens. It was hard to find a job in construction, really hard. You went to look for a job, and there were five hundred people, but they only had fifty jobs. When they found out you'd come from Eastern Europe, they didn't hire you. They just gave you a strange look. That was hard.

As the years passed, I got more involved in the construction business. It was all exploitation. Pure exploitation! We worked from dawn to dusk. By that time no one knew we'd come from Eastern Europe. We learned to fit in; we didn't tell anyone we'd come from abroad. We weren't stupid; we just didn't tell anyone. What mattered then was your value as a worker, how well you did your job. If you worked harder than the next guy, then they hired you. That's what I learned. And I learned something else, too. A man hires five people, *they* work, and *he* earns the most money. The five of them are working for him, and he just pays them a little. That's capitalism; that's the system. I figured it out right away, and I said, "I'll become a capitalist too, like them." And I did in no time. My education helped a lot. I knew how to read house plans, so I quickly mastered the business and became number one.

I often thought about going back to Hungary, but later when I was making good money, I said, "It's different there. Here you can accomplish something. There you can't." I realized that I was better off here in Greece. You have to work hard here, but you can accomplish a lot more. In Eastern Europe you didn't have the same opportunities. Everything belonged to the state. Here you could become a rich man. If I were still a day laborer, I'd be worse off here in Greece. But I started my own business, I bought wood and equipment, and I made contacts with engineers and people with money. I joined their circle and seized every opportunity I could. If you have what it takes, you can make it. That's the way it is in Greece.

---

## Maria Bundovska Rosova[4]

*Maria, or Mare, as she is known informally, Rosova, a Macedonian refugee child, was born on March 11, 1940, in a village known as Trnaa in Macedonian and Prasino in Greek. It lies in the hills above the Prespa Lakes just east of the main road from Florina to Kastoria. Maria's husband Georgi was born in a village only fifteen miles away; he is also a refugee child. After they arrived in Canada in 1961, Maria worked as a medical technician in a hospital. Georgi obtained a Bachelor's Degree in civil engineering from the University of Toronto and spent most of his career working for a company that built large industrial complexes all over the world. Maria and Georgi are both retired now and live comfortably in an attractive suburb of Toronto. They have three sons, all university graduates, and eight grandchildren.*

### Civil War

My mother had three brothers. One was killed at the age of 19 in 1942. His name was Alexander—that's why they named my sister Alexandra. He was a little shepherd boy. He and another guy found a land mine. His friend said, "I know how to open this stupid thing." They thought it was a toy, but it exploded, and my uncle was torn in pieces. The other guy was very badly wounded. He lived for an hour, but no doctors, no nothing. So two young guys, they died.

In 1946 and '47 we had no salt; it was forbidden. As a kid I can remember. Salt was very important, even the animals wanted salt. It was a small village, and we were mostly self-sufficient. We had sheep, goats, and stuff like this. When they forbid salt, it was just for punishment. My aunt went to Lerin, to Florina, with other ladies from our village to purchase some salt. The police caught them in the next village. They confiscated the salt and gave them a really nice beating. Apparently my uncles in Canada knew that sugar and salt were going to be scarce, so they sent a parcel with a bag of sugar, a bag of salt, and a bag of coffee. Unfortunately it all spilled on the way, so we couldn't use any of it.

Just before we left, there were two murders in our village. When it's a civil war, you don't know which side to take. One side is killing the other. There were two guys; one was the mayor, and the other was his assistant. They were both killed. Later on I found out from my uncle that apparently a lady had come from the neighboring village. The assistant suspected she was bringing messages, so he searched her. As a woman, to be searched, she felt very violated. So she told her brother, who was with the partisans. They came during the night and pretended that they were the monarchist army. Right then they killed him, and after that his children were kinda revenging on the villagers. It was a mess. This is a picture that stays in my head.

### Departure

The airplane flights were coming more and more and more. In 1948, on March 11, I turned eight years old. The order was for the children to be evacuated. My mother was one of those group mothers, *omadarhisses* as they were called. From the village there were two married women with children, my mother and Aunt Lena, and three single women. They were chosen by the village committee. They said, "It's best to send the kids away. The airplanes are coming. We don't know from day to day what's going to happen. It won't be forever; it will just be for a short time." It wasn't: "Either you send them, or you'll be tortured." It wasn't forced; it was just, "Let's escape. The situation's getting worse and worse, and the children will be gone just for a few months. They'll come back soon." No one expected it would be a lifetime.

My mother didn't want to go because my father was fighting with the partisans. In '46 and '47, he was in Yugoslavia. He went to Belgrade with the Macedonian movement, and my mother didn't want to leave her parents, her home, and everything and just take off and go. But her father persuaded her. He said, "This is the worst of the storm. I would advise you just to take your children and go, because otherwise you'll be taken by the Greek Army and sent somewhere to the islands or to prison because your husband is with the partisans. Or else you're going to be taken into the partisans yourself. You have no other choice. This way at least you'll go with the children."

So from our household it was my mother, the two of us—my sister and myself—and my three cousins. My uncle was in the army too; it was only the two women at home, my mother and my aunt. So my aunt was the only one left in the house. It was just before Easter, Lenten period, and I remember the mothers sending the kids off, like to a camp, with whatever they had—boiled eggs, a chicken, a little lamb, or some pastries.

There were a few families whose children stayed in the village. It wasn't like you saw them dragging children out of their parent's arms. People from the village—the committee—had organized it. I remember my poor grandparents. I was their first grandchild. It was dusk; my grandmother was hugging me, and she said, "*So zdravie da odite.*" That means, "May you go in good health." That was the last time I ever saw my grandmother.

### Crossing the Border

We went down the road from Lerin to Kostur; then we took the road that branched off to Prespa. It was evening. Slowly we went to a village in Prespa, and we slept in the homes of the children who had left just before us. The next morning we had to get up early in the dawn so we wouldn't be spotted by the airplanes that were constantly circling around. They said, "Okay, get the kids ready." So we got up. No breakfast, no nothing. There were some thick forests, so they said, "Let's hide here in the shade." We were hungry, screaming, and crying. Finally they brought something for us to eat. It was already dark, and we were walking on some narrow mountain paths, just for the sheep or the goats.

We reached Dupeni on the other side of the border in Yugoslavia. Those villages over there were just like ours. No radio, no television. You couldn't get any messages. They didn't say, "Oh, the kids are coming!" Nobody knew. We were among the first to arrive. Where could they accommodate us? The school was full, so they put us in barns with just straw. It was March, and the winds were cold. We were just like little mice, squeezed in one close to the other.

Then, I remember, they put us in some trucks with canvas covers, and we went to Bitola. My father had left some money there with a relative of ours in case his wife came. My poor mother! They said, "This is the money that your husband left." But she had so many kids, what could she buy? She was looking for bread, but there wasn't much. So she bought some roasted chickpeas and raisins for the kids. They gathered us in Brailovo, a few kilometers north of Prilep. They had those big pots like the army. The kids were sick; some were very nauseous. We're talking little children. And everything was so disorganized! One hand didn't know what the other was doing. It was a gathering place. So many, many children!

### Journey through Yugoslavia

Then they started putting the kids onto trains. God knows how they were dividing them up. By age? By village? Some kids from our village went to Romania; some went to Bela Crkva in Vojvodina, in Yugoslavia. The next day it was our turn. We went inside, but my mom stayed outside. I didn't know what to do; I didn't know how to get to my mom. I was crying, and I said, "Give me my little hanky!" You find an excuse, you know, a child just makes up an excuse. And my mother said, "Oh, Mare, here it is." So this guy just grabbed the little hanky from my mom and gave it to me. He pushed me inside the train, and then he pushed my mother out. She fell. So they took us away, and we ended up, me and my sister, in Bulkes in Serbia. My mother and my Aunt Lena, they just left them behind; they didn't send them with the children. They tore us apart. Eventually they sent my mother with other kids who were coming from Kostur, like Georgi, my husband. She didn't go through Bulkes; she went straight to Czechoslovakia.

We ended up in Bulkes. We were sleeping in some houses that were left by people of German origin. There was a lot of corn in the attic and a lot of pigeons who would go and eat the corn in the evening and make a lot of noise. The older girls would say, "Vampires!" and I would be so scared. I remember they had one big dining room, and they made us some dandelion greens. That was first time I ever tasted them; they were very bitter. And they gave us sugar cookies. I held mine in a little serviette and went to look for my sister. I was eight; she wasn't even five. And I think I'm in my village and that everyone knows who my sister and I are. Here I am, looking for her so I can give her my cookie, and that stupid cookie crumbled. There was nothing left, and here I'm crying, "Alexandra! Alexandra!" Then fortunately a lady who was a group leader from a neighboring village and knew me and my sister took me and said, "Mare, here she is," to calm me down.

Meantime my mother went to Mikulov, a detention center for refugees in southern Czechoslovakia, with another group of children. They said to her, "Don't worry! Your children are going to be there." But we weren't there; we were in Bulkes. Eventually journalists started coming from Bulgaria and asking, "What's going on?" So the ladies started telling them everything: "They split us up, so we don't know where our children are." They made lot of commotion; they started complaining to the Czech authorities.

### A Yellow Dress

A few weeks later we were put on the train to Czechoslovakia. While we were going through Hungary, they sprayed us with some kind of powder for disinfection and lice. Then we arrived in Mikulov. My mother was looking to see who came. She spotted us from far away. I was holding my sister tight by her hand. My mother waved at us and called us by name. She was dressed in a shocking yellow dress with red flowers—carnations—that was sent from God knows where. They took all their clothes. My mother never wore a dress like that; she always wore the traditional village outfit. That dress still sticks in my mind. I didn't recognize her because I was feverish, and my eyes were kind of blurry. She couldn't come close to us.

We were taken straight to be bathed. We were undressed, given a shower, all of us—like tiny little fish, and then wrapped in gray cotton blankets. We were examined by medical doctors. I was sick; I had the mumps, so they put me in isolation. My sister and two of my cousins were reunited with my mother, but I was missing. My mother didn't know where I was. She didn't understand the nurses when they told her I was in quarantine. So she went from window to window, looking in from the outside, until she found me. When she finally did, she said "Mare, don't worry! Mom is here!"

*Life in Czechoslovakia*

When we went to Darkov, it must have been June or July. We were now in smaller groups—there were about seventy of us—and we were very well taken care of. We had a garden, and for the first time we ate carrots, cauliflowers, and other vegetables. Some of us had long braids, and they took us to get a haircut for the first time. They took us to the little town, and for the first time I saw those dummies in the window. To me they looked like real people, and I said, "My goodness! How can they stand so still?" It was like being in Wonderland. Every evening we would take down the Czech flag and in the morning put it back up. They taught us a song that I used to sing to my kids. It's a beautiful song. It goes:

> Little stars, good night.
> I'm going to bed now,
> I'm leaving my parents to you.
> Take good care of them
> Because I love them so dearly.

That was the song. It was like our little prayer when we used to go to bed at night. It stayed with me. I don't know if it was a Czech song or if it was specially made for us, but it was a little prayer to calm us because our parents weren't there. That was the first song I remember.

We stayed at Darkov for a little while. Then they started gathering us in a bigger place called Klokočov not too far from Krakow, on the Polish border. We started our schooling in Greek and Macedonian. I was only eight years old. On the chalkboard they wrote Greek, and I was supposed to copy it. I didn't know what it was all about. Then we started Macedonian. That we understood, since most of us were Macedonians. Eventually, when the situation back home didn't improve, they brought Czech teachers into the home. They started teaching us in Czech when I was in grade four. Later we were integrated into the Czech schools. The main language was Czech, then Russian. After school we also studied Macedonian and Greek.

They used to call us "the Greek children." Our Czech caregivers were puzzled; they said, "These are Greek kids, but some of them don't speak Greek, and some of them do. What's going on?" There's a lot of similarity between our language, the Macedonian language, and Czech. That's when they started distinguishing between us. It was a lot easier for us to grasp the Czech language than for the Greek children.

Even though my mother was there in the children's home in Klokočov, I lived just like the other children. My mother wasn't taking care of me; she was working in the kitchen or helping the nurses. So even though my mother was there, my mother, my sister and I weren't living together. We were with the children, and she was with the other ladies. We were separate.

In 1950, my mother found out that her brother had been killed, the one who was in the Greek Army. It was after the war had finished. They were digging trenches near the Albanian border, and one of those trucks overturned and crushed him. Meantime her youngest brother, who was with the partisans, was badly wounded in the thigh. He was treated in Katlanovo, south of Skopje. From there he was transferred to Tashkent.

### Family Reunion

My mother and father were reunited through the Red Cross. My father was in Skopje; he started writing letters to my mother. My mother and father didn't have much of an education, but my father eventually went to night school in Skopje to learn to read and write Macedonian. My mother just knew the Greek alphabet, so she would write Greek letters, but Macedonian words.

In the early '50s, the political situation between Yugoslavia and the rest of the communist bloc deteriorated a lot. It really affected my mother and some other ladies in the children's home who were receiving letters from their husbands, brothers, and other relatives in Skopje. Officials from the Greek Communist Party read their letters. There was nothing political in them, just family news. One day they called my mother in and said, "We're sorry. You have to leave the children's home." When she asked why, they said that the letters from Yugoslavia had a bad influence on the children. They said she was part of "Tito's clique." Because she was getting letters from her husband in Skopje! Where was my mother to go? She said, "Tito doesn't know me, and I don't know him. These are letters from my husband." But it was the '50s, the same thing you had here—the Rosenbergs and the McCarthyism. It was that sick paranoia. What did my mother have to do with Tito? They chased her away from the children's home.

She was complaining of a sore throat, so she went to Opava to have her tonsils taken out, but it was all nerves. Finally she ended up in a psychiatric hospital in Olomouc. Fortunately she received good care there. I said, "Mom, why do you wear those black clothes?" But she wouldn't say anything. She was only thirty-two years old. While my mother was in the hospital, she got a letter from my uncle in Tashkent. I opened it, and it says, "Our brother was killed." So then I knew why she was wearing black. There I am, a child, ten years old. My mother is sick, my uncle is killed, and my father is far away. I thought, "Okay, my mother is going to die and turn into a vampire." I couldn't sleep at night, and I would beg, "Please, just keep a little light on." It affected me emotionally. My poor mother didn't know where to go. She finally ended up in Bruntal, in a factory where they made linen products. She worked there for quite a few years. My sister and I used to visit her at Christmastime or during the summer.

In '56, when Khrushchev went brother-brother with Tito and the situation warmed up a little bit, my mother started doing the papers for us to go to Yugoslavia. With me having all these bad memories as a child going through there, I said, "How on earth are we going to go to that country again?" And I said to my mom, "Let me finish school here, and then I'll go." My father said, "Oh, don't worry. There are schools here in Skopje too." So after I finished grade nine, I moved to an *internat* with my sister. It was mostly Czech students. There were six Macedonian and four Greek girls there. Then on July the 10th, 1957, after I finished grade ten, we went to Skopje, Macedonia.

It was midnight when my father picked us up at the railway station. The next day he said to my mother: "I'll have to take you to register with the police. They'll take you for interrogation to Idrizovo." The prison outside Skopje. "You don't need to say too much," he said. "You say one thing, it's gonna come another thing. Don't elaborate. You went there with the kids. The less you know, the better it is."

I was seven years old when I last saw my father, and then I arrived in Skopje at the age of seventeen, ten years later. I knew he was my father; we had some correspondence. I remember he sent us a parcel with dresses for me and my sister, but to me he was like a stranger. Because she was younger or because it's her character, my sister came closer to my father sooner than I did. I wouldn't even address him as "Father" or "Daddy." I was fortunate that my father was a very kind, very warm man. He was a loving and caring person. After two months he made me feel like we had never been separated.

Life in Skopje was difficult in the beginning, because I was educated in the Czech language, but after five or six months, you get adjusted. In two years I finished a course in medical technology. Then I worked one year in a clinic for the Macedonian government.

## Marriage and Emigration

I met my husband, Georgi, when I was only fifteen and he was twenty. We had a correspondence, and one thing led to the other. In July '57, I went to Skopje; in September '57, he came to Toronto with his family. He sent me a letter, and he said, "How lucky you are to be there, close to our homeland, speaking the same language." Coming to Canada was very difficult for him—a completely different language and culture. After three years he wrote a letter to my father. He said, "I would like very much to marry your daughter." My father replied, "We have been separated; we have only been together for three years. If you want my daughter, I really would like you to come here and take her from my hands, so at least I know who I'm giving her to. I don't want to just send her away as I did before."

Georgi came to Skopje, and we had our wedding. Then we came to Canada. I came in the middle of January '61. It's going to be forty years now. By March of '61, I had already started working at the hospital. I had never taken English; I had taken Macedonian, Greek, Czech, Serbo-Croatian, two years of German in high school, and two years of French. So the patients in the hospital would ask for "the petite brunette from Quebec," because I knew a few French words.

When I came to Canada, I was worried. As a young kid growing up in a communist system, coming to this capitalist system, I was crying. I said to Georgi, "How on earth am I going to go over there to a capitalist country?" He said, "Don't worry! That's only propaganda, you'll see." But it's the fear. Capitalists, poverty, exploitation! I was always looking to find it. But my fears were unfounded! The people I worked with were very understanding and very caring. The only thing I couldn't understand was charging patients for their blood work. In Czechoslovakia and Yugoslavia people had free health care. Thankfully we have universal health care in Canada now.

In the mid-sixties we bought a new house in a brand new subdivision. At the same time our second son was born. That was when the air traffic started to get worse. Whenever I took my new baby for a walk and I heard an airplane fly over, I felt the fear that I had as a child. I always felt like throwing myself on the stroller to cover my child. For me a plane was still a tool of bombardment and murder.

*In 1976, Maria's father died at the age of sixty in Skopje. Maria, Georgi, and their three children, Peter, 14, John, 10, and Chris, 6, traveled to Skopje to attend his funeral. Then they decided to go to Greece and visit the villages where she and Georgi had been born.*

### *Return to Trnaa*

When we went to Trnaa, a lady said, "What would you like?" I said, "Nothing. Just a bottle of water." I gathered some wild flowers that were growing in the garden of our old house, and when I returned to Skopje, they had already dried out. I went to put them on my father's grave, and I said, "You couldn't go to your village, to your birth place, but I brought something for you from there." I put the flowers on his grave and poured some water on it so he could have a drink. I remember going to see my grandma's house in Trnaa. My mind knew that she'd been dead for a long time, but just being there I got angry. I said, "You promised me that you would be here for me. And here I am coming to visit you, and you're not here."

We went to Kostur, to a little motel that somebody from Canada was building. There were only four beds, so I slept with Chris, the youngest one. I remember the dream I had. We were walking, and the airplanes were coming. But I'm a mother now. I have a child, and I'm squeezing that little boy close to me. Suddenly he says, "Mama, you're choking me." And, excuse me, he wet the bed. Finally I came to myself, from the nightmare I had, and I said, "Thank God, Chris! We're alive. We're okay, and even if we're wet, we can change our clothes."

It was a nightmare. It was the first time we'd gone back home, and I'd seen some soldiers there. All that brought back memories of '48, of leaving the village, but now I'm dreaming. We're leaving; the airplanes are bombarding us. I'm a child leaving, but at the same time I'm a parent. I have children, and I'm squeezing the kid beside me. I'm hiding him from the airplanes. I could just feel the airplanes; they were circling over us. And suddenly he woke me up. It was just a dream. Thank God!

*In 1986, Maria and Georgi visited their villages for a second time. Georgi had just completed a yearlong assignment in South Africa, where he had supervised the construction of a large mining complex. Maria visited him in Johannesburg, and on their way back to Toronto, they flew to Athens and then Thessaloniki. There they rented a car and drove to Skopje to visit Maria's mother and sister. When they attempted to reenter Greece at the border crossing at Gevgelija, the Greek official examining Maria's Canadian passport noticed that she had been born in Greece.*

### *Crossing the Border Again*

He's looking at me, and he says, "You were born in Greece. Why don't you speak Greek?"

"I left when I was very young," I say.

"When did you leave?"

And I say, "1944."

And he says, "What kind of name is Bundovska? Where is Trnaa?"

So I look at him. Coming from South Africa when it was apartheid, I saw how even the black people there had more rights than we did here. And I thought to myself, "You bastard! You intimidated my grandparents. You intimidated my parents. But you are *not* going to intimidate me." I look him straight in the eyes, and I say, "Sir, I'm sorry. I did not choose my name; I did not choose my parents; I did not choose the place I was born. I've been a citizen of Canada for over thirty years, and it is not some banana republic. The Canadian consulate is right here in Salonika. You can get all the particulars you need. There's no point for you to intimidate me here like this."

"Go!" the guy says angrily.

And I smile and say, "Thank you. You have been very kind."

They'll do anything to intimidate us. I didn't say anything to Georgi, because Georgi would say, "You always have to speak up your mind." Georgi is kind of obedient. But with me, when it's not right, I like to speak up my mind.

### Life in the Diaspora

Our son Chris got married in the summer of 2000. My mom called at 7:30 in the morning to congratulate us. She started crying, and she said, "I wasn't there when they were born, and unfortunately I'm not there now when they're getting married." And then I say, "Mom, the kids all have good jobs here; they're professionals. What if I was over there, and they didn't have jobs or they were in the army? See what happened there. The whole country has collapsed. With us it was the Civil War that scattered us all over the place; now it's reality. See how many parents are over there whose children can't find jobs. Now they're coming here or to Australia. Life has changed. We have to look at the positive things."

In Lerin now everybody talks to you in Macedonian; they're not afraid. Greece is not the wild dog it was before. Now it's under the European Union. With the internet, with telecommunications, the roads are open, and people can travel. I'm fortunate that I'm in Canada. My children were born here; I have eight grandchildren. I'm still involved with our church, the Macedonian senior home, and the Daughters of Macedonia.

I don't believe in any enemy; you create your own enemies when you start labeling people. I remember when we went to our reunion in Skopje in 1988, our declaration was, "Let no child experience what we did. Let no parents long for their children as ours did." Look at Yugoslavia, which was the envy of all Eastern Europe. Isn't it a shame? We're at the threshold of a new century. It takes a long, long time to give birth to a child and raise him into a man or to build a house, but it takes only a split of a second to destroy what it took centuries to build. Like Dubrovnik. How beautiful it was!

Look at me! After fifty-two years, the tears are still coming. If we can find a common language, we'll find we have a lot more in common than things that divide us. We don't hate anybody. We have to learn from the past so we can have a better future for our children and for generations to come.

# FIVE

# Children of the Paidopoleis

## Efterpi Tsiou[1]

*Efterpi Tsiou was born in 1935 in Likorahi, a village whose inhabitants were all Greeks, located high above the Sarandaporos River valley in the foothills of Mount Grammos a few kilometers from the Albanian border. In the 1970s, Likorahi was relocated to a more accessible site right next to the new road from Kastoria to Konitsa that had just been built along the valley floor.*

*Efterpi is a tall, thin woman who has dressed in black ever since her husband died many years ago. Unlike most village women her age, Efterpi does not cover her hair with a black kerchief; she wears it in a long gray braid that hangs down to the middle of her back. Efterpi's thick glasses do nothing to dim the liveliness of her bright blue eyes. Of the twelve children born to Efterpi's mother, only six were alive when the Civil War began. Because Efterpi's parents were wealthy and supported the Greek government, and because Likorahi was under communist control for extended periods of time, Efterpi's family suffered greatly during the Civil War.*

### Civil War

During the Civil War many people in Likorahi were killed. Some poor villagers betrayed others just because they were wealthy, because they had storerooms full of wheat. They made up excuses; they said that that people were cutting telephone lines or passing documents from the partisans to the army. They were just looking for excuses to kill people, and they found them.

One family had to leave their daughter at home in bed alone. I remember it as if it were yesterday. She was sick, and they couldn't go take care of her because they were afraid the army would arrest them. So my mother sent me once a day to give her water until she finally died.

The partisans were such fanatics. They killed my father, my father-in-law, and five or six other people in one day. They strung them up and beat them. I didn't see it with my own eyes; my mother described it to me. The partisans put rocks on their backs while they were hanging there. They hung there until they died. Then the partisans cut them down and buried them in the fields behind the village.

*In October 1947, just before the outbreak of the Civil War, Efterpi's parents were able to send her to the paidopoli that Queen Frederica had recently opened in Konitsa. It was housed in a former agricultural school, a large two-story building of light brown stone that still stands on a terrace below the town in a grove of tall, dark cypress trees.*

### Departure

It was like a summer camp. They took children for two or three months and then sent them home. But the Civil War broke out, and we had to stay there. The fighting started, and the villages were cut off. The roads were closed; we were trapped in Konitsa. They didn't send us home because they didn't want the partisans to take us away.

The president of the village said, "Who'll go first?" To tell you the truth, it was a question of who your friends and relatives were and how many children you had. If you had lots of children, two would go. If you had fewer children, only one would go. If you were poor, one would go even if you only had two. The president and the village council chose us. They enrolled twenty-five boys and three girls. It was a big deal for the girls to go with the boys. I'd never been to school. My father didn't let me go in Liko-rahi. When he registered my older sisters for school, he said they were two years older than they really were so they'd finish sooner. He needed them to work in the fields and take care of the animals. I was younger, and they kept me at home. Even though I was little, I cooked, I washed clothes, and I folded blankets. I wanted to get out of the house, but my parents made me stay home.

In '47, our parents took us to the paidopoli. A big army truck came, and they put us inside. We'd never ridden in a truck; we'd never even seen one before. They put us in the back of the truck with our mothers. The trucks drove through the mud and rocks in the riverbed. We were crying and throwing up all over the back of the truck. We spent the night at the inn outside Konitsa. The next morning we arrived at the paidopoli.

We saw the tall building and the big windows. We were used to small houses with little windows. We were in terrible shape—woolen skirts, woolen socks, and homemade village shoes on our feet. They gave us showers and cut our hair. We were crying and shouting, "Don't cut our hair!" It was full of lice; that's why they cut it. I cried a lot because I had really long hair. I was proud of it. I had two long, thick braids down to here. When my mother saw me later with my hair cut, she cried too. "You cut my little girl's hair!" No one could have recognized us when we came out of those showers.

## The Battle of Konitsa

We had a good life there; that's the truth. We had a regular schedule—milk in the morning, a meal at noon, something sweet in the afternoon, and another meal in the evening. Then they showed us a movie. But we were shut in; we didn't have any contact with our parents because of the war.

When my mother left me at the paidopoli, she kissed me. That was it. I remember it as if it happened yesterday. My father used to go to Filiates with his sheep. He came to the paidopoli in the spring, and I remember he brought me a pencil. He cut it in half and sharpened each half at both ends. "This is for you," he said. "I cut it in half so you won't lose the whole thing all at once." Then he kissed me. I never saw my father again. Two months later the partisans killed him together with my father-in-law and seven other men.

When the partisans began to withdraw and the road was open, some villagers came down to Konitsa. They told the director, and she called us in one day. "Children," she said, "it's wartime, and we hear good news and bad." We were always worried about our parents, but we never had the courage to ask the director or the women who took care of us if they had any news from them. The director said, "Unfortunately, Tsiou has lost her father." But she didn't tell me that the partisans had killed him. Later I learned how they killed him from other villagers who came to the paidopoli. They said that the partisans hung him up, and beat him, and left him to die. My relatives never even found out what happened to his body.

When the battle of Konitsa broke out, we were trapped in the paidopoli. The partisans wanted to attack Konitsa and capture us so they could take us behind the Iron Curtain. But officials in Konitsa and the director of the camp realized what was happening and notified the authorities in Ioannina, so they sent lots of soldiers. A terrible battle took place; it lasted eight days. The partisans surrounded the town, but the army didn't let them capture us. We lay on the cement floor in the basement for eight days with one blanket to cover us and two figs a day to eat. They didn't let us stand up. The director blocked the windows with sacks of flour. Finally the army won, and the partisans withdrew. We were liberated. We went outside and raised the blue and white flag. Queen Frederica came on the third day and congratulated us for surviving all that time.

We didn't return to Likorahi; the government wouldn't let us go back. There was no transportation, and they didn't want the partisans to take us away. After the war, three or four big trucks came and took us to the Paidopoli of Saint Eleni in Ioannina. Two days later, they brought us to Ziro, where we stayed for six months. Then fighting broke out between the partisans and the army at a monastery nearby. Army trucks came again and brought us to Preveza. They put us on an old navy boat. The partisans had destroyed the bridges over the canal at Corinth, so we had to go all the way around the Peloponnese to get to Athens. One night the boat broke down in the middle of the ocean. It was dangerous. They turned on the sirens, and within a half an hour another boat came. It tied up to us and towed us all the way to Piraeus. When we got off the boat, there were more army trucks. They always put us in army trucks; we never went by bus. They took us to the Paidopoli of Saint Andreas in Rafina outside Athens.

### Life in Rafina

We had a good time at Saint Andreas. There was an upper area for girls and a lower area for boys. The queen came once with Constantine, her son, and we played "slaves." I hit Constantine, and he cried. We were the same age. The children said, "She hit Constantine! She hit Constantine!" The queen said, "He's fine." We let him play with us, but he shouldn't have hit us. We were girls, and he was a boy. So we kicked him out, and made him go play with the boys.

To tell you the truth, I felt like the queen was my mother. I respected her; I still do. I'm grateful to her as our benefactor. She saved us then; she was there for us. We had no mother, no father, no brothers. She took care of us all those years while we were at Saint Andreas.

Every day was the same: school, dormitory, homework; school, dormitory, homework. But we went to lots of parades—October 28th, March 25th. They always asked me to carry the flag because I was tall and had long hair. I took pride in that. I got along well with the teachers. I respected them, and they appreciated me. What can I say?

We went on lots of field trips. We went to the Acropolis, to museums, to foundries. We wore uniforms with little white collars. Our rooms were in little houses. Each room had four beds—bunk beds, top and bottom. Usually they put the older girls on the top and the younger girls on the bottom. The boys lived in a big building. It had one huge room with fifty beds in it. We didn't have anything of our own, though; everything belonged to the paidopoli. We didn't have any money, either. Who would have given it to us? Our parents? We only had what the institution provided. Everything was the same. They gave us coats, uniforms, shoes, and socks, and they gave us underwear. They brought us all our clothes in one big bundle— ironed, disinfected, and folded. We didn't get to wear the same clothes all the time. I didn't like that, to tell the truth, so I wrote my name in all my clothes. When they brought our clothes, I searched through everything until I found my own.

The daily program went like this: In the morning we woke up, washed our faces, combed our hair, and went to the dining room. Then we drank our milk, ate our bread and jam, and went to school in lines with our teachers. As soon as school was over at one or two o'clock, we went back to the dining room and had lunch. Then we went back to our rooms to rest. In the afternoon a young woman taught us sewing and embroidery. The girls who finished elementary school and didn't go on to high school worked with her. They learned some skills so that later in life they could mend a sock, as the saying goes. These were necessary skills for a girl to get by.

I finished elementary school in '49. After elementary school, they sent you to technical school, or to high school if you were a good student. They chose me, another girl from our village, and some boys. The boys they sent to Volos; they sent the girls to Larissa.

*All these years Efterpi had no direct communication with her family. While she was still living in the paidopoli in Konitsa, she learned from fellow villagers that in 1948 many families from Likorahi, including her own, had been forcibly evacuated by the partisans to Albania. From there her younger brother and sister, together with twenty-five other children from the village, were forcibly taken by the partisans against their parents' will and sent "behind the Iron Curtain" to Czechoslovakia. In 1949, Efterpi's mother and older brother and sister returned secretly to Likorahi, without permission from Communist Party officials. Efterpi's mother had been afraid her two older children would be drafted by the partisans and sent back to Greece to fight. She had to leave all the family's sheep and goats behind in Albania. In 1954, Efterpi's younger brother and sister returned to Likorahi from Czechoslovakia. Her oldest sister, who had married before the Civil War began, remained in Likorahi with her husband throughout the war.*

### Return to Likorahi

In 1950, my older brother was working in Trikala. Twice my mother sent him to bring me home. I didn't want to leave the paidopoli in Larissa. I remembered the old life we'd lived when I was a child and all our suffering. I didn't want to go back to the village. The first time and the second time I refused to leave, so my mother sent my brother a third time. The director said, "I'm sorry, Tsiou, but when your mother asks for you, we can't insist anymore." I cried like a river. I wanted to stay in school, but my brother came again so I had to leave. It seemed to me at the time like the director was expelling me from school.

My brother sent me by bus to Ioannina. From there I came to Konitsa. My mother's brother happened to be there. He recognized me and brought me to Pirsoyianni. My brother-in-law, the teacher, and the village president, were there. I was a young girl; I was embarrassed. I didn't speak to them at all. Not a word.

When we arrived in Likorahi, they took me to my mother. I was shocked to see her again. I didn't even recognize her! My mother cried, but I just stood there unmoved. I didn't feel any emotion; I didn't remember her. I was furious because she took me from the paidopoli and brought me back to the village.

"What's for breakfast?" I asked my mother the next morning.

She was poor and didn't have anything—no milk, no eggs, nothing.

"We'll cook some beans for lunch. " she said. "We'll eat then."

"But now, for breakfast," I said, "what is there to eat?"

Everyone in the village heard about that: "Efterpi said, 'What is there to eat for breakfast?'" That was the gossip.

I was ready to explode. My mother had a bad temper. I knew she was poor; I knew she was a widow. But she was impossible to live with. She was always complaining, so you had to do whatever she wanted. I was totally inexperienced. She sent me to work in the fields. What did I know about hoeing? There I was hacking at clumps of dirt all day. In the evening—tears! I was so upset I couldn't eat; I couldn't do anything. "What's the matter?" she asked. "Nothing." I just cried. I couldn't say anything. What could I say? She forced me to come home.

I came back from the paidopoli with one pair of shoes. My mother couldn't afford to buy me another pair, so I wore homemade village shoes tied together with pieces of string. Your heels came out of them, and the soles of your feet hit the ground. There were thorns and rocks everywhere.

Hoeing, weeding, and harvesting. We suffered a lot; we were poor. We worked hard, and we didn't see much in return.

My mother sent me to my older sister's to help her husband plow their fields. He had an iron plow, not a wooden one. UNRRA gave iron plows to the refugees who'd been repatriated. America sent them a lot of things. One day my sister came home from the fields and found me crying. She told my mother.

"I came home and found Efterpi in tears," she said.

"Why were you crying?" my mother asked.

"Why shouldn't I?" I said. "I'm crying for my misfortune, for my miserable life. It's all your fault! You took me out of school. I was happy there. And what did you do? You brought me back to Likorahi to work in the fields! You're my mother; I love and respect you. But why did you bring me home? What kind of life do I have now?"

### Marriage

There was more to come. So-and-so wants to marry Efterpi; so-and-so does too. There were six or seven young men in the village and no young women. They'd all been drafted by the partisans and killed in the mountains or evacuated to Eastern Europe. The young men all looked the same to me. How could I decide which one to marry? But my mother's complaining was unbearable.

One day a man was walking by on his way to the fields. I hadn't seen him before; I didn't know who he was. "Do you see him?" my mother asked. "He's the one who's been asking for you, the one whose uncle comes by every day trying to arrange a marriage. He's the one you'll marry." So I said to myself, "Him? Him!" I was caught between a rock and a hard place. Do you understand?

My mother made the decision. We got engaged, and then in January 1951 we got married. I lived with my mother for three months; then she married me off. My husband was a villager; it's the truth. He didn't know any other life. I'm not blaming him. He couldn't offer me any help with my education. I was just a girl. My husband wanted a wife, and he found a wife.

So I became a shepherd. We had twenty-five sheep. The pasture was far away—an hour from the village on foot.

"Today," my husband said, "we'll go out with the sheep."

So we went out with the sheep. In the evening we loaded the mule with wood.

"Go home," he said, "so you won't have to spend the night in the hut."

But how could I find my way home? I'd only been back in the village for three months.

"I can't find my way home," I said. "I'll get lost."

"Don't worry," he said. "The mule will lead you home."

And it did. It brought me right back to the village.

Later I had three daughters. Out in the fields all day, hoeing, weeding, and harvesting. I raised three daughters in the dirt, in the furrows of the fields. We hung the cradle in a tree and went to check it in the morning, at noon, and in the evening. I'm amazed I survived. I raised my daughters the best I could. I was determined to give them a loving home and to educate them so they could leave the village and escape the misery and the hardships I endured.

*Efterpi's three daughters finished elementary school in Likorahi and went on to high school in Konitsa. The oldest boarded with a family in town; the other two lived in a dormitory run by the Orthodox Church. Efterpi and her husband made great sacrifices to educate their daughters, and all three graduated from high school. One works as an accountant in Ioannina, another works at a hospital in Larissa. The third was a student at the University of Ioannina, when she died suddenly at the age of twenty-three.*

### Living with Our Enemies

Four or five years ago my uncle, my father's sister's husband, came back from Czechoslovakia. I was out in the stable when he walked by. He recognized me, and I recognized him. He said "Efterpi, my niece, how are you?" That's how he spoke to me. I didn't say anything. I didn't speak to him. He was responsible for my father's death. After he killed my father, he left the village and went to Albania. When someone asked him about my father's death, he said, "You have to separate the wheat from the chaff."

I never spoke to him. He died a year later, and I never spoke to him. He spent years behind the Iron Curtain. My father's sister fought with him her whole life. "You killed my brother!" "You killed my brother!" That's what she said, till the day she died. But I never spoke to him. I may have sinned, I may be at fault, but I just couldn't speak to him. I couldn't open my mouth and say, "How are you, Uncle?"

The people who came back from Eastern Europe were our enemies, the enemies of our family. Not all of them, just some of them. The children weren't to blame. How could they have been responsible? They didn't know anything. We have an obligation to speak to them, to welcome them into our homes. It was the adults, the party leaders, who were to blame. When a man lives here, and you see him every day, and when you know he killed your father and left six children orphaned, how would you feel? How could you stomach him after that?

I don't have any problems with his son; he's my cousin. He was in Eastern Europe. When he returned to the village, he came to my house for dinner. "Efterpi," he said, "I'm leaving. I'm going far away. They'll need the Red Cross to find me." Someone had spoken to him: "For your own good, I'm telling you. Leave! You're innocent; you shouldn't have to pay the penalty. But your father's police file will ruin you. You'll never find a job; you'll never have a life." And that's what happened. He went to Brazil. No one heard from him for forty years. Then last year, when he needed some government documents for his children, he came back. After all that time.

### Setting a Good Example

When I returned from the paidopoli, I wanted to set the best example I could for all the women in the village. And I did. In spite of all our disadvantages and all our poverty, I sent my daughters to elementary school dressed like dolls. I patched up the old clothes from America that UNRRA gave us, and I sent my daughters off to school with dignity and self-respect. They looked better than any other children in the village. Everyone said, "Efterpi knows how to do this and that. Let's go ask Efterpi." I'm not boasting. I wasn't taught how to weave or make dresses at the paidopoli; I learned on my own. I came back, and I taught all the women here in the village.

At the paidopoli I wanted to study. It's not that I didn't like sewing and weaving, but I wanted to study. I wanted to become an educated person. None of the other village women had gone to elementary school. To tell you the truth, they were so backward they didn't even know how to dance. They were never free to learn, to grow, and to live.

---

## Traian Dimitriou[2]

*Traian Dimitriou was born in 1934 in a Slavic-speaking village of four hundred people known as Leskovec in Macedonian and Leptokaries in Greek, located ten kilometers southeast of Florina at the foot of Mount Vitsi. Traian entered elemen-*

*tary school in 1940, but the school soon closed when the violence of World War II completely disrupted village life.*

*After the Civil War ended, Traian finished elementary school in Leptokaries and then attended high school for a few years in Florina. In 1954, he emigrated to Toronto, where one of his aunts had settled in 1927. Now Traian lives in Aigincourt, a residential neighborhood northeast of the city center. He is married to a Macedonian woman from the Florina region and has two grown children. A former employee of the Toronto Transit Commission, Traian has long been an active member of the Macedonian-Canadian Human Rights Committee.*

### Civil War

When the resistance groups took over, there was a sort of happy feeling that now socially things would be better. The Macedonians felt that they would be partners in whatever system took over, with their identity being protected. But unfortunately this did not happen. This was a very difficult time with a lot of murders and killing and suspicious things—knocks at the door. The population was terrified.

Leskovec was in an unusual place. We were very close to the government-controlled areas. As soon as darkness fell, the partisans were there, but during daylight hours we were very vulnerable to the government troops. The population there was definitely suppressed, there's no doubt, especially the Macedonians. They were not trusted; they were third-class citizens. In many cases they were taken by armed men to clear the highway with their ox-driven carts in case there were mines. So they would get killed clearing the roads. I know that for a fact because I have seen it.

There were times in '47 when the population was terrorized because suddenly the Greek government forces would come into the village and beat everybody up. About fifty men from my village were beaten so hard they couldn't walk. One of them said, "You are recruiting for Markos [Vafiadis, commander general of the Democratic Army]. By beating me you are making me to go over to their side." And they beat him up some more.

*Traian's parents sent him to live with his older sister, who was married and lived in Pesočnica (Ammohori in Greek), a village in the plains much closer to Florina that was under government control. There Traian would be safe; he would also be able to attend school. Pesočnica was only five kilometers from Leskovec, so Traian and his parents saw each other frequently. Unfortunately Traian was back in Leskovec visiting his parents the day the Greek army evacuated fifteen children from the village to protect them from the partisans and the violence of the Civil War.*

*Departure*

My father and people in the village that were in the organizations knew that children were being sent to Eastern Europe. Actually there were Macedonian partisans who told our fathers to remove their children from the village to a safe area under government control so they would not be taken to Eastern Europe. There was conflict between the Communist Party and ethnic Macedonians on this. The Macedonian partisans didn't want the population to be moved outside the country. They said, "Send the children somewhere—to go to school, to your relatives—but make sure you don't lose them. Do everything you can to keep the children here."

I didn't know what was happening. I had gone to Leskovec for a visit, and all of a sudden the whole area was being surrounded by government troops. But most of our children in Leskovec had already gone to other villages that were considered safer. Leskovec was actually in a no-man's-land. The children in the partisan-controlled areas, of course, ended up in the Eastern countries. If I'd been in Pesočnica that day, this would never have happened to me.

I was in the house when they came to take me. They spoke to my parents: "We're evacuating the children. It's for their own good. They'll be going to school; they'll be safe." But the fact is, we were taken by force. My parents couldn't understand it. They refused, both of them. They told the soldiers, "There's no reason for this. He doesn't live here; he goes to school in Ammohori. You consider that a safe area." The soldiers were armed; they hit my parents and said, "Stay back!" My poor mother! She pushed the soldiers away; she fought them. I was afraid to do anything because they could shoot you right there on the spot. I felt terrible, but I couldn't do anything. I didn't want my parents to be in danger. If I'd said, "I'm not gonna go," I figured my parents would be shot. And so they loaded us on the trucks and took us to Florina.

In the truck it was terrible. We were there with the soldiers; kids were crying. We didn't know where they were taking us; we had no idea. We heard about the children being taken by the other side. We figured it was the same thing, but we didn't know. It was not a happy thing. We were terrified, really terrified. I never slept all night.

We were afraid about what they were going to do to our parents. The soldiers sorted us out in Florina. Most of the kids went to Solun, Thessaloniki in Greek; some of them went to the Paidopoli of the Holy Trinity and some to Saint Dimitrios. To be honest, you were devastated, mentally devastated. You don't sleep, you're worried, you're not well fed, and you have these strange people over you. You don't know what's going to happen to you or to those you left behind.

Somehow I found myself with a number of other boys, and we were taken all the way down to Athens. Then we went on a ship, a Greek naval vessel, from Piraeus to Leros. I remember the boat ride; it was a very rough sea. We had to go down below because the waves were splashing on the deck. I thought, "We'll never come out of this alive." They said, "We're going to send you to school. You'll be able to communicate with your parents. You'll swim there. You'll like it very much." All kinds of positive things. That's what they said.

### The Royal Technical School of Leros

It wasn't pleasant. There was always that unknown. What happened to my parents? What did they do to them? We tried to communicate by writing letters, but our letters were being censored. They were very dry. We never wrote anything, just "We're fine," and this and that. We tried to avoid writing, "I don't like it here. I don't like the food. I miss you very much." Then we found out from the others "Oh yeah, there's censorship. Why did they call that guy in? He must have written something in his letter." You find this out through the rumor mill. Sometimes we didn't receive any letters for a long time. Apparently our parents were writing to us, but we didn't receive every letter. This is what I found out after I came back.

It was an Italian base. The buildings were all fenced in. They had villas and date trees, which we had never seen. It was organized just like the military. We were all in "units" and "groups" with "unit leaders" and "group leaders." Every morning and every evening we had to stand in front of our bunks. Outside it was prayers, reports, roll calls, and awards for children who behaved well.

It was strict discipline, actually. We used to get up very early in the morning, just like in the military. They'd come out there with whistles, the whole works. You exercise, you make your beds, and then you wash. There wasn't enough water, and they didn't have proper showers. Maybe every Saturday or something. Then the water ran, but there was no hot water, so you had to wash in the sea. The sewage system didn't work. They had all these latrines right by the sea, right in front of the buildings. It was terrible.

The food wasn't really that great. Many times kids would complain and wouldn't eat it. But what are you gonna eat? There was nothing else. And you couldn't go out and buy food; you didn't have any money. They never paid you anything, nothing at all. You had to survive just like that. After I got familiar with the place, I actually managed to do things that most of the children couldn't. I spent a lot of time in the library, and I managed somehow to be accepted in the public school. Breakfast was just a chunk of bread and a cup of tea. Then we would all assemble outside; there were prayers, the national anthem, the raising of the flag. After that we either went to school or we went to work in the shop—they said it was to learn, but actually it was to work.

I went to school in the mornings. When we finished school, we had lunch—a chunk of meat sometimes or beans, very little. There was a siesta after that, and if you weren't quiet, you ended up cleaning the latrines just like in the military. Then you made your bed again, and you cleaned up everything. In the evening we were more or less free to walk around or go swimming, but swimming was very dangerous because that particular area was polluted. Sometimes we had films or lectures. Then it was time to go to bed.

We didn't have many possessions. I actually made myself a suitcase out of wood. Too bad I didn't keep it. I felt pretty proud of it. I kept all my stuff there under the bunk. Our bunks were the military type, one on top of the other. Our mattresses were filled either with straw or wood shavings. We had a couple of military blankets, those grey nondescript ones. Most of the uniforms we had were actually old recycled military stuff.

I missed home, and a lot of others did, too, but being exposed to other people opens your horizons. You have to look at the positive side. In spite of all the obstacles, we managed to exchange ideas, to do different things. In some ways it was good. I'm not going to say that it was all negative.

### Being Macedonian

The environment was very politicized because the people there were nationalists. They tried to imbue us with patriotism. We were kept separately in a milieu where you had no choice but to communicate in Greek. We couldn't speak another language. Of course they didn't call it Macedonian in those days because it was the style to call the Macedonians "dirty Bulgarians." So "Macedonians" became "dirty Bulgarians," "traitors," "Slavs," or "communists." They used all kinds of derogatory terms, but we knew who they were talking about.

The whole thing was aimed more or less at your parents. When you returned, you were to be the torchbearers, the people who would save the fatherland. "Never mind what the older people do," they said. "They're stupid; they're backward." They were always downgrading our background. They tried to humiliate you by identifying you with that group, on the one hand, and to make you feel superior to them, on the other hand. But it didn't work for us; to us it was propaganda. We were much older, and we would just sort of glance at each other and wink and say, "Oh, yeah. Sure. A lot of crap is being said." That's how it was done. We knew what it was; we didn't pay much attention.

It was very difficult to find people that were Macedonian by background. You didn't know; you became suspicious of this person and that person. The positive thing about it was that the group of people we finally got to know were Macedonians. None of them ever squealed. We used to meet in different areas and speak our language, but nobody knew that was happening. There was only one guy . . . he knew Macedonian but he wouldn't speak it. But he never told anybody, to his credit.

I managed to speak Macedonian within days of my arrival actually. I met somebody from one of the villages very close to mine. I don't know how; I think it was his accent. And there was this other guy from Drama; his whole family had gone to Bulgaria. He missed his village and his friends so much that he just walked to the border, but he got caught by the Greek military and sent to Leros. Of course he didn't speak a word of Greek. Nothing. A lot of the others were making fun of him because he would say "Atena" instead of "Athena." He couldn't say "th." I actually befriended the guy, and he became like a magnet because he spoke Macedonian.

Through him I found a number of people who were ethnic Macedonians. Once I cracked a joke half in Greek and half in Macedonian. It's a real Macedonian joke. This guy heard it, and he just started laughing like you've never heard in your life. That's how the whole thing started. The support group was very good.

I didn't feel that I was being punished; I felt that I was being indoctrinated. I had to comply with the people around me. But I remembered what my mother told me when they took me away. She said, "I don't mind you going to school, but I know what they do in the schools. You'll never be able to learn your own language, and you'll turn against me, because they'll remold you." My father said the same thing. "Ke ve pretopat." In Macedonian that means, "They'll melt you down; they'll put you in a mold." I said, "I'm not going to turn against you. You're my mother." And I kept that in my mind all the time. My identity was very important to me at that period. I missed my parents; I missed my family. I missed my place of birth to the point where it hurt very much.

*In the fall of 1949, Traian's parents were successful in convincing government officials to let him return home early. They argued that they had been evacuated*

*from Leskovec and were living in Pesočnica (Ammohori), which was under gov-
ernment control and had a functioning elementary school.*

### Return to Leskovec

They called me in once, and to my surprise, they said, "You'll be leaving
soon. You're going home." Boy, I couldn't wait! I got my suitcase, all the little things I had, and I said good-bye. Of course, parting with people wasn't
easy. But at the same time, I was going home. I still remember when I was
on the train and I first saw Florina. It was just indescribable; it felt so good
to be home.

I got off at the station at Ammohori. Tears were coming down my
mother's eyes. People were staring at us, wondering what was happening.
"Look," I said. "They didn't remold me. I took whatever I could take for my
advantage. And the rest," I said, "it's me." She couldn't believe they hadn't
destroyed my spirit. She thought I would have turned against them, just
like the Nazi youth. That's exactly how she put it. She said, "I was afraid
that your character would be completely destroyed, your identity gone.
That you'd be remolded and turned against us and your people." Then she
said, "I can see it didn't happen to you." I feel proud of that.

Some children returned to Leskovec from the queen's camps in 1950,
when the village was resettled; others in 1951. Some of the younger children, especially the girls, had changed. They looked down at their own
people and thought of themselves as being more cultured, more educated.
They had been assimilated; they had become Hellenized. Some of them
never spoke Macedonian again.

We ended up staying in Pesočnica, in Ammohori, all winter. The next
spring some of the men went to the village and spent the night, but they
were not allowed to repatriate yet. It was very difficult. That summer everybody went back for the harvest. The village wasn't burned; it wasn't destroyed. The houses were dirty like people had stayed in them—troops or
partisans. A lot of stuff had been looted.

The immigration had already started. Many people left for Australia;
some came here to Canada. Probably a third of the people left, and it
started from there to go downhill. They said there was no hope for us in
the village. Even though we returned, we felt oppressed. There was no future. People were still in jail; they were still being questioned. People were
arrested as soon as they came back. They just wanted to return to their village and carry on with their lives.

## Kostas Dimou[3]

*Kostas Dimou was born on June 20, 1940, in Vovousa, a small village in the central Pindos Mountains of Epirus. Kostas now lives in a fashionable apartment in the old section of Ioannina. He worked as an agronomist for the Ministry of Agriculture in Ioannina until his retirement in 1996. His wife is a high school teacher, and his daughter studied art conservation in Ravenna, Italy.*

*Kostas speaks articulately and precisely about his childhood. He is eager to defend the directors of the paidopoleis against the charges of sexually abusing the children in their care that have been leveled against them by the authors of two recently published books. Kostas kept a diary when he was young, which may help explain the remarkably detailed account he is able to offer of his childhood years. He hopes one day to write a book of his own about his experiences in the paidopoleis.*

### Civil War

The partisans were in the village; the army soldiers were on the opposite hillside. A partisan with a machine gun was running in the snow. The soldiers saw him, got him in their sights, and fired. He pretended they'd killed him and just lay there motionless, so the soldiers stopped shooting. Then one of his comrades—without a cap, his hair flying—bent down over him to see if he was still alive. A few minutes later the man with the machine gun started rolling over and over in the snow until he fell into a ravine. From there he made his way to our house. He set up his machine gun on the second floor, on the balcony. The partisans in the village were shouting up to him. "Shoot, Spiro! Shoot!" Bam! Bam! Bam! "A little more, Spiro!" Bam! Bam! By evening the battle had ended. The army never entered the village; they never captured Vovousa.

The first time they bombed our village, my older brother Vasilis, my younger brother Zisis, and I were grazing our goats in a field. It was about ten o'clock in the morning, in June. We saw two or three planes coming toward us. They had bombed the village and were flying away right over our heads. We could see the pilots' faces. They dropped a bomb from a height of a hundred meters. I don't know why. We felt the bomb fragments hit the branches of the trees where we were hiding; then the trees caught fire. Those were horrible experiences.

I remember when a detachment of partisans gathered us all together in the yard of the Church of Saint George. "Who wants to go abroad?" they asked. A man named Dimos Nollas, who now lives in Venezuela, said to his father "I want to go." His father scolded him. I didn't say anything to my parents; I didn't want to leave. No one was willing to leave. In other words, it wasn't what they call a *paidomazoma*. No *paidomazoma* took place in Vovousa. The partisans didn't take anyone by force. I remember. They asked, "Who wants to go?" and no one went.

In our village we spoke Vlah; my mother tongue was Vlah. I hardly spoke any Greek at all until I was eight years old. I started school in '46. In first grade, our teacher spoke Greek to us; I didn't understand a thing. I was afraid she'd ask me a question, and I wouldn't be able to answer. I was terrified; I was a very sensitive child. I spent three years—'46, '47, and '48—in the first grade. My mother was from a cultured family; she loved learning. Her brothers in Romania were well educated. I remember she said, "My children will always be blind." When she said "blind," she meant "uneducated." That comment wounded me to the depths of my soul.

### Father's Death

During the Civil War my father's family was the victim of both the Greek Army and the Democratic Army. My grandmother, my father's mother, was a woman, a mother, just like Eleni, Nicholas Gatzoyiannis' mother. In less than two years she lost three relatives. Her daughter Kiratza and her husband Zisis were killed by the Democratic Army, the partisans. They were executed; they were interrogated and then executed. Then in 1949, a few days before the end of the Civil War, my father was killed by the Greek Army.

They were conducting cleansing operations, and a group of soldiers were coming down from Elatohori toward Vovousa. My father didn't leave with the other villagers; he stayed behind by himself to plant our fields. The soldiers were coming down the hillside. They said, "Halt!" As I learned later, my father asked if he could go down to the river to get his coat. But he ran away and hid in a cave near the river. He did what any normal person would do; he was afraid. The soldiers went looking for him, and when they couldn't find him, they realized that he was hiding somewhere. They found him in the cave, and they executed him.

When my mother returned to the village—she was in Ioannina at the time—no one had found my father's remains. So she lived with the false impression that he was still alive, that he'd escaped and was living in Eastern Europe. A few years later, though, the Aoos River flooded, the water level rose to the place where they had executed him, and his bones came to the surface. A villager found them and told my mother, and so she went and collected them. At that point she finally believed that her husband was lost. That's the story of my father's death.

In 1982, after so many years, in a city in Macedonia—I don't want to identify it by name—my cousin Yiannis, a businessman who owns a construction company, was talking with one of his employees.

"Yianni," the employee asked, "where are you from?"

"From Vovousa," my cousin replied.

"Vovousa?" the employee said. "We killed a man there during the Civil War."

And he described the precise details of the execution. My cousin immediately understood what had happened.

"Do you know who that was?" Yiannis said. "That man and my father were brothers. I was named after him. I was born three years after his death."

"Yianni," the employee said, "do you want to know who it was that killed your uncle? He's from a village in Macedonia. I know his name. If you want, you can go meet him."

My cousin told me all this. After a good deal of thought, I decided I did not want to meet the murderer of my father. I am not interested in who the murderer of my father was. I am interested in institutions. What I believe is important is that my father was a victim of the Civil War. My father was killed by the Greek Army, by the Greek state. I never want to know the name of his murderer, because he was a victim too. If I ever learn his name, then the whole myth of the Civil War collapses. My father was a victim of the Civil War.


### A Vow

My father loved me. He took me wherever he went; I was his right hand. He often went . . . the partisans often took him on forced labor details to carry the wounded and build bridges. In the summer of '48, the partisans took him and some other men to the village of Ziakas for the harvest. One day, my mother gave me the donkey to take some things to my father and bring back supplies. We left Vovousa for Ziakas early in the morning. As we were going through a big forest of beech trees, we came to a partisan camp. "Halt!" After the head of our group explained who we were, we set off again for Ziakas. It was an eight-hour trip. In the afternoon we came to a spring and stopped to rest. Ten meters away in an open area underneath a pine tree we saw the body of a soldier that the wolves had dug up. Two or three women from my village went over to the body. They found his wallet—not to steal it, just to see who he was. I saw the women opening a letter. Maybe it was a photograph, I don't know. The women were crying and singing a lament. Were they lamenting his lost youth? Had they seen a photograph of his children? His wife? Had they found a letter and read it? Even now my hair is standing on end.

For years this incident continued to haunt me in my dreams. From 1948 to 1992, I had the same nightmare every night. I dreamt I was there at the spring. Every time I knelt down to drink, I woke up. In 1992, I happened to visit the same place during an excursion with some friends. I immediately remembered the whole scene—the body, the women, the lament. After that, the nightmare stopped. I made a vow to hold a memorial service at the spring, to honor the souls of all the people who died in the Civil War. All the people, on both sides of the war.

I returned home to my mother with the supplies. My father stayed in Ziakas. A few days later the Greek Army came and took us—not by force, for heaven's sake, whoever wanted to go. They took us to Ioannina. I went to the paidopoli. When my father returned from Ziakas, he asked my mother, "Where are the children?" "They left," she said. My father was furious with her for letting us go.

All the children in Vovousa wanted to go to Ioannina. For us Ioannina was a dream, just the way America is for Greeks. My father had other plans for us, other dreams. He wanted to send us to Moscow—yes, to Moscow— for an education. And instead of Moscow, I ended up in the paidopoleis of Queen Frederica. But the dreams of my father and mother were fulfilled. I got an education.

### Departure

One morning my mother sent me to my aunt's house. She was my father's sister; her husband had fought with the partisans and then gone to Tashkent. From there he'd gone to Venezuela and disappeared. It was a beautiful sunny day in September or October. My mother sent me with a little cup to get some yogurt. On my way, I saw my aunt's two children, my cousins, all dressed up and ready to go to Ioannina. My aunt gave me the yogurt. Then, as I was running home, I fell and spilled it. But I picked it up off the ground and ate it. When I got home, my mother spanked me.

I spoke to her in Vlah. I said, "Thanasis and Marigoula are going to Ioannina with the army." My mother went and asked my aunt, to make sure I was telling the truth. Then she dressed my brother and me up, and in the blink of an eye we were off with the army to Ioannina. My father was still in Ziakas. If he'd been at home, he never would have let us go. No one took us by force; we wanted to go. That's important; I want to emphasize that.

We set off with the army. We reached the crossroads—one road goes toward Ioannina, the other toward Larissa. It's the place where we bid farewell to people who are leaving. It's called *Anathema* ["Curses"] because that's where mothers and children, husbands and wives, say good-bye. When men left the village to work in Romania, their wives would accompany them that far. They'd stop there at the high point in the road and watch as their husbands disappeared in the distance. They'd say, "*Anathema se xeniteia!* [Curses on foreign lands!]." That's why it's called *Anathema*.

The women and children were all riding horses; the soldiers told them to. One soldier paid me a compliment. "Good for you!" he said. "You're walking like a real man." I was very proud of myself, an eight-year-old boy walking like a man. Even though they begged us to ride, I refused. I wanted to show them I was a man.

We spent the night at a place called Tsoka Rosa. It was a beautiful warm evening. The soldiers cooked us spaghetti in meat sauce, as much as we could eat. When I lay down to go to sleep, I began to cry because I missed my mother. In the middle of all the excitement, I missed my mother. The next morning we set off for Greveniti. One soldier was smoking. As soon as he threw away his cigarette butt, I picked it up and took a few puffs.

About noon we arrived at a bridge where I saw my first truck. I didn't know what it was. I heard the roar of the truck engine and thought there was a man under the hood. I tried to see who was making all that noise inside. We got in the army trucks and headed down toward Ioannina. One woman from the village threw up. We reached Ioannina that evening, and they took us to the Child Welfare Institute. We spent about three months there together with children from other villages.

### Two Beautiful Eyes

Then we went to the Paidopoli of Saint Eleni. An uncle of mine, my mother's cousin Kostas, was with me. He lives in Australia now. He took care of me; I was eight, and he was fourteen or fifteen. When they brought us to Saint Eleni, they separated us. They kept the younger children there and took the older ones to the Paidopoli of Saint Constantine. When I learned that Kostas had left, I felt a lump in my throat; I couldn't swallow. I remember that night we had spaghetti with lots of sauce and pieces of beef. All the other children were eating, but I was so upset I couldn't eat. I was looking off into space and thinking, poking at the gristle with my fork. Just then, a young woman, a girl eighteen or twenty years old, saw me. "Why aren't you eating? What's the matter?" She came over to me, touched me on the back of the neck, and gave me a kiss. I remember that well. I looked up, and I saw two beautiful eyes full of sympathy. And now, after all these years, I think of the verses of Cavafy:

> Those gray eyes will have lost their beauty—if she's still alive;
> That lovely face will have grown old.
> Memory, preserve them for me as they were then.

At the paidopoli I was a real rebel. For days I tried to escape. I couldn't stand that environment. I finally found an escape route, and I said to myself, "OK. Where shall I go?" My mother had stayed in the village by herself, and my father's brothers in Ioannina had their own problems, so I had nowhere to go. Little by little the system assimilated me.

There were children from villages all over Greece, kids of all shapes and sizes. We were village children, children of the Civil War, who just happened to end up together there. I was in the first grade. Somehow I learned Greek like a sponge. Something else that's strange. . . . I left the village in '48 and returned there for a visit in '55 after seven years in the paidopoleis. I had completely forgotten how to speak Vlah; just like that. I had forgotten Vlah in seven years. Isn't that strange?

One other observation, and I want to stress this. It's a lie that they filled our heads with propaganda. There was no propaganda. Sure, at a superficial level there was, but there were *some* things they had to tell us. They said Frederica was our mother. OK, we accepted that. But given the circumstances, the right wing found Frederica an appropriate person, and they made use of her. If it hadn't been Frederica, it would have been someone else. They had to have someone. In fact, she accomplished a great deal. She could have done more, of course. But we weren't exposed to any harmful or alienating propaganda. The slogans didn't really influence us at the time or later in our lives.

### Attempted Return

The end of the Civil War was a period of transition. At the end of the school year, in the summer of 1950, I was about to enter the third grade. That's when the repatriation process began. It was an emotional time. The director called each child into her office individually and asked what his family situation was—if his parents were still alive, if he could go back to his village. My mother was still alive, and no one had told me that soldiers had killed my father. The director called my brother Zisis and me into her office.

"Dimou, what are you going to do?" she asked.

"I have a mother and a father," I said.

"Do you want to go back to your village?"

"Of course I do."

I suspect now that the director had heard that my father had been killed, but she pretended not to know. I told her to put us on the list of children who were going home. They sent a whole fleet of army trucks to take us. They filled each truck with children from one village. We set out for the villages northeast of Ioannina: Vovousa, Greveniti, Makrino, et cetera, et cetera.

We left on a Sunday morning I think. I had a premonition that I wasn't going home that day. I didn't know anything for certain; I just had a feeling. I said to myself, "I'm not going to my village today." We went to Baldouma and waited at a coffeehouse there. Parents from Vovousa came to pick up their children. My brother and I waited until five o'clock in the afternoon. We had some canned food, but I was so anxious I couldn't eat anything. That evening we went back the same way we came—back to Saint Eleni. My mother didn't want to take me because my father had been killed. That's why she left me at the paidopoli.

A few days later, in June of 1950, together with children from the Paidopoli of Saint Pavlos in Larissa, we were taken in an army truck to Ziro.

### Life at Ziro

The staff at Ziro were exceptional; they were educated, sensitive human beings. Every evening in the dining hall they read to us, from 1951 through 1954. One teacher, Hristos Gerekos, read the whole *Iliad* to us. He acted it out for us as if he were on stage. I may have read the *Iliad* a hundred times since then, but I'll never forget the way he read it to us.

We had another teacher from third grade until sixth grade, Mr. Giogas, from northern Epirus. In third grade I was an average student; I didn't pay much attention to my work. In fourth grade we were supposed to sit completely still with our hands folded. We were studying grammar; we were learning about contractions. I heard the word "contractions," and I took my pencil and wrote it down in my notebook: "contractions."

"My boy," Mr. Giogas said, "what are you doing?"

"Sir," I said, "I heard the word, and I wrote it down."

"You see, children," he said, "Dimou is not a good student, but he tries."

From that day on, I was a totally different student. I just took off. In fifth and sixth grades I was one of the best students in the class.

The queen came to Ziro in June of 1953. We really looked forward to her visit; it was an important event. Why? Because she was the queen. She was like our mother. Sure, that's what they told us—nothing more, nothing less. Nothing about evil communist bandits or anything. She was the queen, our second mother. We couldn't wait for her to come. She kissed a few children. I had my picture taken with her then, but I lost it. She wasn't as evil as some people made her out to be—at least in my experience. But I was only thirteen. She wasn't a witch or anything like that.

The last time I went back to Ziro was in 1977. It was still operating as a paidopoli. They had taken down some of the buildings, but I found the one I'd lived in. I remember the rooms; I remember the beds. I lay down on the same bed I'd slept in as a child. I went there like a pilgrim to pay my respects.

### Mother's Death

My mother died of cancer on May 29, 1952; she was thirty-eight years old. They didn't tell me anything at the time. At the end of October, on Saint Dimitrios' Day, my aunt, my father's sister, came to Ziro; her son was in the paidopoli too. In their letters they'd said that my mother couldn't write me herself because her hand was bothering her. So I asked my aunt, "How's my mother?" That flustered her; she said, "Her foot is bothering her." I thought, "What's the connection between her hand and her foot?" And I grew suspicious.

I wrote a letter to my aunt in the village. She was my mother's first cousin; she lives in Australia now. "Greetings," I wrote. "How is my mother?" As if I believed she was alive. I still wanted to believe she was alive. Her brother said, "We should write the boy the truth! We can't keep lying to him." So my uncle sat down and wrote me the truth, the whole truth: "Kosta, your mother died. . . . " And he sent me a photograph. I've gotten over it now. During her last days in the hospital in Ioannina she had her picture taken. I still have the photograph. On the back my aunt had written: "May 31, 1952." And below that: "Your ill-fated mother, who is no longer alive, kisses you."

My younger brother Zisis was sitting at another table watching me. When we received letters at Ziro, we were thrilled because they usually contained money. But Zisis saw that I was upset. We met outside the dining hall; it was April 2, 1953. I told him the truth, and the two of us drank that bitter cup alone. It was Ash Wednesday. We Orthodox sing funeral hymns on Good Friday. That afternoon I had the strength to go to the rehearsal for the Good Friday service. I sang, "All the nations offer a hymn at your tomb, dear Christ." I knew what it meant. I was lamenting the death of Jesus Christ, but inside I was lamenting the death of my mother. That evening in church as we sang the hymns, my brother and I cried.

"What's the matter?" Miss Marika asked.

"My mother died," I said.

And she kissed me. Moments like that are unforgettable.

*Elementary school students in the paidopoleis who received grades of eight or above on a scale of ten were sent to the Paidopoli of Saint Dimitrios in Thessaloniki to attend secondary school. Kostas left Ziro when he finished elementary school in the summer of 1954. Ten to fifteen other children from Ziro went with him to Saint Dimitrios.*

### Education in Thessaloniki

At Saint Dimitrios 150 of us slept in one big room. It was like the army, with bunk beds one on top of the other. We were all eager to learn; we loved to read. They turned off the lights at ten o'clock, but we kept reading—not just schoolbooks, but other books we were interested in, for pleasure. I'd take one of the little tins that our shoe polish came in and fill it with cod-liver oil—they gave us cod-liver oil because it had lots of vitamins. Then I'd cut up one of my shoelaces and use it for a wick.

We wore special clothes, a uniform—a jacket, a sweater, and a shirt. Pants and shoes. When I entered the university, I wore those clothes for six months until I could afford to buy new ones. Fortunately that didn't bother us. Before we bought our new clothes, someone saw us all together and said, "Excuse me, do you boys work for KTEL?" KTEL, the bus company. In other words, "Are you ticket takers?" I was insulted, but I was never jealous of anyone.

Of the forty-six students in our class, only one had an average of seventeen [out of twenty]—Hristos Venetis. Now he's a cardiologist in Athens. He is from Lia in Epirus, the same village as Nicholas Gatzoyiannis. Six of us had an average of sixteen; we were all promoted to the next grade. We entered school in the fall of '55 as usual. A month later a directive came down from Frederica that all students with an average *below seventeen* had to return to their villages. Those of us who had nowhere else to go stayed at Saint Dimitrios. I spent two months there learning to be a cobbler. They expelled me from high school! I was going to be a cobbler! It was a crime, a crime committed by Frederica and the paidopoleis. That's when I began to form a negative opinion of Queen Frederica and her ladies.

Then they changed their minds again and decided that all children with an average of *sixteen or above* could continue. So on November 19, 1955, we went back to school. I remember the date. That was the most difficult, the most upsetting, period of my life. I was only fifteen, but I took it very seriously. They expelled me from high school! In any event, we went back to school after a two-month interruption. We studied really hard, and by the end of the year all six of us had averages of eighteen, nineteen, or twenty. That's when the teachers realized that the children of the paidopoleis were exceptional students.

During high school the paidopoli paid all our expenses. I shouldn't be ungrateful. But when we entered the university, they gave us seven hundred drachmas a month and one suit. After that, we were on our own. If you couldn't afford to continue your studies, that was your problem. But fortunately we were all well prepared and strong, and no one was left out on the street. We sweated blood and tears to complete our education and become human beings. I graduated from high school in 1960 and entered medical school. My first year went fine, but I couldn't afford it. So I was forced to take the examinations for the school of agriculture and start all over.

For three years, from 1961 to 1964, I couldn't sleep at night. I only ate at noon in the student union, once a day. For three years I never ate a meal in the evening. I went to bed hungry, just a piece of candy, but I finished all my homework. In 1964, when I began to eat an evening meal, I started to fall asleep right away. In spite of all that, I never lost hope. I knew that better days would come.

### Allies of the Queen?

Unfortunately the officials of the Royal Welfare Fund, Frederica's circle, didn't take education seriously; they didn't really invest in the education of the children. An educated person may become a leftist, it's true, but he certainly won't be ungrateful. If someone tells you, "I educated you," you'll say, "Yes, you educated me, but I don't embrace your politics." It would be ungrateful not to thank your benefactor. The Royal Welfare Fund's goal was to produce craftsmen who would make an immediate contribution to society. It didn't invest in the intellectual life of the children. As an individual I express my gratitude for everything it gave me. It showed me the way, but I followed it myself.

The royal family was doing fine until 1964, when King Paul died and Constantine ascended the throne. That's when Frederica began to meddle in politics. Things reached a climax with the rupture between the palace and the political leadership. The institution of the monarchy and all the people around Frederica were taking a lot of fire from everyone. That's when they said, "Where can we find allies? Let's ask the children." At the time I used to go to Saint Dimitrios every so often to see my old friends. One day, the director of the paidopoli said to me:

"Kosta, why don't all you *paidopolites* get together and issue a statement in support of the queen and the king?"

"Excuse me?" I said. "*Now* you remember us? I spit blood in order to get an education. If you want our support, you should have earned it."

# PART THREE

# Ethnographies

# SIX

# Refugees, Displacement, and the Impossible Return

The journey creates us. We become the frontiers we cross.

—Salman Rushdie (2002, 351)

In an important review article on the anthropology of refugees, Liisa Malkki argues that the interdisciplinary field of "refugee studies" has been characterized by a sedentarist perspective according to which people living stationary, settled lives constitute both the norm and the ideal (1995a). From this perspective, it is people's attachment to a fixed geographical location that not only gives their lives meaning, but also enables them to construct a clearly defined identity based on their relationship to a single place called home. Malkki observes that many scholars working in the field of refugee studies make the assumption that identities "can only be whole and well when rooted in a territorial homeland" (1995a, 511).

As a result of this sedentarist bias, refugees have often been viewed as powerless victims who have experienced a loss of both culture and identity.[1] According to Malkki, "much of the policy oriented, therapeutic literature on refugees tends to share the premise that refugees are necessarily a problem" (1995b, 8). More precisely, refugees present a problem for what Malkki has called "the national order of things" (1992, 25), the fundamental principle of nationalism according to which people who share a common culture and identity should live together in a single place. From a nationalist perspective, refugees have been pathologically uprooted (Malkki 1992, 32); they represent "matter out of place" (Douglas 1966, 48). Their

An earlier version of portions of this chapter appeared in Loring Danforth, "'We Crossed a Lot of Borders': Refugee Children of the Greek Civil War," *Diaspora* 12 (2): 169–209.

repatriation, their return to their homeland, is, therefore, the only cure for their pathological condition, the only way to solve the "refugee problem" and restore the "national order of things" to its original state of purity.

This sedentarist approach is clearly unable to deal satisfactorily with the globalized world of the early twenty-first century, a world in which refugees, transnational migrants, and members of diaspora communities are constantly on the move, a world in which virtually instantaneous communication by fax, email, and cell phone is widely available. In order to provide deeper insights into the lives of increasingly mobile people, Arjun Appadurai (1996) and James Clifford (1997) have proposed a more cosmopolitan alternative to this sedentarist approach. They have demonstrated the importance of subverting the "national order of things" with its functionalist assumption that people are naturally rooted in territorial homelands (Malkki 1995a, 511). This cosmopolitan perspective focuses on the global rather than the local, on displacement rather than emplacement, and on mobility rather than stability (Breckenridge et al. 2002).

More specifically, Appadurai has introduced the notions of "global cultural flows" and "ethnoscapes" (1996, 33) to help anthropologists focus their attention on the lives of people who have become "moving targets" in an increasingly globalized world (Breckenridge and Appadurai 1989, i). James Clifford has also effectively opposed the localizing strategies of earlier forms of anthropological analysis by encouraging the study of people who are "out of place." Concentrating on "routes" rather than "roots," "traveling" rather than "dwelling" (1997, 1–13), Clifford suggests a model for the ethnographic analysis of the "global space of cultural connections and dissolutions" (1988, 4).

While this shift from a sedentarist to a more cosmopolitan perspective has been very productive, it has in some instances been carried too far. In an extreme form, this cosmopolitan perspective can lead to the privileging of mobility to the exclusion of stability. It can result in an overemphasis on movement and a failure to acknowledge the continued importance of permanent homes in the lives of many people throughout the world. As Malkki suggests, "the idealization or romanticization of exile and diaspora can be just as problematic for anthropology . . . as is the idealization of homeland and rooted communities in works of refugee studies" (1995a, 514).

Rather than simply rejecting a sedentarist perspective and replacing it wholesale with a cosmopolitan one, we suggest that it is necessary to integrate the two perspectives, for only in this way is it possible to remain sensitive to the many forms that the relationships between identity and place may take in different people's lives. The need for a synthesis of these two perspectives is suggested by Appadurai's image of a textile in which the warp of stability is "everywhere shot through with the woof of human motion" (1996, 33–34).

By avoiding an oversimplified, dichotomous choice between sedentarist and cosmopolitan perspectives, by refusing to privilege either perspective to the exclusion of the other, we are able to recognize several important truths. Both mobility and sedentariness have their costs and their rewards. Leaving home may be experienced in some cases as deprivation, in others as liberation. People driven from their homes may lose the identities they had, but they inevitably gain new identities based on the losses they have experienced and the ties they have established to their new homes.

Recent contributions to the anthropological study of "place" and "home" are also useful in understanding the world of refugees who seek to live meaningful lives that incorporate both experiences of departure, separation, and nostalgia for the past, on the one hand, and experiences of return, reunion, and hope for the future, on the other. Feld and Basso's book *Senses of Place* presents detailed ethnographic studies of the meaning of place in a variety of cultures. The contributors to this volume explore "the experiential and expressive ways places are known, imagined, yearned for, held, remembered, voiced, lived, contested, and struggled over" (1996, 11). The essays in Olwig and Hastrup's collected volume *Siting Culture* examine the cultural significance of place by analyzing the relationships between place and identity in order to understand people's "simultaneously continuing and changing multiple attachment to places" (Hasager 1997, 185). These "geographies of identity" (Lavie and Swedenburg 1996) are particularly complex and interesting when experiences of displacement and deterritorialization have fractured the relationship between people and the places they use to identify themselves. Refugees are constantly engaged in a process of constructing and reconstructing their identities by attempting to situate themselves in relationship to the places—real and imagined, near and far—that give meaning to their lives.

"Homes" and "homelands" are among the most significant places people use to define who they are. From a sedentarist perspective, "home" is a single, fixed location, a place of birth, associated with parents, childhood, and the past. Several anthropologists, geographers, and literary critics, however, have recently challenged this overly sentimental conception of "home."[2] They argue that in many cases—particularly in the case of refugees—the notion of a singular, permanent home needs to be problematized in order to be replaced by a more sophisticated understanding of home as a "moveable concept" (Bammer 1992, vii). From this perspective a person can "be at home" in more than one place.

Refugees in particular have multiple loyalties to the many places they call "home." They not only have important ties to the locations they actually inhabit; they also have equally, if not more important, ties to the far-away places they may once have inhabited in the past or may long to return to at some point in the future. The importance of imagined or remembered homelands leads to a disjuncture that requires ethnographers to acknowledge "the unyoking of imagination from place" and attend more carefully to *the work of the imagination* as a constitutive feature of modern subjectivity" (Appadurai 1996, 3, 58, emphasis in the original).

The anthropological study of "home" has focused almost exclusively on the spatial dimension of the concept. "Home" is usually regarded first and foremost as a place that exists in a specific geographical location. It is crucial, however, to keep in mind the temporal dimension of the concept of "home." As Edward Relph has pointed out, places "have a distinct historical component," since "time is usually a part of our experience of places" (Relph 1976, 3, 33). If we understand places as culturally meaningful locations, it is inevitable that with the passage of time a given location will become a different place. The place called "home," in other words, can and will change location over time. "In that sense," Stuart Hall has written, "there is no going 'home' again" (1993, 362).

## Narratives of Separation, Exile, and Family Reunion

The isolated mountain villages of northern Greece are generally considered the epitome of sedentary communities whose inhabitants are deeply rooted in the soil they till, while Eastern Europe during the Cold War has long been regarded as a closed world where freedom of movement was tightly restricted. In addition, the Iron Curtain separating Greece from its neighbors to the north, constituted an insurmountable barrier between "the Soviet bloc" and "the free world." In fact, these communities were much more cosmopolitan than these images suggest. In the early twentieth century, the villages of northern Greece were the source of labor migration to Romania, France, and the United States.[3] Refugee children themselves managed to cross the Iron Curtain, sometimes more than once, as refugees, repatriates, and tourists. They also moved frequently both within and between the countries of Eastern Europe as they attempted to rejoin other members of their families who had been scattered by the violence and turmoil of the Civil War.

An elderly political refugee observed that no matter how long he lived, his new home would always be a foreign country. "The place where you live," he said, "never becomes your home, your native land" (*opou zeis, den patrizeis*). This comment, which Dimitris Gousidis chose as the title for his book on Greek political refugees in Eastern Europe (1975), stands as a bitter refutation of the widely known Greek proverb, "The place where you live, *that* is your home, *that* is your native land" (*opou zeis, ekei patris*). This elderly refugee creatively transformed a traditional Greek proverb promoting a cosmopolitan perspective so that he could assert the applicability of a sedentarist perspective to his own experience.

The first-person narratives of refugee children from the Greek Civil War also affirm the truth of important aspects of the sedentarist discourse on refugees. Refugee children *were* tragically uprooted from their villages in northern Greece; they *did* spend difficult years in exile in children's homes in Eastern Europe deprived of the love and care of their parents and grandparents. For many refugee children, their departure from home *was* unimaginably painful. A Greek refugee child from the district of Evros described a scene she has never been able to forget: a group of mothers from her village running desperately behind the truck that was taking their children away, across the border to Bulgaria. A Macedonian woman who accompanied a group of twenty-five refugee children from a village in the Prespa area described the moment of departure this way:

> March 24th! That was a day villagers will remember forever, the day we took the children from their mothers! Tears! Kisses! The children clung to their mothers like leeches. We couldn't tear them away.

Accounts such as these testify to the relevance that sedentarist discourse has for understanding the experiences of refugee children of the Greek Civil War. They were victims of violence they were powerless to stop; they were linked to their homes and families by ties of geography and kinship. Many of them were unable to return to their villages. All of them experienced a long exile abroad that was for many "a living death."[4]

Narrating their life stories as adults, refugee children emphasize their experiences of separation and loss, as well as the feelings of sadness that sometimes swept over them. For them, the Civil War never ended; it has continued to haunt them, to cast a shadow over their entire their lives. Mare Kondova, a Macedonian refugee who now lives in Skopje, said that she never married because she left part of her heart in her village in Greece. In order to marry a man, she felt she had to be able to give him her whole heart. "Even if I could go to Greece now," she said, "what would I have? My house? No! My land? No! I don't even have my parents' graves!" Some refugee children seem to have spent their whole lives searching to find a replacement for what they have lost. A Greek refugee from Thrace said, "I lost my mother. I've been searching for her ever since, but I know I'll never find her. She's gone. A dream that's disappeared."

Sedentarist discourse on refugees, therefore, is not false, as these accounts clearly show. It does not, however, present a full picture. The life stories of refugees are replete with contradiction, ambivalence, and paradox; they complicate this sedentarist discourse in important ways. As Relph points out, attachment to a place is not always positive, and being "at home" may be an "oppressive and imprisoning" experience (Relph 1976, 41). In such situations, leaving home may be liberating, a life of exile may offer a new world of opportunities, and family reunions may painfully demonstrate the impossibility of reestablishing social bonds broken by years of separation.

The Greek Civil War transformed the villages of northern Greece from homes where children led difficult, but safe and secure lives into battlefields of random violence and sudden death. Homes were bombed, children were wounded playing with unexploded shells, and parents were killed by mortar fire from surrounding hills. Under such conditions, it is not surprising that many parents and children saw the evacuation programs organized by the Communist Party and the Queen's Fund as both blessings and tragedies.

Refugee children themselves had a wide range of responses to the difficult dilemmas they faced. Their responses illustrate the tensions that result from conflict between sedentarist and cosmopolitan perspectives. Mirka Trpovska, a Macedonian from the Kastoria region, remembered the partisans telling the children in her village, "You'll go [to other countries] where they'll give you cocoa, chocolate, caramels, and white bread. . . . You won't stay there long. You'll come back again as soon as the Civil War is over." Mirka begged her mother to let her go, but her mother hesitated. Mirka was her only daughter. In the end, though, Mirka's mother gave her permission to leave.

Some children argued with their parents about leaving. Lazo Kondov, a Macedonian from a village west of Florina, was fifteen years old in March 1948. He wanted to go to Eastern Europe with the other children because he was afraid of the bombs that fell on the village every day. All his friends were going, and he didn't want to be left behind in the village with the old people. But his stepmother refused to let him go. She sent her own three children, but not Lazo, not her stepson. She needed him to take care of the animals. A year later the whole village was evacuated, and Lazo and his family fled north to Yugoslavia. Lazo is still angry at his stepmother for preventing him from leaving the village with the other children and getting a good education in Eastern Europe. He knows that if his own mother, his real mother, had been alive in 1948, she would have let him go. She would have loved him enough to send him away.

Most refugee children have positive memories of the years they spent in Eastern Europe, and they are grateful to the people and the governments of the countries that took them in. Their evacuation to Eastern Europe opened a whole new world for them. They received clean clothes, ample food, proper medical care, and a good education. They had their first encounters with electricity, automobiles, and trains; for the first time in their lives they slept on beds with sheets, went swimming, saw movies, and played sports.

Refugee children talk about all the doors that opened for them, all the educational and cultural opportunities they received. In Prague and Budapest they were exposed to the worlds of literature and art, museums and opera. Years later, many refugee children remember their time in Eastern Europe as the best years of their lives. One refugee said, "We became human beings, people of the twentieth century"; another said simply, "We became *kosmopolites*, citizens of the world." These positive accounts confirm the validity of a cosmopolitan perspective in which home is "a moveable concept" (Bammer 1992, vii). They do not in any way, however, refute the equal validity of a sedentarist perspective, in which separation from home and family is a traumatic and tragic experience.

Many refugee children admitted that while they missed their parents a great deal, their absence became less painful as they adjusted to their new lives in Eastern Europe. "Slowly, with time, the wound healed, and we forgot our parents," said one refugee. The ambivalent feelings refugee children developed toward their absent parents are poignantly conveyed by the troubling experience of another refugee child who was attending a summer camp in Czechoslovakia in the summer of 1949.

On Sunday when the parents of the Czech children came to visit, I'd run away and hide in the woods so I wouldn't see them. One time, when the parents of a Czech friend of mine came, he said, "Come here! My parents want to meet you." They offered me something to eat, but I was embarrassed and didn't take anything. Then my friend's mother asked me if I missed my mother. "No," I said, "I'm a big boy. I don't miss my mother."

I can't imagine what she thought of me. Maybe I really felt that way; maybe we were taught to be strong and obey the party and not to feel. . . . to think that mothers are for little kids. I don't know. Whenever I think about that, even now, it's difficult for me. I don't understand how I could have said that. That was the tragedy of our relations with our parents.

Refugee children always referred to the young women who accompanied them during their evacuation and cared for them in Eastern Europe as "mothers." Vančo Angelkovski, a Macedonian refugee from the Kastoria area, described seeing his mother again for the first time in Poland in the early 1950s. He recognized her right away, but his younger brother Ilya didn't. When Vančo introduced Ilya to his mother, Ilya said, "You're not my mum. My mum is over there," and pointed to the "mother" who had cared for him since he had left his home in 1948. A "mother" from a village near Florina accompanied a group of children that included her own one-year-old son to a children's home in Czechoslovakia. Sitting in her apartment in Toronto, she said, "All the children called me 'mother'; my own son did too. But the other children knew that we were 'foreign mothers' (*xenes manes*)."

Just as refugee children addressed unrelated women as "mothers," later in their lives they referred to the country where they had been raised as "a second homeland" (*defteri patrida*). At the reunion of the Association of Refugee Children from Aegean Macedonia in Skopje in 1998, Mirka Sarova, a Macedonian "mother," travelled with thirty of her former "children" to the home in Bela Crkva in Vojvodina, Yugoslavia, where they had lived together for many years. Mirka described this visit in exactly the same terms that refugee children use to describe their visits to the villages of their birth. They went back to see the house where they had spent their childhood, to drink the water and eat the bread that had nourished them when they were young. At a reception held in their honor at the children's home in Bela Crkva, Mirka gave a short speech. "We are not guests here," she said. "We were children in this home; we lived here for ten years. We are not in a stranger's house; we are in our own home."

During the years they lived in Eastern Europe, refugee children went through a process of reterritorialization. They constructed new homes, setting down new roots in what had until then been a foreign land. It is ironic that while refugee children were establishing second "homelands" in Eastern Europe, an important component of the education they were receiving from the Communist Party was "*patridognosia*," the history and geography of their homeland, Greece. A third grade reading book used by children in Eastern Europe contained a poem entitled "Homeland," which began, "I live far away from my homeland. I know it only from maps."[5] A Greek refugee child from the Grevena region who spent over twenty years in Czechoslovakia described feeling "nostalgia for Greece, his unknown homeland."

Another Greek refugee child, who was evacuated to Bulgaria and then to East Germany, where he settled permanently, described his ambivalent feelings about the Greek language and Greece as a place to call home: "I like to hear Greek, and I like to speak it. But it's not my language. Everyday life in Greece is different. I can't get inside it; I haven't lived it." When asked where he feels at home, he replied, with some hesitation, "Here, in Halle. I've lived most of my life here. People know me here; this is my village. My village found me here. A person can live anywhere." These comments illustrate the twofold process through which a foreign land becomes home and home becomes a foreign land.

Refugee children were reunited with their parents in many different places—the Toronto airport, the train station in Skopje, and the villages where they were born in northern Greece. Their accounts of these reunions demonstrate the disturbing truth that just as strangers can become "mothers," mothers can also become strangers. Two aspects of these accounts stand out: the inability of parents and children to recognize each other, and the difficulty of reestablishing close personal ties after an extended period of separation. Maria Dragouli left home at the age of two in 1948 and returned seven years later. When she saw her mother again for the first time, she didn't recognize her. Maria said to her, "You're not my mother," and chased her away with rocks. Another child refused to believe that the man who had come to meet him in Thessaloniki was his father until the man, his father, showed him that he was missing the index finger on one of his hands (Georgitsa-Papadimitrakopoulou 1997, 590–91).

Conversely, parents sometimes failed to recognize their children. A seven-year-old refugee fled his village and walked eight kilometers to the Yugoslav border. When he came back from Poland ten years later and saw his mother again for the first time, she didn't even cry or give him a hug. For several months she showed no tenderness or affection toward him at all. Then one day she told him to take off his shirt. She wanted to see if he had a small white birthmark the size of her fingernail; she wanted to see if he was really her son. When she saw the birthmark, she began crying and tearing her hair and shouting: "It's him! It's him! It's my son!"[6]

Risto Kalkov, a Macedonian refugee child who left his village near Kastoria in 1948 when he was six, spoke the wrong language when he saw his mother again for the first time in Skopje eight years later. Risto never spoke Greek in his village—no one else in his family did either, but he learned Greek, as well as Macedonian, in Tulgheș, a large children's home in Romania, where Greek was the official language. That's why, when he stepped off the bus in Skopje and embraced his mother, the first words he spoke to her were Greek. Risto's mother looked at him strangely and in Macedonian asked his sister (who had remained with her in Greece) if Risto were really her child. She couldn't believe he was her son because he was speaking Greek. She had no idea he'd learned Greek in Romania. Risto's sister asked him in Macedonian, "Why are you speaking Greek?" He replied, "I thought you spoke Greek." But he was wrong. They didn't speak Greek at all. Not a word.

Many refugee children spoke painfully about their inability to respond to their parents in an emotionally appropriate way when they were first reunited with them. When she arrived in Skopje after many years in Romania, Dimitra Boneva saw her mother for the first time in the prison in Skopje where she was being interrogated. Dimitra remembers her mother running toward her and crying, "I'm your mother! Don't you recognize me?" Dimitra recognized her, but couldn't respond. "I didn't move. I felt love for my mother, but not for this woman. This woman was a stranger (*xeni*) to me. She opened her arms and just stood there. I didn't open my arms or give her my hand. Nothing. She was crying; I was like a stone." One Greek refugee child was reunited with her mother in Czechoslovakia when she was nineteen, six years after she had left her village. "I couldn't call her '*Mamá*' because I hadn't said the word for years. I didn't know whether to say '*Mamáka*,' '*Mamá*,' or '*Mána*' (Mommy, Momma, or Mom). I didn't know how to say it! It took me two or three years of calling her '*Mitera*' (Mother) in order for me to feel close to her."[7] Another child, who argued bitterly with her mother after they were reunited in Greece in 1961, told her bluntly, "Romania raised me, not you."

These comments demonstrate the need to integrate a sedentarist and a cosmopolitan perspective in order to understand fully the experiences of refugee children of the Greek Civil War. Home is not a single, fixed location, and a place that once was home can cease being home when it is engulfed by war. While leaving home certainly evokes feelings of pain and loss, it can also provide opportunities to create meaningful new identities through constantly changing relationships to a multiplicity of places.

## The Impossible Return: Place, Home, and
## Identity among Macedonian Refugee Children

The meaning of "home" and the relationship between identity and place are central themes in the life stories of all refugee children from the Greek Civil War, both those who have returned to Greece and those who have not. While some young refugee children, both Greek and Macedonian, were repatriated in the 1950s, the vast majority were not allowed to return until after the fall of the right-wing military dictatorship in 1974. Before then, the experiences of Greek and Macedonian refugee children had been very similar: none of them had been able to return to their homes. Then in 1982, with the passage of legislation specifically allowing only those political refugees who were "Greeks by birth" to be repatriated, the paths of Greek and Macedonian refugee children diverged quite sharply.

Since they were not allowed to return to Greece, the vast majority of Macedonian refugee children remained in Eastern Europe, settled in the Republic of Macedonia, or emigrated to Canada or Australia. Many of them have a strong Macedonian national identity based on powerful emotional bonds that link them to the villages of their birth in northern Greece, which many refugees have not seen since 1948 and may never see again. These villages constitute what Salman Rushdie (1991) has called "imaginary homelands," places kept alive through memories of the past and hopes for the future.

Many Macedonian refugee children have done well economically and professionally. They have become engineers, surgeons, and university professors working in Skopje, as well as translators, nurses, and accountants living in the suburbs of Toronto and Melbourne. Many of them married other refugees, have well educated children, and are now grandparents. Their life stories, in other words, have what they consider to be "a happy ending."

The Macedonian refugee children who left Eastern Europe for Canada and Australia in the late 1960s and early 1970s experienced what could be called "rediasporization" (Clifford 1997, 248), when the initial diaspora that was created in 1948 was expanded with their emigration overseas. Although many had to restart their professional careers from scratch, almost without exception they felt positively toward their new homelands and have come to identify with them in many ways. They frequently attributed their positive attitude to the explicitly multicultural policies of the Canadian and Australian governments and to the fact that as a result of these policies they felt completely free for the first time in their lives to assert their Macedonian national identity. One refugee said that coming to Canada was the best decision he'd ever made: "We're proud to be Canadians. . . . Whenever I go to Europe, I always say, 'I'm Canadian.'" Another refugee, who has lived in Melbourne for thirty years, said that when he and his wife were traveling through Western Europe they identified themselves as Australians. When they saw the kangaroo on the tail of the Qantas 747 that was taking them back to Australia, they said, "That's ours."

With the normalization of relations between Yugoslavia and the other countries in Eastern Europe in 1955, many refugee children with a Macedonian national identity were able to move to Skopje and rejoin other members of their families. At this time the government of the Yugoslav Republic of Macedonia officially encouraged Macedonian refugees from the Greek Civil War to settle there. It recognized them as "a considerable human resource" because of their high level of education and professional training (Brown 2003, 31).

Macedonian refugee children who settled in Skopje in the late 1950s and early 1960s expressed conflicting opinions about the Republic of Macedonia as their homeland. They said their decision to move there from Eastern Europe had been motivated by a desire to "return to their homeland (*tatkovina*)" and to live as close to their villages in northern Greece as they could. One refugee who came to Skopje in 1957 after spending nine years in Romania and the Soviet Union attributed her decision to "patriotism." She felt that by coming to the Republic of Macedonia she was coming home. It didn't matter to her whether she lived in the republic or in northern Greece. For her the border between Greek Macedonia and Yugoslav Macedonia didn't exist; all Macedonia was her homeland.

Other refugee children, however, had very different experiences. They said that as "Aegean Macedonians" (Macedonians from "Aegean" or Greek Macedonia), they had been discriminated against by "Vardar Macedonians" (Macedonians from "Vardar" or Yugoslav Macedonia). Sometimes they were called "Greeks," but even when they were called "*Egejci*" (Aegeans), they interpreted it as an insult. As "*Egejci*," they felt like foreigners, like second-class citizens, or even worse, like "Gypsies." They were subjected to negative stereotypes and jokes, and they were accused of being stingy, clannish, and receiving special treatment—apartments, jobs, and pensions— from the Macedonian government.

Worst of all, they still felt like refugees. They had identity cards that defined their legal status as "foreigners without citizenship" (*stranci bez državjanstvo*; Monova 2001, 186; 2007). One refugee remembered arriving in Skopje to look for a job. "What do you want?" people asked. "Get out of here! Go back to Greece!" Another refugee remembered being laughed at in elementary school in Skopje for her "Aegean accent," the local dialect she had learned growing up in Greece. When she had been a foreigner in Czechoslovakia, no one had made fun of her accent. Referring to Yugoslav Macedonia, another refugee just said, "That part of Macedonia isn't really my home." Macedonian refugees arriving in Skopje in the late 1950s particularly resented the fact that they were often interrogated for days by the Yugoslav secret police at the Idrizovo Prison on the outskirts of Skopje. They were suspected of being "Stalinist spies" because they had recently arrived from Eastern European countries that remained under the Soviet sphere of influence.

Macedonian refugees with strong nationalist tendencies resented Tito's policy of "Brotherhood and Unity," with which he attempted to create a broader, more inclusive Yugoslav identity and limit expressions of Croatian, Serbian, Albanian, and Macedonian nationalism. They said that people in the Yugoslav Republic of Macedonia had become "Yugoslavs" or "Serbians" and that under Tito people couldn't be "real Macedonians." They even referred derisively to Yugoslavia as "Serboslavia." One refugee complained, "It was dangerous to say that you were a Macedonian, not a Yugoslav. I didn't feel completely free." For these Macedonian refugees, the Republic of Macedonia began to feel much more like a real homeland when it became an independent country in 1991.

Perceptive Macedonian refugee children acknowledged both of these contradictory perspectives and seemed to accept the ambivalence of their situation. When Dotčka and John Lappas were married in Tashkent in the former Soviet Union, they decided to "return to Macedonia." Dotčka described an experience John had shortly after they moved to Skopje in 1967:

> He goes to the bus, and he hears everybody speaking Macedonian. He says, "I feel so good. I never heard so many people speaking Macedonian." Then you feel at home—when everybody surrounds you, welcomes you, and understands you. Oh, for sure there were difficulties too, because the native Macedonians there, the *Vardarci*, they were thinking, "Who are those *Egejci*? Why did they come to our country? Why did they take the best apartments and the best jobs?" That sort of hurts you.[8]

Like other people whose identities have been shaped by experiences of displacement and deterritorialization, Macedonian refugee children have left "a trail of collective memory about another place and time"; they have created "new maps of desire and attachment" (Breckenridge and Appadurai 1989, i). These sixty-year-old men and women, many of whom have lived half their lives in the Republic of Macedonia, Eastern Europe, Canada, or Australia, continue to define themselves as *"deca begalci"* (refugee children). Their identity, in other words, is inextricably linked to the villages in northern Greece where they were born, villages with Macedonian names like Bapčor, Smrdeš, and V'mbel, many of which no longer exist. These villages were destroyed during the Greek Civil War, and nothing remains of them now except the hollow shells of a few houses and a ruined church or school. Even those villages that *do* still exist cannot be found on maps. They now have Greek names, like Pimeniko, Kristallopiyi, and Moshohori. Many of them have been settled by Greek-speaking Aromani (Vlahs) and Greek refugees from Asia Minor. They are no longer the Macedonian villages the refugee children remember from their youth; they have become "foreign" villages, Greek villages.

One of the most effective ways Macedonian refugees have been able to keep alive memories of their lost homeland is through the publication of "memorial books" (Slyomovics 1994, 1998), that is, histories of villages of their birth that no longer exist either because they have been destroyed or because their former inhabitants were forced to flee. In these memorial books, Macedonian refugee children reconstruct as texts the villages of their homeland. They do so as a political gesture whose goal is to perpetuate Macedonian geography and history and reinscribe them upon what is now territory of the Greek state (Slyomovics 1994, 162–63). Publication of these Macedonian memorial books, therefore, constitutes an act of resistance against the Greek state's efforts to destroy evidence of a Macedonian past within its territory.

Memorial books written by Macedonian refugee children from northern Greece have been published in Skopje, Toronto, and Melbourne.[9] Each one documents in impressive detail the history, geography, and local culture of the author's natal village. Maps show the location of the houses of all the families of the village. Kinship diagrams trace seven or eight generations of important village families. Old black-and-white photographs of married couples and extended families from the 1920s contrast with color photographs of dances and picnics held by associations of emigrants from the village in Canada and Australia in the 1990s. Photographs taken periodically from the 1930s through the 1990s chronicle the destruction of the village during the Civil War and the gradual decay of the ruins that were left, like the frames of a slow-motion film in which the village seems to disappear before your very eyes. Sentimental poems attest to the emotional ties villagers and their descendants still feel to their lost homeland. Special place in these memorial books is always given to stark photographs and short obituaries of villagers killed during World War II and the Greek Civil War.

Most Macedonian refugee children living abroad have accepted the impossibility of returning to settle permanently in the villages of their birth. Many of them, however, would like to regain legal title to the houses and fields their families left behind. Their property was confiscated by the Greek government after the Civil War and in many cases is now occupied by their relatives or by strangers who were settled there by the Greek government. Some Macedonian refugees talked wistfully about being able to spend summer vacations in their ancestral homes. Others recognized the purely symbolic value of owning the houses where they were born. For these refugees, "the impossible return" (Van Boeschoten 2000) occupies a central place in the imaginary geography of their identity.

Macedonian refugee children who *have* been able to visit the villages of their birth have often experienced powerful feelings of alienation and loss. These visits confirm Stuart Hall's observation that "the places to which [displaced people] return will have been transformed out of all recognition" (1993, 363). When they finally reached the villages where they had been born, refugees often felt "out of place"; they felt like "strangers" (*xenoi*). They realized that they had very little in common with the people living there. When Macedonian refugees addressed the present inhabitants of their villages in Macedonian, the villagers replied in Greek, a reversal of Risto Kalkov's poignant experience of mistakenly addressing his mother in Greek instead of Macedonian when he was reunited with her in Skopje.

Often, Macedonian refugees who returned to their villages in Greece were harassed by the local police. They needed to obtain special permits because they were entering a restricted security zone near the border. For the same reason, they were told, they couldn't take photographs; they were also warned not to talk politics. Understandably, their visits often provoked conflict with their relatives who had remained in the village and now occupied their houses and farmed their fields.

Dimitra Boneva was evacuated from the village of D'mbeni when she was only eight years old. After nine years in Romania, she moved to Skopje to rejoin her family. Then in 1979 she returned to D'mbeni for the first time:

> I went to the priest. The church and two houses are the only buildings they didn't destroy.

"Please," I said to him, "I have two brothers and a sister. I have a grandfather and a grandmother. They all died here. May I go and light a candle in their memory?"

"Go ahead," he said.

"I can't," I replied. "You plowed up their graves. You plowed them up! I want to know where you put their bones so I can go and light a candle. But since I'll never know that, could you at least open the church for me so I can light a candle where they were baptized?"

"Go ahead," he said. "I'll be right there."

"Thank you," I said.

I waited for four hours in front of the church, but he never came. I was in tears; I got in my car and left. I never returned. I don't ever want to go back.

Macedonian refugee children constitute a global community of people who are now in their sixties, many of them grandparents, many retired and living settled lives in Skopje, Prague, Toronto, and Melbourne. But they still identify themselves as refugee children from Aegean Macedonia. In this way, they demonstrate the strength of the ties that link them to their homes in northern Greece, homes they no longer inhabit, homes to which they may never return.

## "We Came Back like Angels and Found Ourselves in Hell": The Repatriation of Refugee Children in the 1950s

The experiences of Macedonian refugee children who settled permanently abroad contrast sharply with those of refugee children, both Greek and Macedonian, who returned to their villages in the 1950s. For these two groups of refugees, the relationships between their "homeland" and "foreign lands," between the world of everyday reality and the world of the imagination, are reversed. The villages of Macedonian refugee children the Greek government has not allowed to return to their homes are "imagined places," and the cities of Eastern Europe, Canada, and Australia are "lived spaces" (Paerregaard 1997, 55), while for repatriated refugee children, Prague, Budapest, and Warsaw exist only as objects of memory and desire, while the villages of their birth, where they now live, are all too real.

The narratives of refugee children who returned to Greece in the 1950s convincingly refute the sedentarist and nationalist myth of traditional refugee discourse in which repatriation is a cure for pathologically displaced people. These stories show how easily people can become strangers in their own homes and thus demonstrate the impossibility of a genuine return. In addition, they illustrate the fact that for refugee children repatriation to the villages of their birth involved the loss of the identities and the homes they had established in Eastern Europe. In many cases, this new loss was just as painful as the original one they experienced when they were evacuated from Greece in 1948.

Many refugee children who were teenagers in the mid-1950s when their parents sought their repatriation did not want to return to Greece. They preferred to remain in Eastern Europe and continue their education, marry someone of their choice, or pursue a career. According to several refugees, children under eighteen were required to return to Greece if their parents requested their repatriation, even if they themselves preferred to remain in Eastern Europe. Refugees over eighteen, who were legally entitled to stay there, often agreed to return to Greece only because they felt an obligation to their parents who desperately wanted them to come home. Pressure from their teachers and officials of the Greek Communist Party to stay in Eastern Europe was rarely able to counter pressure from their parents to return to Greece.

In 1956, Jim Merakis, a Macedonian refugee child from the village of Psarades in the Prespa area, was a fourteen-year-old student in Hungary when he received a letter from his father asking him to return to Greece. His aunt, who was also in Hungary at the time, told him not to. Jim was too young to remember the poverty and isolation of his village, but she wasn't. He obeyed his father and returned to Greece. Several years later, though, he left again and moved to Canada, where he lives now. Jim's brother-in-law Makis Nitsiou had also been evacuated from Psarades to Hungary, but his father, who had studied in Belgrade and worked in the United States, dealt with the issue of his son's repatriation more sensitively. In 1957, he sent Makis a letter in which he wrote, "I am sending you your passport so that you can return to Greece. But I want to emphasize that while your past was ours, your present and your future are your own." Reflecting on his father's letter many years later, Makis said, "I realized that he was giving me the freedom to decide myself. I knew that he loved me and that he always wanted me near him, but he knew that he couldn't give me the kind of life I deserved in Greece." So Makis decided to stay in Hungary. He became an engineer and lives in Budapest still.

Leaving the cities in Eastern Europe where they had spent five or ten years was difficult for many refugees. They had to say good-bye to other refugee children they had lived closely with, to their "mothers," their teachers, and their Polish, Hungarian, or Romanian friends. They were leaving an independent life in a world of educational and professional opportunities for both men and women, to return to a poor mountain village and a home that many of them barely remembered. The journey to Greece by train was often a frightening one. Some young refugees threw books of Macedonian history and poetry out the train window as they approached the Greek border. They had been taught to fear the "fascist" soldiers who greeted them at the Greek border, so they were surprised when the soldiers offered them candy instead of the beatings they expected. Some children were afraid to eat the candy because they had heard stories in Eastern Europe about children being poisoned when they returned to Greece. They had been warned not to call anyone "comrade," but it was a hard habit to break, and the word slipped out sometimes while they were being interrogated by Greek military intelligence officers in Thessaloniki.

During these interrogation sessions, refugee children were asked about their lives in Eastern Europe. How had they been treated? Had they received good medical care? Had they been given enough to eat? What had they learned in school? When one young Macedonian refugee said he had studied the 1903 Ilinden Uprising, which had been fought to establish a free and independent Macedonia, the officer angrily told him to forget about all that nonsense. A thirteen-year-old Macedonian boy was asked if he believed in God. He had never been taught anything about God and thought it was a joke. So he said, "Sure. He's up on the roof catching mice." But it wasn't a joke, and the Greek officer hit him in the face.

Between 1950 and 1952, the first five groups of refugees—524 children in all—were repatriated to Greece from Yugoslavia (Georgitsa-Papadimitrakopoulou 1997, 577–631, Ristović 2000, 99–117). The children stayed at a paidopoli in Thessaloniki for several days while they were being interrogated. Then they were either met by their parents or sent home to their villages. The overtly religious and nationalist nature of the reception to welcome these "children of Greece" back to their homeland elicited some touching responses from the young refugees, who had grown up in a very different world. Many of them spoke no Greek at all. One child was heard singing the Greek national anthem in Macedonian. Another, when asked if he wanted a Greek flag, said yes, he did; but he wanted a red one, not a blue and white one. When the archbishop of Thessaloniki greeted the children, many of them refused to kiss his hand and threw away the crosses he gave them. They just laughed when he tried to teach them how to make the sign of the cross (Georgitsa-Papadimitrakopoulou 1997, 583–84).

Some Greek refugee children who were repatriated to the villages of their birth in the steep mountain valley of the Sarandaporos River valley along the Albanian border in Epirus described the intense feelings of isolation and alienation they felt at their return. Fifty years later their voices were still tinged with bitterness and regret as they talked about their decision to return to Greece. It was the biggest mistake of their lives. Everything "was turned upside down"; their world "was ruined." As one refugee put it, "It would have been better to shoot me than to send me back to live in my village."

Their lives in Eastern Europe had been characterized by a significant degree of independence, but now they were expected to obey their parents and subordinate their own needs to those of their family. As a result, their relationships with their parents were often strained. Repatriated refugee children were also shocked by the poverty and backwardness of their villages. They had left a world of sidewalks, movies, and dances and returned to one of muddy paths, donkeys, and arranged marriages. In comparison with the people of Prague and Warsaw, the villagers they encountered were "barbarians" who "lived like animals." They had no electricity or running water, ate with their hands, and didn't wear pajamas or sleep on beds with sheets. While he was brushing his teeth the first night after his return, one young refugee was asked by his father, "What are you doing, sharpening your teeth?"

Many refugees found it difficult to perform the hard physical labor that was expected of them when they returned. They were completely unfamiliar with the agricultural and pastoral jobs they were assigned. Two sisters who had just returned from Hungary were forced to yoke themselves to a plow and pull it themselves because their family had no draft animals. When a fifteen-year-old girl returned to her village from Yugoslavia, her mother pointed to the family donkey and said "That's your job."

Young men and women faced different challenges upon their return. In many ways, young women encountered even more oppressive conditions than young men. Parents were much less likely to let their daughters leave the village to pursue a career than their sons. Young women were expected to go to church every Sunday, but they didn't believe in God. And worst of all, they faced the prospect of an arranged marriage with a village man they hardly knew and considered an ignorant shepherd or farmer. Maria Panayiotou had studied music in Poland and loved to play the accordion. When she returned to her village along the Albanian border in 1956, her father ripped up her diploma. "What are you doing with an accordion?" he said, "That's for men, not for you." Several years later during a village wedding, she borrowed the accordion of one of the band members and played a few songs. Her mother-in-law was so angry she refused to speak to her for a week.

Issues of dress and appearance had a much greater impact on women than they did on men. Women couldn't wear pants without being accused of looking like guerillas. They couldn't wear their hair permed as they had in Eastern Europe; instead they had to wear kerchiefs over their head like other village women. Eleni Liourou returned from Hungary to her village in Epirus in 1961 at the age of twenty-two. When she married a village shepherd a short time later she wanted to wear a white wedding dress, the kind they wore in Budapest, but her mother-in-law insisted she wear the traditional village bridal outfit. After her marriage, Eleni's new husband cut up all the dresses she'd worn in Hungary because he thought they made her look like a prostitute. Describing her repatriation to Greece many years later Eleni said, "We came back like angels and found ourselves in hell."

Young men who returned from "behind the Iron Curtain" were closely monitored by the police and denied employment and educational opportunities because they lacked the necessary "certificate of loyalty." Their passport applications were often rejected, and when they were drafted into the army, they were given the most undesirable assignments. They were treated like second-class citizens, and they felt completely alienated from the village life they had returned to. In the late 1950s, for example, the coffeehouse in the village of Likorahi in Epirus was full of refugees who had returned from Eastern Europe. All the young men from Poland sat playing cards and speaking Polish at one table. Another table was occupied by young men speaking Hungarian; another by young men speaking Czech. "It was like the Tower of Babel," one refugee observed. Until, that is, the police told them all to stop speaking "communist languages."

Many male refugees found village life so unbearable that they left their homes a second time to begin new lives somewhere else—Athens, Western Europe, Canada, or Australia. Sotir Ničev, a Macedonian refugee child from the district of Florina who had been evacuated to Yugoslavia, had a promising career as a professional soccer player in Belgrade. He scored the winning goal for his Partisan youth club in the final game of the Marshall Tito Cup in May 1952. Then he received notification that his widowed mother had arranged for his repatriation to Greece. Sotir desperately wanted to pursue his soccer career in Belgrade, but he had promised his father before his death that he would take care of his mother and his sisters. Life at home in his village proved impossible for Sotir. He couldn't speak Greek, he was harassed by the police for wearing his Partisan warm-up suit, and he refused to show the necessary respect to Greek authorities. A few months later Sotir's mother arranged for him to leave for the United States to join an uncle who had lived there for many years (Naumoff 2003).

Some young men who returned from Eastern Europe were sent to the Royal Technical School of Leros either at the initiative of their families or with the encouragement of local authorities. Nick Pavlou, a Macedonian refugee child who lives in Toronto, returned to his village near Florina from Romania in 1958 at the age of seventeen. With the help of a wealthy uncle he entered high school in a nearby city, but he was expelled when school officials searched his trunk and found copies of a Greek communist newspaper, some books by Lenin, and notes that Nick had taken in Macedonian. After he returned to his village, the police asked Nick if he wanted to go to Leros to learn a trade. He didn't see any future for himself in the village, so he went. For the next ten years Nick continued to have problems with the authorities and never found a job. In 1970, he left Greece and emigrated to Canada.

Other young men, however, remained in their villages where they continue to live today. Stavros Lazaridis is one of these doubly displaced people who are caught between two worlds and who will never be fully "at home" in either. He is an exile in his own village. His repatriation to Greece was not a return; it was a second departure, one that in many ways was more alienating and disruptive than the first.

Stavros was seven years old in March 1948, when he fled on foot across the Albanian border and the mountains that loom tall and dark above the village of Kallithea where he was born.[10] He was seventeen in 1958 when his father made arrangements for his return to Greece. Stavros had been studying music in Poland. He had learned to play the piano; Chopin and Liszt were his favorite composers. A music teacher Stavros respected a great deal told him not to go back to Greece. Stavros tried to explain to him why he had to return to Greece by reading him his favorite line from the *Odyssey*—book 9, line 34: "Nothing is sweeter than a man's fatherland and his parents." This was the first book Stavros had bought in Poland—the first book he had ever owned in his life—a bilingual Polish-ancient Greek edition of the *Odyssey*. Stavros could only read it in Polish, because he'd never had a chance to study ancient Greek.

When Stavros returned to Kallithea, he brought two suitcases with him. One was full of clothes; the other was full of books. All the old women in the village gathered at his house to welcome him. He didn't recognize his mother, so he asked a friend to step outside with him for a minute to tell him which one she was. Stavros soon realized that he didn't want to spend the rest of his life in Kallithea, but his father was a strict man and insisted that he stay. When Stavros tried to run away to Athens with a friend, his father called the police, who caught them as they were about to board a bus and brought them back to Kallithea. Later Stavros tried to get a passport so he could return to Poland, but the Greek government wouldn't issue him one since he hadn't completed his military service. He wrote the date he was refused a passport to return to Poland inside the front cover of his copy of the *Odyssey*.

Stavros' father used his influence to have Stavros appointed village secretary. In this way he made sure that his son would stay in Kallithea. Stavros' mother was always complaining that he burned so many candles reading late into the night that she didn't have any left to light in church. With some money he had saved, Stavros bought a tape recorder and some cassettes of classical music. All his friends told him he should throw those away and buy some Greek folk music. Once Stavros went to the International Fair in Thessaloniki and bought several books at the Polish exhibit. When he returned to Kallithea, someone informed on him, and the police called him in to ask why he was reading books from a communist country. In 1957, he told a group of village children about *Sputnik*, the Soviet satellite that had just been the first to orbit the earth. Someone overheard him and told the police; they warned him not to spread communist propaganda in the village.

Now Stavros loves to watch Polish television shows on his satellite dish. He often thinks about his favorite music teacher in Poland and his first girlfriend, a tall, dark-haired Polish girl, who sat next to him in school. He recently bought his first car and would really like to go back to Poland to see if he could find them. He realizes the sad irony of his situation: when he was studying in Poland he always dreamed of returning to Greece, but since his repatriation he has dreamed of going back to Poland. Stavros knows now that it would have been better if he'd stayed in Poland; that's where he spent the best years of his life.

The image of a young Greek refugee in Poland citing the *Odyssey* to justify his desire to return to Greece would seem to confirm the validity of sedentarist and Greek nationalist discourse, which glorifies the repatriation of Greek refugee children as necessary to restore the "national order of things." The fact that he read the *Odyssey* in Polish, however, the fact that he was exposed to the world of Homer through the Polish educational system, completely undermines the validity of this discourse. If Stavros had not become a refugee in a foreign land, it is unlikely that he would ever have read Homer or come to appreciate the meaning of this passage. After all, the sweetness of home is best understood by Odysseus, Stavros, and other exiles, as is the bitterness—and the sweetness—of foreign lands.

The estrangement felt by Stavros Lazaridis and other repatriated Greek refugee children after their return to Greece also challenges this traditional sedentarist and nationalist discourse. It demonstrates that a return home is never fully possible. With the passage of time not only does home become a different place, but refugees themselves become different people. That is why repatriated Greek refugee children like Stavros often lived like exiles in their own homes.

## "One Foot in Greece and the Other in Germany": The Repatriation of Refugee Children in the 1970s and 1980s

The experiences of refugees who were repatriated to Greece from Eastern Europe in the 1970s and 1980s were significantly different from those of refugees who returned in the 1950s. For decades, refugee children who came back to Greece as adults had been "burning with desire to return home"; for years their dinner parties had ended with the toast *"Kali patrida!"* (To our beautiful fatherland!). And yet, when they were finally able to return to Greece, their encounter with their *patrida* was often bittersweet (Van Boeschoten 2000, 137–38). For most of the refugee children, now adults with families and careers, the Greece they found on their return did not look at all like the idealized image of Greece they had nurtured during their childhoods. Instead of being reunited with their "mother fatherland" (*mitera patrida*)—a common, if somewhat paradoxical image suggesting that Greece, the fatherland, is a loving mother—they returned to find that their birth mother had been replaced by a cruel stepmother, that their mother fatherland, in other words, had become their "stepmother fatherland" (*mitria patrida*).[11]

When political refugees began to return to Greece in significant numbers after the fall of the military dictatorship in 1974, they encountered a society that was much less conservative and much less dominated by anticommunism than it had been for the previous seven years of military dictatorship or in fact since the end of the Civil War. Even after the restoration of democracy, however, Greek society was still extremely polarized, and the legacy of the Civil War very much alive. For several years after 1974, many former refugee children were met with hostility and prejudice when they tried once again to establish new homes, this time in the country of their birth. They were accused of being Slavs, communists, and enemies of the Greek state; they were asked why they had come back to Greece and taken jobs away from Greeks.[12] Their fellow villagers were afraid that their presence would reopen old wounds, that they would go to court to try to regain title to property that had been confiscated by the government and occupied by their relatives who had remained in Greece.

When Anthi Markou, a Greek refugee child from the Florina region, returned to Greece in 1976 at the age of thirty-seven, she and her family settled in Athens. Someone vandalized their car; it still had Hungarian license plates on it. Their neighbors called them "dirty Bulgarians" and told them to go back to Bulgaria. After she returned to Greece from Hungary, Ourania Topali, a Greek refugee child from the Evros region of Thrace, said she was treated like a second-class citizen. Once someone at work told her, "I would have preferred a Greek in your position." Ourania was furious. "Do you mean to imply that I'm Hungarian?" she asked. "If you can show me anyone here in Greece who is more Greek than I am, I'll cut off my head." No one ever dared call Ourania "Hungarian" again.

After the end of military rule in 1974, the Greek government was still reluctant to allow the unconditional return of political refugees, restore their rights as citizens, or even grant their requests for short visits (L. Papadopoulos 1999, 100–14). Associations of Greek political refugees in Eastern Europe mounted a campaign to persuade the Greek government that finally, twenty-five years after the end of the Civil War, they should be allowed to return to Greece. They sought "political amnesty," "the annulment of the unconstitutional laws" that had blocked their repatriation, and "the right to return to their homeland as equal members of Greek society" (Gousidis 1975, 14).

Many political refugees expressed their dissatisfaction with the "degrading and humiliating terms" under which they had previously been allowed to return, requirements that they declare their national identity as Greeks, renounce left-wing political beliefs, and sign statements of repentance and remorse (Gousidis 1975, 30–35). They also stressed their loyalty to the Greek state and the excellent education and professional training they had received in Eastern Europe that would enable them to make valuable contributions to Greek society. A political refugee who had become a sculptor in Budapest said, "We're not bandits with knives in our mouths ready to go down to Greece and slaughter people. We're well respected people ready to offer our services to our homeland" (13).

On December 29, 1982, these demands were finally met when the newly elected socialist government of Greece issued a ministerial decree announcing "the free repatriation and restoration to Greek citizenship" of all political refugees who were "Greeks by birth." According to this decree, after filling out a questionnaire at a Greek consulate in their country of residence, political refugees would be issued travel documents allowing them to return to Greece. They could then apply for the restoration of their Greek citizenship.

Before deciding whether to return to Greece on a permanent basis, many political refugees made a preliminary visit to determine whether Greek authorities would recognize the educational and professional credentials they had earned in Eastern Europe and whether they could continue to receive their pensions after they moved to Greece. They wanted to investigate the employment possibilities and the living conditions in the cities where they planned to settle. They also were interested in learning how they would be received in the villages where they had been born.

Many refugees were amazed to see how much economic growth Greece had experienced since the Civil War and how much higher the standard of living there was. They had left isolated mountain villages after almost a decade of war and were now returning to a rapidly modernizing country that had recently become a member of the European Union. Their decision to return to Greece was greatly influenced by the fact that in the 1980s living conditions in Greece were significantly better than they were in Eastern Europe, where economic growth was stagnant, inflation was widespread, and the standard of living was deteriorating. As children growing up under communist regimes, they had heard only negative things about capitalism, but when they arrived in Greece they were able to compare the two systems themselves. It took many of them some time before they were able to adjust. As one Greek refugee who returned to Greece late in his life put it, "We lacked the shrewdness you need to survive in a capitalist system. We were as innocent as lambs."

The two factors most responsible for the differences between the experiences of refugee children who were repatriated in the 1950s and those who returned in the 1980s were the political and economic conditions they encountered upon their arrival in Greece, on the one hand, and their age difference, on the other. After paying a short, but moving, visit to the villages of their birth, most of the refugee children who returned in the 1980s decided to settle down in cities where they could find good jobs and continue the careers they had pursued in Eastern Europe. For this reason, they did not experience the extreme culture shock that confronted refugees who returned in the 1950s and settled in more remote areas of northern Greece.

Repatriation decisions made in the 1950s were not made by the refugee children themselves, but by their parents. At that time, because their *parents'* homes were the villages of northern Greece, the homes of the refugee children were there as well. In the case of refugees who returned to Greece in the 1980s, the situation was precisely the opposite. These refugees, now adults, were fully responsible for making the decision to repatriate. What is more, many of them now had children of their own whose interests they had to consider in making their final decision whether to return to Greece.

Greek refugee children who returned to Greece in the 1980s had lived most of their adult lives in Eastern Europe. They had assimilated more fully into the societies in which they lived and had developed a stronger sense of identity as Poles, Hungarians, or Czechs. When they returned to Greece as adults, they did not experience the shock of moving from a sophisticated urban environment to an isolated mountain village, but they did experience the feelings of alienation that come from having more than one home and not feeling completely comfortable in either. A refugee child who returned to Greece as an adult and settled on the outskirts of Athens said that if her children had stayed in Hungary any longer they would have become Hungarians. She said that she herself had almost begun to feel like a Hungarian too. Even after her return to Greece, she still felt like an outsider, a *xeni*. Nothing tied her to Greece anymore; she didn't remember anything about it at all. Greece was no longer her "home."

Eleni Milona, a refugee child who was evacuated from her village in Evros when she was ten years old, grew up in Bulgaria and East Germany. In 1989, she retired from her job as an optician in West Germany and returned to Greece. She and her husband bought property and built a house in the city of Alexandroupolis, but they kept their apartment in Berlin. Eleni's husband needed to work a few more years there before he could receive his pension, and their children and grandchildren still lived there as well.

> I have one foot in Greece and the other in Germany, but one day we'll have to make a decision. We can't dance at two weddings. It's either here or there. . . . I'm still not 100 percent here in Greece. We want to go to Greece, so we can finally be Greeks. We have German citizenship, because we thought it would be better for the children, but we feel more like Greeks. Both our feet need to be together in one place.

Eleni Kiriazi, who was also born in Thrace and raised in Germany, disagreed: she wanted one foot in each place, not because she felt at home in both countries, but because she did not feel at home in either. "We're birds of passage. Wherever we go, we will always be strangers (*xenoi*). Once you've left your country, your roots are gone."

Eleni Milona, Eleni Kiriazi, and many other Greek refugee children who returned to Greece in the late 1970s and 1980s are struggling to resolve the conflicting ties that link them to the two places they call home. They are people who, in Appadurai's words, must "deal with the realities of having to move and the fantasies of wanting to move," people whose lives "transcend specific territorial boundaries and identities" (1996, 34, 49). They must balance their own needs with those of their children; they must also reconcile the practical questions of citizenship and economic security with the more emotional issues of personal identity and sense of home. Even though they want to stand with both feet in one place, even though they want to have one unambiguous identity, one permanent home, they may not be able to. Their evacuation in 1948 and their repatriation some thirty years later have permanently complicated their lives. They may always have to stand with their feet in two different places.

## The Many Meanings of Home

Macedonian refugee children who settled in Eastern Europe, Canada, and Australia and refugee children who returned to Greece have very different identities. All former refugee children have one or more places they call home, but the meanings they attach to the term vary. Many of the Macedonian refugee children who have not been allowed to return to the villages where they were born are proud to call themselves "refugee children from Aegean Macedonia." By using this term they stress that their real homes remain the villages of their birth. For them, being refugee children is still a central component of their identities, as their narratives of separation and loss, nostalgia and desire, suggest. They are still refugees because they are not allowed to return to Greece. They continue to identify themselves in terms of their relationship to their lost homeland, to define themselves as victims of the tragedies they experienced as children. This is the fundamental fact that distinguishes the experiences of Macedonian refugee children from those of their Greek counterparts; this is the fact that has transformed them from temporary refugees into permanent exiles (Ballinger 2003, 183).

In "Reflections on Exile," Edward Said has pointed out the intimate links between the language of nationalism and the condition of exile. Exiles, he writes, feel "an urgent need to reconstitute their broken lives, usually by choosing to see themselves as part of a triumphant ideology or a restored people" (2000, 177).[13] In their first-person narratives many Macedonian refugee children identify themselves as victims who have become heroes. They have created for themselves what Malkki (referring to Hutu refugees from the 1972 genocide in Burundi) has called "a heroized national identity . . . as a people in exile" (Malkki 1995b, 3). From this perspective, Macedonian refugee children are heroes because they retained their Macedonian national identity in the face of persecution by the Greek government; they survived their tragic experiences during the Greek Civil War, and they went on to live successful and meaningful lives. In this way, they have "located their identities within their very displacement, extracting meaning and power from the interstitial social location they inhabited. Instead of losing their collective identity, this is where and how they made it" (Malkki 1995b, 16).

Being "refugee children from Aegean Macedonia" not only gives Macedonian refugees from the Greek Civil War a meaningful identity they can be proud of, it also gives them a political cause that many of them have dedicated their lives to—preserving the memory of their lost homelands and defending the human rights of the Macedonian minority of northern Greece. The life stories of Macedonian refugee children that follow this internal logic are fully consistent with Macedonian nationalist discourse. Their experiences can be legitimated, their tragedies openly mourned, and their successes publicly celebrated. Their collective narrative is an important episode in the Macedonian national myth of a people struggling to preserve its language, culture, and identity against the hostile and more powerful nations that surround it.

As Said reminds us, however, triumphant narratives about victims transformed into heroes are "no more than efforts to overcome the crippling sorrow of estrangement." Exile, Said continues, "is the unhealable rift forced between a human being and a native place, between the self and its true home: its essential sadness can never be overcome" (2000, 173). It is this fundamental sadness that forms another, contrapuntal component of Macedonian refugee children's identities. In their narratives this sadness often takes the form of anger and frustration at the Greek state's refusal to allow them to return to the villages of their birth. A Macedonian refugee child who lives in Budapest used a powerful kinship metaphor we have heard before to give voice to this anger: "For me, Greece is just a stepmother. If she were a real mother, she would have tried to get *all* her children back!"[14]

Another way in which Macedonian refugee children express the sadness of exile is through narratives about their lost childhood. They claim they are still children because they continue to feel as adults the pain and loss they experienced as children. They say they still feel like children because they have never stopped trying to recover their lost childhood. A sixty-one-year-old refugee who saw her mother for the last time when she was five years old said, "I wish I could just have the chance to give her a hug and sit on her lap again, to get all those things I missed as a child." Another woman who left her village when she was eight said, "People can say I'm an old woman, but deep inside I've remained a child."

Refugee children who *did* return to Greece express similar feelings of loss and sorrow, but since they are no longer exiles, this pain no longer occupies a central place in their identities. Their present lives are not defined by their lost childhood or their heroic refugee identity, they are defined by a return, a "homecoming," that failed to fulfill its promise. The disappointment they felt when they returned to Greece can be attributed both to the poverty of their home villages and to the way they were treated by their fellow villagers and by representatives of the Greek state.

Refugee children occupy very different positions in Macedonian and Greek national discourse. While Macedonian refugee children play an important role in the Macedonian transnational national community, refugees who were repatriated to Greece are little more than awkward reminders of a controversial and painful period in modern Greek history. In addition, since the fall of communism in 1989, any positive memories they may have of their lives behind the Iron Curtain are no longer shared by others either in Greece or in their former host countries. These memories are simply "lost objects" of history.

Refugee children who were repatriated to the villages of their birth in the 1950s never became members of a transnational, cosmopolitan diaspora. What is more, from the sedentarist perspective that has dominated international legal discourse and the official discourse of the Greek state, they ceased being refugees the moment they returned to Greece. From this perspective, repatriated refugee children no longer had a distinct identity as refugees; they were only "former refugees," or "repatriates" (*epanapatristhendes*). According to Greek nationalist discourse, their repatriation eliminated the pathological condition that characterized their status as refugees by returning them to their homes and restoring the "national order of things" to its original state of purity. The children of Greece had returned to their homeland. Their repatriation was a cause for national celebration, just as their evacuation had been a cause for national mourning.

The official discourse of the Greek state, however, differed markedly from the actual treatment that refugees repatriated in the 1950s received upon their return to Greece both at the hands of the government and the Greek public. In Greek nationalist discourse, in 1948 they were innocent victims of "a crime against the Greek race," but when they came back to Greece, they were "children from behind the Iron Curtain." They were treated like second-class citizens; they were interrogated, refused passports and "certificates of loyalty," and denied both educational and professional opportunities. As Slavs, they were no longer members of the Greek nation, and as communists, they were enemies of the Greek state. These two identities coalesced to justify acts of exclusion that in turn fostered a strong sense of alienation from mainstream Greek society.

The discourse of the Greek state also contrasted significantly with the personal experiences of the repatriated refugee children themselves. Most refugee children who identified themselves as Greeks or Macedonians in 1948 continued to do so when they returned to Greece in the 1950s. By the time of their repatriation, however, they had also constructed new identities based on their experiences in Eastern Europe. In many ways, therefore, these repatriated refugee children were not "children of Greece" returning to their homeland; they were "children of Eastern Europe" arriving in a foreign land. They were children of Poland, Hungary, and Czechoslovakia who had been repatriated, sometimes against their will, to the unfamiliar world of Greek mountain villages. Many of them did not experience their arrival in Greece as a return, but rather as a second departure, a second displacement, often more traumatic than the first. It was as if they were "coming from one exile to another" (Araidi 1985, 7–8, cited in Lavie and Swedenburg 1996, 57); as if they were living now as exiles in their own homes.

More significantly, this second displacement, which the refugee children experienced upon their "repatriation" to Greece, could never be publicly acknowledged as such. The sense of loss and alienation they experienced when they left their homes in Eastern Europe had to remain private; the nostalgia they felt for their lost childhoods there had to be suppressed. These feelings, these aspects of their identity, were not legitimated in any way by official Greek discourse because they refuted the validity of the sedentarist and nationalist assumptions on which it was based. The positive experiences the refugee children had in Eastern Europe, like the negative experiences they had upon returning to Greece, could never be reconciled with the ideals of loyalty to family and homeland. Unlike Macedonian refugee children who were never able to return to Greece, refugees who were repatriated to Greece did not acquire a positive collective identity with which to construct meaningful lives as national heroes in a transnational diaspora. Instead, they acquired a stigmatized identity that made their efforts to construct new lives in Greece even more difficult than it would otherwise have been.

Both refugee children who never returned to Greece and those who did feel a desire to retain ties to their lost childhood homes, whether these homes are the Greek villages where they were born or the children's homes in Eastern Europe where they grew up. These childhood homes, however, are located securely in the past. In that sense, to quote Salman Rushdie again, "the past is a country from which we have all emigrated" (1991, 12). We can never return to our childhood, even if we *can* return to the *place* we called "home" when we were children. The passage of time transforms our childhood home into a foreign place, whether we can physically return there or not.

Now that the Iron Curtain is no more and most of the countries where the refugees grew up have joined the European Union, it has become much easier for them to maintain ties both literally and imaginatively to the different homes of their childhoods. The relatively high standard of living enjoyed by refugee children in the diaspora has made it possible for many of them to return as pilgrims and tourists to the villages of their birth. Those who are unable to do so (as well as whose who are) participate in the construction of "imaginary homelands" by joining the many village and regional associations that play such an important role in the social life of the Greek and Macedonian diaspora communities. Similarly, for the refugees who returned to Greece and live in an urban environment, it is now much easier to travel in the opposite direction. Many have second homes in Berlin, Warsaw, or Prague, where they spend part of the year. It is much more difficult for repatriated refugees who live in rural areas to return literally to their second homes in Eastern Europe and to maintain ties to the cities where they lived. With the development of modern communication technologies, however, they can still remain in touch with their "imaginary homelands" through satellite TV and the Internet.

In spite of the differences that separate them, both refugee children who never returned to Greece, and those who did, have multiple identities constructed from their attachments to multiple places. One refugee said, "Many times, to tell you the truth, I don't know who or what I am. I hear a Macedonian song and remember my grandmother. . . . I hear a Polish song and remember my youth." Another said, "For us the Civil War never ended. . . . It continues to haunt us. We never settled down; we don't have a homeland anywhere." Comments like these, made by refugee children who remained abroad and by those who returned to Greece, express "the anguish of cultural displacement and diasporic movement" (Bhabha 1992, 142). All the refugee children of the Greek Civil War lost one home, one identity, one life, but they gained others. To this day, they remain precariously balanced on the border between the two.

# SEVEN

# Communities of Memory, Narratives of Experience

*Tiheroi mesa stin atihia* (Fortunate amidst Misfortune)

—Title of a book by Mihalis Raptis, a refugee child from Epirus

The evacuation of children from northern Greece by the Greek Communist Party and the Greek government's demand for their repatriation marked the first major international confrontation of the Cold War. After the unsuccessful attempts of the International Red Cross to repatriate the refugee children in the late 1940s and early 1950s, the Greek government soon lost interest in them. It was afraid that they might have been "contaminated" by the "communist virus" and dehellenized. The refugee children were "forgotten"; they became a taboo topic excised from the public memory of the Civil War. During the "years of stone," as the aftermath of the Civil War is often referred to, official memory in Greece was controlled by the victors.[1] Right-wing nationalist versions of history dominated all public discourse. In other Western European countries resistance to the occupying Axis powers was glorified as a heroic struggle that served to legitimate postwar democratic regimes. In Greece, however, the predominantly left-wing resistance was banished from public memory. Official commemorations of the Greek Civil War legitimated the eventual rise to power of the anticommunist right, while supporters of the left were condemned as traitors to the nation.

The spectacular changes that have swept over Greece and the rest of Europe during the last three decades have thoroughly transformed the context in which public memory is shaped. These changes have created a new intellectual space in which the history of the Greek Civil War has been revisited. The end of the Cold War has also created new tensions on both the domestic and the international fronts. The arrival of large numbers of migrants from Eastern Europe and the international conflict over the proper name of the newly independent Republic of Macedonia dominated the Greek media in the 1990s and influenced the ways in which Greeks have come to understand their recent past.

This was the context in which the refugee children of the Civil War re-emerged as a controversial topic of public concern. In 1981, only a few months after the Panhellenic Socialist Movement, PASOK, came to power, novelist Elli Alexiou, a leading member of EVOP, the committee responsible for the education of the refugee children in Eastern Europe, was interviewed on state television. This was the first time since the end of the Civil War that the left's perspective on the evacuation program had been publicly aired in Greece. Alexiou's interview provoked angry reactions from the traditional Greek right. A leading conservative newspaper called it a "provocation of communist propaganda," and the issue was hotly debated in the Greek Parliament, where a socialist minister insisted that conservatives had no right to mourn the fate of these children since for so many years they had denied them the right to return to Greece (Gionis 2006).

A few years later, in 1983, the controversy was given new impetus with the publication of *Eleni*, the best seller by Greek American journalist Nicholas Gage, in which he attributed the execution of his mother by the partisans in 1948 to the fact that she had refused to send her children to Eastern Europe and had instead secretly organized their escape to government-controlled territory. Gage's book was seen by many as a return to the anticommunist propaganda of the Cold War and a setback for the process of reconciliation. It provoked a scathing response from a left-wing journalist, Vasilis Kavvathas, whose book, *The Other Eleni* (1985), received no international attention, but played an important role in public debates over the issue in Greece. More recently, the fate of the children hosted in the paidopoleis of Queen Frederica has also emerged as a controversial issue in which two conflicting versions of the past—right and left—bitterly confront one another. Two novels and a television program presenting negative depictions of life in the homes have recently provoked angry reactions from former residents.[2]

Finally, the "memory war" over the fate of the refugee children is closely linked to what has been one of the most sensitive issues of Greek diplomacy since the early 1990s: the Macedonian conflict, a complex set of problems that involves the international recognition of the Republic of Macedonia and the acknowledgment of the existence of a Macedonian minority in northern Greece. From the perspective of Greek nationalists, the resolution of this "unfinished business" of the Greek Civil War constitutes a threat to Greek national identity and the territorial integrity of Greece.

In this chapter and the next we analyze the life-history narratives of refugee children and explore the relationship between the construction of their memories, on the one hand, and the master narratives that dominate the public arena, on the other. Then we explore the politics of this "memory war" by presenting ethnographic analyses of specific communities and events in which memories of the evacuation program have played a major role in the construction of collective identities. This focus on the "politics of memory" places our analysis at the heart of a major academic debate over "war memories."[3]

We offer new insights into this debate by moving beyond the two world wars and the Holocaust (the focus of most studies of war memories) into the Cold War and post–Cold War periods and by looking at these conflicts from a transnational perspective. One of the major puzzles posed by the "memory war" over the fate of the refugee children is why this Cold War conflict has taken on such heightened significance now that "communism is dead" and the language of nationalism has been replaced, at least partially, by a global discourse on human rights and multiculturalism. Is this conflict just a complex replaying of Cold War ideologies, or is it a response to new challenges in the context of the "new world order?" We will return to this crucial issue in the final pages of the book. In light of the evidence presented here, we argue that although the rhetoric deployed on both sides repeats ideological patterns of the Cold War, it is used for different purposes and in a different global context.

## Memory and Narration

Battles over the memory of the evacuation of refugee children of the Greek Civil War involve polarized master narratives in which opposing sides each claim a monopoly on the "historical truth." The children were either "refugees" or "hostages," "saved" or "kidnapped," "educated" or "indoctrinated," "Hellenized" or "Slavicized." Each side asserts its own version of the historical truth, and in the process, individual experiences that do not fit either of these two master narratives are conveniently "forgotten" and condemned to oblivion.

More importantly, this memory war has largely ignored the first-person voices of refugee children themselves. The children of the Greek Civil War, the very object of these contested memories, have been cast as "innocent victims" with no agency of their own. The multiple ways in which they remember their own lived experiences and the meanings they attribute to them in the present have been omitted or excluded from the two opposing master narratives that have come to dominate both scholarly and popular discourse on the subject. And for good reason. The complex, multilayered private memories of individual refugee children are often at odds with the monolithic view of history presented in official discourse; they undermine the claims to absolute truth this discourse promotes.

The discrepancies that exist between public and private memories do not mean that we should read the children's stories primarily as oppositional narratives, consciously challenging the truth of hegemonic accounts. Nor does it imply a clear-cut dichotomy between official public memories and unofficial private ones. Memories are not shaped independently of the temporal or spatial contexts in which they are formed. As people try to make sense of their lives, they may integrate parts of the master narratives available to them into their own life stories. They may respond to these master narratives by "confiscating" them and actively using them for their own, often very different, purposes. As refugee children grew into adults in Toronto, Budapest, Skopje, and villages in northern Greece, they were drawn into public debates over the politics of memory. Conversely, these debates penetrated the private narratives that the refugee children presented to us during our research.

In this chapter we focus our attention on the role of memory in the formation of individual subjectivities—on what Sherry Ortner has called "the ensemble of modes of perception, affect, thought, desire, fear and so forth that animate acting subjects" (2005, 31)—by exploring the subjective truths expressed in the first-person narratives of refugee children of the Greek Civil War. These subjective truths, as well as their complex relationships to the master narratives that play a crucial role in the "memory wars" of the public arena, are a necessary counterpart to the politics of memory in public discourse that is the subject of chapter 8.

Our analysis of these first-person narratives focuses on the commonplace elements in the narrators' self-representations. According to Luisa Passerini, such self-representations "reveal cultural attitudes, visions of the world and interpretations of history, including the role of the individual in the historical process" (1987, 19). We explore cultural themes in the life stories of children who went to Eastern Europe and of children who went to the paidopoleis by looking at the ways refugee children have structured their narratives and the meanings they attach to their lived experience. We identify shared patterns of memory both within and between these two groups.

In part 1, we made use of oral testimonies to reconstruct the multiplicity of experiences lived by the refugee children evacuated from their villages in 1948. Oral memories are a valuable complement to written sources and help fill in significant gaps in the historical record. These narratives also offer insights into the process through which historical actors construct meanings and identities in the present. Because of the ambivalent nature of memory, pointing simultaneously toward the past and the present, the interpretation of these narratives raises important theoretical issues. Can people recall experiences exactly as they lived them? If not, how and why are these experiences transformed? How do individual memories relate to the recollections of other people in a community and to official master narratives of the past? What is the difference between remembering and narrating past experiences? How can we explain the fact that some aspects of our past are forgotten, while others stay with us in the form of incessantly repeated memories?

The pioneering work of Maurice Halbwachs has been an influential source for scholars interested in the social construction of memory. In a famous passage from *Les cadres sociaux de la mémoire* (The Social Frameworks of Memory), published in 1925, Halbwachs points out that when we read again as adults one of our most cherished childhood books, we may find to our surprise that we are unable to reexperience the vivid impressions the book made on us when we were young. Halbwachs attributes this inability to relive our initial experiences to the fact that they have been displaced by our later experiences and by the total set of ideas that we hold about society in the present. Our inability to relive these childhood experiences is also linked to the fact that we now belong to different social groups than we did when we were children, and to the fact that individuals within these groups (family members, work colleagues, or members of a political party) may have different ideas about the social and natural worlds to which they belong (Halbwachs [1925] 1994, 83–88). The complexes of ideas maintained by social groups are what Halbwachs refers to as "social frameworks of memory."

The major insight Halbwachs has contributed to the study of social memory is that people remember, not as isolated individuals, but as members of social groups. These groups provide the frameworks that make it possible for individuals to remember and interpret their past. Both the social groups to which we belong and the social frameworks of memory they provide us with change over time. The meanings we attach to our past experiences are determined to a significant extent by our present situation. Memory is, therefore, selective and variable. It is a process rather than a "thing"; a process through which the past is reconstructed and constantly updated in light of developments in the present (Halbwachs 1992, 1994).

Halbwachs' work on social frameworks of memory is a useful starting point from which to approach the memories contained in the life stories of refugee children from the Greek Civil War. Children who were evacuated to Eastern Europe and those who were evacuated to the paidopoleis became members of different social groups when they were separated from their families and placed in new environments. In this way, they were exposed to different social frameworks of memory. For both groups, political ideologies played a central role in their new lives. These experiences framed their memories in important ways. This is not, however, a straightforward, unilateral process. People from the same village who went to the same home in Eastern Europe or to the same paidopoli may have very different memories of their experiences there, because the way in which social frameworks of memory shape individual memories is also a product of subjectivity and individual agency. This insight emphasizes the significance of the interaction between individual, private, and unofficial memories, on the one hand, and collective, public, and official memories, on the other.

Personal memories, however, are not only determined by the present, as Halbwachs seemed to believe. More recent research has shown the importance of "cultural scripts," that is, preexisting cultural narratives according to which people make sense of their experiences and structure their memories (Ashplant, Dawson, and Roper 2000, 34; Green 2004; Petersen 2005). These cultural scripts may be linked to the immediate social environments of particular individuals, but they may also include elements from the master narratives circulating in the nation as a whole. For example, accounts in school textbooks of the Ottoman practice of *devshirme* (the *paidomazoma*) or family stories about prewar emigration to the United States may have influenced the ways in which children "remembered" their departure from their village in 1948. While it is true that the present shapes the meaning of the past, it is equally true that the past shapes the meaning of the present.

Cultural scripts like these play an important role in the transformation of personal memories into public narratives. The relationship between experience, memory, and narration is a complex one. It is dominated by a tension between lived and retold experiences (Rosenthal 1995), the tension, in other words, between the former self as social actor and the present self as narrator and author of a particular life story (Skultans 1998, xii). In this transformation, the relationship between experience and narration is not always straightforward. Events may be invested with a meaning they did not have when they were initially experienced, or they may be transformed into a mythical tale that contradicts history, but that expresses the meaning of the event in subjective terms (Portelli 1991).

The narration of a life story, therefore, becomes an important tool in the formation of the narrator's social, cultural, and political identities in the present. This is, of course, primarily an individual process; each narrator constructs a life story in his or her own manner. At the same time, however, the life stories of individuals with a shared past also contain recurrent themes and common memories. These common memories are important clues that contribute significantly to our understanding of the narrators' present identities and their readings of the past.

## Communities of Memory

Just as personal narratives play an important part in the formation of individual identities, group narratives contribute significantly to the formation of collective identities. In times of violent disruption of daily routine, shared experiences may shape a whole generation, especially a generation whose members lived through tragic events in their formative years. The horror of World War I, for example, created among young soldiers a "community of experience" that marked them off from earlier generations.[4] Halbwachs (1997, 129–30), as well as more recent scholars of memory, has defined "communities of memory" as groups of people—the inhabitants of a village, war veterans, the survivors of a massacre, exile communities—who share common experiences and shape their memories through daily face-to-face interaction and acts of remembrance.[5]

The members of a community of memory, whether they actually live together or not, try to make sense of their past and thus contribute to the formation of their identity through the act of narration. In this way, they attempt to establish control over the memory of certain events and to legitimate their actions both in the past and in the present. By doing so, they set themselves off from others who did not live through the same experiences or who have interpreted these experiences differently. The construction of identity, the creation of meaning, the maintenance of boundaries, and the recognition of community are key concepts that contribute to our understanding of the memories kept alive by these communities.

It is important to focus on the multivocal and often contradictory nature of memories that exist within the same community of memory. Contrary to what Halbwachs (1997, 129–30) claims, individual members of a community of memory do not always remember their shared experiences in the same way. Alternative versions of the past may emerge in the narratives of different individuals, challenging or contradicting the "approved" version of the narrators' own group. Since memories are shaped not only by common experiences in the past, but also by experiences later in life, one original community of experience can break up into different subgroups and develop into distinct communities of memory.

It is important to understand the processes through which communities of memory are formed. As Roger Bastide (1970) has shown, not all communities of memory are defined exclusively in relationship to a single place, nor are they shaped by shared experiences alone. Their members can be linked to each other through transnational bonds to form a community of interests, thoughts, or feelings (Connerton 1989, 37). Particularly relevant in this context are the theoretical contributions of Arjun Appadurai on the cultural consequences of globalization. In *Modernity at Large* (1996, 1–23), Appadurai discusses the creation of "communities of sentiment" extending beyond the level of the nation-state, the increased role of imagination as a social practice, and the formation of "diasporic public spheres." In these new settings, communities of memory can be transformed into *global* "imagined communities" (Anderson 1992).

Here we distinguish between two different, but often overlapping, types of community of memory—experiential communities of memory and political communities of memory—each of which is associated with different kinds of narrative, operates in different arenas, and has different goals. In experiential communities of memory, narratives are mainly structured by lived experience, shaped by private actors in intimate social settings (family gatherings, group meetings, or oral-history interviews), and are intended to make sense of the narrators' lives. In political communities of memory, narratives are mainly structured by political ideologies, mediated through public arenas (commemorations, exhibitions, conferences, websites, or electronic discussion lists) and directed toward political action in the present. In her study of two groups of Italians from northern Yugoslavia who were divided by World War II, one that emigrated to Italy and the other that remained in Yugoslavia, Pamela Ballinger identifies them as two communities that "have been continually (re)constituted through practices of remembrance and contests over history which actors phrase in terms of singular and exclusive historical truths" (2003, 268). In other words, political communities of memory are shaped by the past as it is reconstructed in the context of a politicized present, rather than by the past as it is reconstructed from shared personal experiences.

Members of experiential communities of memory develop close social networks among themselves in order to share their memories and experiences. Jay Winter (1999) uses the metaphors of "fictive kinship" and "families of remembrance" to describe the bonds that united survivors of World War I. Refugee children from the Greek Civil War also employ the language of kinship to describe the bonds that unite them to other refugee children; they often say, "We were all brothers and sisters." Greek refugee children from the Evros region, who grew up in East Germany, meet every summer in the village of Dadia in Thrace. Eleni Milona is one of them. When she spoke about the reunion in Dadia, she switched from Greek to German, the language that evokes the close ties she feels toward the other refugee children who grew up in Germany together. "We're closer to these people. We can talk to them, tell them things only they can understand. That's because we had the same experiences, the same fate. It wasn't such a good fate, . . . but we made something of our lives, and we're satisfied."

Mare Kondova, a Macedonian refugee child who is now a professor of applied mathematics at the University of Cyril and Methodius in Skopje, was looking at some recent pictures of her three Greek "sisters" who had lived with her in a children's home in Poland. One of them still lives in Poland; the other two live in Canada and Bulgaria. For over forty years they have corresponded with each other, usually in Polish. Three of the four girls had lost their fathers during the Civil War. Mare explained—half in English, half in Greek—how the support they drew from each other had joined their lives forever.

> [*In English.*] We didn't miss our parents that much. All the children were my brothers and sisters, all together. Because there were so many of us, we were strong. We survived; we remained normal. [*Switches to Greek.*] I can talk to those girls about what we went through, and they understand. Nobody else does. You just can't open your heart to anyone.

These accounts contain several themes that identify Eleni and Mare as members of a specific community of memory. Both women stress their identity as refugee children. Although they have different national identities and although they speak different languages, they use almost the same words to mark themselves off from others who "don't understand" because they did not have the same childhood experiences. Both women say that the childhood experiences they shared played a crucial role in giving meaning to their lives. While Eleni locates this meaning in the children's ability to overcome a tragic fate and lead productive lives, Mare stresses the strength they found to survive the loss of a parent and live "normal" lives. By pointing out that their lives were meaningful in spite of all the hardship they endured, Eleni and Mare seek recognition that their parents' decision to send them to Eastern Europe was a sensible and appropriate course of action. Finally, through the bonds they feel toward people of other nationalities, as well as through the different languages they speak, the stories of Eleni and Mare show us that the communities of memory they belong to are transnational and diasporic in scope.

The personal narratives of refugee children contain memories that are based on experiences they shared during their formative years—departure, separation, repatriation, and migration. These memories, however, are also based on strong peer bonds developed during their lives in the children's homes. In this sense, they can be described as belonging to a community of *experience*, just like young soldiers of World War I. Yet not all of these children belong to the same community of *memory*. When the refugee children became adults and left the homes where they had grown up, their original community of experience devolved into multiple communities of memory, as they joined different social groups and their memories were reworked in the context of different social frameworks of memory.

The experiences these refugees shared as children created the bonds that link them together as adult members of an original community of experience. These bonds led people like Eleni Milona to attend reunions in Dadia; they transformed coffeehouses in small mountain villages into "Towers of Babel," with a different Eastern European language spoken at each table. These bonds also led repatriates living in Athens and Thessaloniki to return to their villages every summer and spend evening after evening talking about their childhoods in Poland and Czechoslovakia (Van Boeschoten 2005). In fact, shared childhood memories enabled refugee children to accept other refugees whom they had never met and who lived on the other side of the globe as members of the same community of memory. In this way, the original community of experience was transformed into several different transnational communities of memory.

Not all refugee children, however, belong to these communities of memory. For some, their refugee past is no longer relevant to their present identities; it may even be perceived as an embarrassment. Some of the early male repatriates moved to Athens and became part of a community of construction workers; others emigrated abroad and became part of diaspora communities. Among those who returned to Greece, some have become fully reintegrated into Greek society and seem to have closed the book on their refugee past. Other refugee children, who remained in Eastern Europe, chose to "forget" their past association with the Greek Communist Party after the fall of communism and the end of the Cold War.

The lifting of the Iron Curtain and Greece's entrance into the European Union offered new opportunities for refugee children to set up transnational businesses in the fields of commerce and tourism. In this context, holding a Greek passport rather than an Eastern European one or a laissez-passer indicating refugee status became a distinct advantage. Since the 1990s, the Greek government, concerned with the increasing number of immigrants entering the country, has strengthened its efforts to improve ties with the millions of Greeks living abroad. Former political refugees are now seen as part of a broader "Greek diaspora." Some refugee children living in Eastern Europe have been attracted by the material advantages associated with this new identity and are, therefore, less interested in maintaining contact with a community of memory that focuses on their refugee past.

Children who spent part of their childhood in paidopoleis have been less inclined to form communities of memory. Although they too were deeply marked by their experiences during the Civil War and although they developed strong peer bonds among themselves as well, most children spent only a short period of time in paidopoleis. In spite of the fact that the Queen's Fund encouraged them to stay in their home villages after their return, many former residents of paidopoleis decided to migrate to Athens or abroad, where their childhood memories of the paidopoleis were no longer relevant. The formation of communities of memory among these children was also inhibited by the fact that today the paidopoleis are associated with orphanages and poverty. In this way, the identity of being a former resident of a paidopoli (a "*paidopolitis*") became stigmatized. For successful professionals, childhood experience in a paidopoli was often no longer relevant to their present lives; it was an experience they preferred to forget. Other former residents of paidopoleis, however, have fond memories of the time they spent there and still feel connected to people who shared this important part of their lives.

## Narratives of Experience

One way in which we construct our subjectivities as meaningful selves is by composing life-history narratives based on recurrent themes and repeated memories. Maurice Halbwachs saw repeated memories as building blocks through which we create our identities. While the experiences on which these memories are based remain the same, their meanings may change as our identities change. These memories come to resemble ancient stones that are incorporated into new buildings (Halbwachs [1925] 1994, 89).

In this sense, the patterns of memory analyzed here represent a snapshot of meanings attributed to past experiences at a specific point in the lives of the refugee children, the late 1990s and the early years of the twenty-first century, a time when many of them were approaching the end of their professional lives and the events they had lived through were a matter of vigorous public debate.

Given their repetitiveness, their symbolic meaning, and their performative nature, these recurrent themes can be understood as "tropes" (Fernandez 1986) that refer to experiences used by narrators to give meaning to their lives. More specifically, they constitute what John Borneman (1992) has called "experiential tropes," a concept he introduced to analyze the life stories of two generations of citizens of East and West Berlin. This approach is particularly relevant for our analysis of the life stories of refugee children from the Greek Civil War because of the way Borneman links these experiential tropes to both hegemonic master narratives and the concept of generation.

> Tropes achieve their full meaning not at the individual level, but as part of a generational gestalt. Because they are themselves of indeterminate meaning, their potential polyvocality allows for different individuals with dissimilar experiences to utilize the same trope to figure a life story. It is only in their relation to the totality of a life, however, in their *emplotment* over time, that they become meaningful through regular appeal to *master narratives*. (Borneman 1992, 7, emphasis in the original)

The life stories on which this book is based are presented as a journey, a journey through time and space, with both a starting and an end point. The end of this journey—the present, the point at which the life story is told—plays a crucial role in shaping the narrative, because it is the lens through which the entire story is interpreted. A story full of pain and suffering may have a happy ending, or it may be told as a story of loss and failure. Along this journey there are crossroads—points at which difficult decisions had to be made. There are also significant focal points—objects, emotions, power relations, and moments of reflection—that organize these life stories into coherent narratives by integrating the experiences that refugee children consider important in their lives. Because of the crucial role shared experiences play in individual life stories—often expressed through "experiential tropes"—we call these accounts "narratives of experience." Here we analyze four recurrent themes that constitute such focal points. We attempt to convey the underlying meaning of each theme by making short vignettes from these life stories "speak to" larger issues (Geertz 1973, 23). We indicate whether these themes occur in only one community of memory (children evacuated to Eastern Europe or children taken to paidopoleis) or in both. Finally, we relate the underlying meaning of each theme to the contested memories of the master narratives that dominate public discourse on the *paidomazoma*.

### Departure Stories

Departure stories play a prominent role in the life-history narratives of refugee children because the meaning they give to this crucial moment is linked to the ways in which they have come to reflect upon the course of their lives as a whole. Two different narrative devices are used to link these memories of departure to the present identities of the narrators. The first involves a "mother's last words" trope, which can be found in narratives of children taken to Eastern Europe and in those of children taken to paidopoleis. Refugee children remember that their mother told them to get an education, come back to Greece, or never set foot in the village again. In some cases, their mother's last words are represented as marking out a trajectory for their entire lives, a journey that would lead them away from traditional village life into a modern urban world. In other cases, a mother's last words are used to legitimate the narrator's present national identity. For example, two refugees with strong Macedonian identities, one taken to a paidopoli, the other to a children's home in Romania, have never forgotten the last words their mothers said to them: "Don't let them remold you!" and "Don't forget your language!"

These "last words," spoken in what must have been chaotic and upsetting circumstances, are invested with new meaning later in the lives of refugee children, who interpret them as crucial advice to guide their future or as final instructions they must fulfill. In this way, narratives of departure are used by refugee children to reflect on whether their lives have succeeded in following the plot outlined by their mothers when they left the villages of their birth. In either case, these departures from home are given new meaning, meaning they did not have in 1948. According to this new interpretation, refugee children did not leave their villages to flee the violence of the Civil War; they left to build new futures for themselves in new and very different worlds.

A second narrative device links these departure scenes with the present in a different way. Instead of being embedded in stories of agency, these departures are linked to a notion of destiny. In this trope, narrators draw heavily on memories of previous generations of family members who emigrated from isolated mountain villages and whose destiny it was never to return. In the case of refugee children from the Greek Civil War, however, this traditional notion of destiny is reinterpreted and acquires a new meaning that is linked to their present life circumstances.

Stoya Čapovska, a Macedonian woman who lives in Skopje and has never been allowed to return to Greece, described how she and her friends covered their hands with mud and left handprints on the doors of their homes when they left their village near Kastoria with 150 other children. Years later, Stoya's sister, who remained in the village, told Stoya that their grandmother used to kiss the handprints and cross herself, as if she were greeting an icon of a saint in church. Stoya also remembered another incident that occurred just before she left the village.

> Four girls—Agapi, Eleni, Xanthippi, and I—climbed to the top of the bell tower of the church and sang a song in Macedonian: "Our brothers and sisters are leaving the village." When our mothers heard us, they gathered under the bell tower. After we came down, they asked us, "Why did you climb way up there?" We said we wanted to see our village for the last time. "What do you mean, 'for the last time'?" they said. "You'll return in a few months like little birds. You'll come back when the war is over." But none of us ever did return. One lives in Kiev, one in Canada, one in Poland, and I live here in Skopje.

The night before their departure, Stoya's grandmother told the nine members of her household to gather to share a meal together as a family for the last time. Stoya's mother said, "What do you mean, 'for the last time'? They'll come back again." Stoya's grandmother replied sadly, "When people leave, they never return." And she was right. None of her family ever returned. She lived alone in the village until she "died of grief" several years later. The morning Stoya left, her dog followed her all the way to the border. Two days later, the dog died. Remembering the death of her dog many years later, Stoya said, "Maybe it died of grief, too, just like my poor grandmother."

Stoya Čapovska's description of her departure from her village is organized into four episodes, each of which foreshadows the "impossible return," a theme that dominates her present life circumstances. Stoya and her friends leave their handprints on the doors of their homes; they climb the bell tower to take a last look at their village; Stoya eats a "last meal" prepared by her grandmother; and Stoya's dog dies of grief, just as her grandmother did several years later. A strong sense of destiny pervades this story. All the characters, including the dog, are presented as if they knew that Stoya was destined never to return to her village. Stoya's story conveys a sense of powerlessness that resonates with the master narrative of the Macedonian political community of memory, which attempts to convey the theme of victimization through religious imagery involving persecution and sacrifice of the innocent. In Stoya's personal narrative, however, religious metaphors convey a sense of victimhood directly related to her individual experience as a refugee child. The "last meal" prepared by her grandmother evokes the image of the Last Supper, just as the sense of betrayal the refugee children felt when they realized they would not soon be returning home evokes Judas' betrayal of Christ. Finally, the dog's participation in human grief identifies nature with culture and enhances the meaning of human suffering.

The sense of destiny evoked in these departure stories is not equivalent to the ineluctable workings of fate. It is a much more malleable concept, for in the end destiny can be challenged and even overcome by human agency.[6] Makis Nitsiou, a Macedonian-speaking refugee child who has a Greek national identity, said that when he left his village he performed an old ritual that marked the departure of migrants as they set out on their long journey to a foreign land. The day he left for Hungary, his mother asked him to step in a washbasin filled with water in order to ensure that he would return to the village one day. Makis complied with her wish, thus accepting the destiny prescribed by village custom that he would return to the village of his birth. Many years later, however, when he finally obtained a Greek passport, he decided to defy his fate and remain in Hungary, where he still lives today.

This focus on the agency of the children themselves, as well as on the "mother's last words" trope, which is a common element in the personal narratives of children taken to Eastern Europe and to the paidopoleis, stands in sharp contrast to the master narratives of both left and right, in which refugee children are presented instead as passive victims of fate.

## Refugees and the Material World

Another central theme in the life-history narratives of refugee children from the Greek Civil War is the importance attached to material objects and sense experiences. This theme is characteristic of childhood memories in general, since children, to a greater degree than adults, experience their environment through their senses rather than through abstract thought. It also illustrates the fact that some memories become "embodied memories" when they are inscribed on the body rather than in the mind (Connerton 1989; Seremetakis 1996).

According to Halbwachs (1997, 193), the material objects that surround us in our daily lives are important components of both our memories and our personal identities because they are essential to the creation of stability and continuity. This insight helps explain why one of the most common experiential tropes in the narratives of refugee children from the Greek Civil War is the recollection of cherished objects brought from home to Eastern Europe or the paidopoleis—a small hand-knit bag, a pencil, a knife, a ragged piece of clothing. These memories are significant because they express the children's desire for continuity amid the uncertainties created by their evacuation to a new and strange environment. The refugee children's attachment to material objects from their villages is associated with a sedentarist view of the world, in which memories and identities are fixed to single places and stable objects.

The narratives of refugee children, however, do not *only* convey a sedentarist image of "silent and immobile societies," the phrase Halbwachs (1997, 195) used to express the sense of stability conveyed by material objects. They demonstrate that refugee children also view the world from a more cosmopolitan perspective. In fact, just as home can become a "movable concept" (Bammer 1992, vii) for refugees, migrants, and other people "on the move," so the material objects that give their lives meaning can be replaced by new ones. While some children tried to save their ragged village clothes from the incinerator, others were delighted to see them burn and to be given brand-new track suits in exchange.

As people move from place to place, they discover new objects that come to symbolize new worlds, worlds that are at once frightening and exciting. In the life histories of refugee children, the power of these events is expressed through a second trope that is also linked to the material world, the trope of "first-time experiences." Many refugees vividly recall their first glimpse of the lights of a big city like Bitola or Piraeus. They remember the first time they saw a truck or train; the first time they smelled or tasted new foods. These experiences marked the refugee children's transition from the rural world of their childhood to the urban environment of their adolescence.

Another recurrent feature of this transition is the "nonrecognition" trope. Children taken to Eastern Europe and to paidopoleis recount their arrival at their new homes in similar terms: when they emerged naked from the disinfection center after a haircut and shower, they couldn't even recognize each other. They had undergone a powerful rite of passage that had transformed them from poor children from war-torn mountain villages into prospective members of a modern urbanized society. They had been stripped of their former selves and reborn into a new and unknown world. Refugee children also remember this transition as a passage from a chaotic world of pollution and disorder, full of lice, fleas, and dirt, to a world of cleanliness and order marked by white sheets, good hygiene, and regular schedules. Seen from the adult perspective they would adopt later in their lives, they had ceased to be "matter out of place" and were on their way to becoming "citizens of the world."

Memories of material objects also serve another important narrative function. They enable people to reflect on the social relations embedded in these objects and the dimensions of power that they embody. This function is most evident in a third experiential trope that occurs in the narratives of children who went to Eastern Europe and to paidopoleis: remembered experiences involving pieces of clothing and the dress codes that regulated them. The power relations embedded in this aspect of their daily lives emerge when refugee children describe the resentment they felt toward the uniforms and the shared clothing they had to wear. In some accounts these memories give rise to tales of resistance in which children claimed the right to personal ownership of the clothes they were allotted. In this way they asserted their right to a unique individual identity.

Clothes also symbolize the process of emancipation from traditional village codes of behavior, particularly for girls. In their memories of adolescence, women often represented their entry into a new world of opportunity and independence from the rigid gender restrictions of village life with an account of the way they acquired modern European clothing. These memories contrast sharply with resentful stories women told about their return to their villages, when they had to revert to traditional rural Greek clothing. Chapter 6 presented many examples of the bitterness adolescent girls experienced when they returned from Eastern Europe, but girls returning from the paidopoleis had similar experiences. One said, "I came home with store-bought shoes, but I had to go back to wearing *tsarouhia* again (old-fashioned homemade shoes)." Although the pressure to conform to village dress codes was stronger for girls, boys also expressed dismay at returning from the "civilized" world of the paidopoleis to the "primitive" world of the village. One man who had been living in a paidopoli for many years recalled proudly the uniform and the school bag he had been given for free by the Queen's Fund. When he returned home, his new possessions looked to his fellow villagers like "extraterrestrial (*exoyiina*) objects."

The cultural attitudes expressed in these personal stories about the material world may at first seem unrelated to the politicized master narratives that are contested in the present and that focus on politically charged moral issues. Yet these first-person narratives have clearly incorporated some basic themes from the political ideologies that guided the education of these children on each side of the Iron Curtain. Both the Greek Communist Party and the Queen's Fund, in spite of their diametrically opposed political perspectives, sought to emancipate "their" children from traditional rural Greek culture, introduce them to "modern" habits, and turn them into "model citizens." The life histories of these children, however, also show that this very modernization process emancipated them from the political ideologies that had been instilled in them during their childhood. Their emancipation, as feminists have noted, was both personal and political.

### *Powerlessness*

The life histories of refugee children are often organized around the tension between powerlessness and empowerment, two broad and interrelated themes that are central to these narratives. There is a dialectical relationship between the past experiences of these children and the identities they claim in the present. Their present identities influence the way in which these two dimensions of power are conceptualized in the past, and vice versa. Childhood experiences of powerlessness and empowerment have contributed in important ways to the formation of the refugees' subjective identities as adults.

In a certain sense, all the children who were removed from their villages in 1948 were powerless, since the Greek Civil War was fought by adults, and since in most cases the crucial decisions that affected the children's future were completely beyond their control. This understanding has shaped the way in which refugee children construct their childhood selves as innocent victims. To express this combination of powerlessness and innocence, they often use animal metaphors, comparing themselves to lambs, sheep, or little birds in need of care and protection. In addition to this general notion of victimhood, there are two different clusters of experiences in which the theme of powerlessness plays a prominent role.

The first includes experiences that have provoked deep and permanent personal trauma that cannot always be articulated: the loss of childhood and the death of a parent.[7] These were all permanent losses that could only be partially compensated for by the development of peer bonds in the homes or by the care of substitute "mothers." Learning about a parent's death from a distance and without the consolation of shared grief is often an "unspeakable event." For this reason, although it is a common experience in the narratives of children who were evacuated to Eastern Europe and to the paidopoleis, it has not given rise to a shared mode of expression. It remains, in other words, a common, but not a shared, experience.

Two other traumatic experiences in this cluster do have a common mode of expression, possibly because they took place later in the lives of the refugee children. The estrangement from parents as a result of long separation is expressed in what could be called the "failed recognition" trope, in which narrators recount not only the fact that parents and children did not recognize one another physically, but also that they had actually become strangers to one another. This estrangement from parents is one of the factors that contributes to the trope of the "lost childhood." In these narratives, people try to make sense of the fact that they did not grow up in a family environment. They emphasize the fact that they still consider themselves children. It is as if their lives had been frozen in childhood at the time of their departure from their villages. In the poignant expression of one sixty-nine-year-old refugee child: "We're still children; it's as if for all these years we've been waiting for something to come, but it never has."

The corollary of this "lost childhood" trope is another related trope focused on the notion of a "lost future." This trope expresses the frustrations of early repatriates from Eastern Europe and of some residents of paidopoleis who had begun to taste the excitement of a different future, a future that was abruptly cut short by their return to their village and to a life under the watchful eyes of their parents. Having already lost the childhood they remembered with their parents in the villages of their birth, these children now felt they were losing their adulthood, the independent future they had imagined for themselves as adolescents. These last two tropes are most prominent in the life histories of refugee children who were taken to Eastern Europe; they appear only in the accounts of children who remained in paidopoleis for many years.

A second cluster of experiences that involve the theme of powerlessness is linked to the fact that the "homes" in which the refugee children grew up were the epitome of "total institutions" (Foucault 1979; Goffman 1962), places where children experienced strict military discipline, ideological indoctrination, and a profound sense of depersonalization. These experiences appear in the life histories of refugee children in the form of similar tropes, but the meaning attributed to them varies greatly depending on the narrators' present political perspective. The experience of depersonalization, for example, is often expressed through the "numbers" trope. Upon their arrival at the homes, children received chains with numbered identification tags that they had to wear around their necks at all times. Many refugees still remembered their identification number more than fifty years later. With this trope refugee children were commenting on the fact that when they were "institutionalized," they not only lost their clothes and all their personal possessions, they also lost their names, the most important component of their individual identities.

This "numbers" trope is often associated with other images that evoke scenes from the Holocaust, such as accounts of refugee children travelling from Bitola to Eastern Europe in boxcars. In some narratives, the association with the Holocaust is made explicit, especially by refugee children who were settled in East Germany, where the memory of the Holocaust was a dominant theme in public discourse.[8] This association with the Holocaust did not mean, however, that the refugee children had reinterpreted their history as one of genocide, as in Greek or Macedonian nationalist discourse. These refugee children had generally positive memories of their time in Eastern Europe; most situated themselves on the political left. They simply used this trope to express a sense of helplessness and loss of personal identity, in contrast to a later period in their lives when they became "human beings."

Refugee children who were taken to Eastern Europe and to paidopoleis express the militarization of their childhood and the strict discipline they experienced through the "We were soldiers" trope. People who had lived in Eastern Europe describe marching in parades through the streets of Warsaw, Prague, and Budapest, carrying portraits of communist leaders like Joseph Stalin and Nikos Zahariadis (secretary-general of the Greek Communist Party), and singing revolutionary songs while dressed like young partisans (see fig. 5 above). They remember clapping hands in the dining room and shouting slogans calling for the victory of the Democratic Army while their soup was getting cold.

Similarly, people who spent their early childhood in paidopoleis remember marching to nearby towns shouting "Long live the King!" and singing songs about the "barefooted partisans" and the Bulgarians, "the hated enemies of Greece" (see fig. 9 above). Some children internalized this sense of rigid discipline so deeply that it continued to shape their lives as adults. One man who spent several years in a paidopoli said, "You had to be obedient, just like in the army." Another remembered, with a touch of irony, that he had been a very unruly child but that when he had gone to a paidopoli he became as docile as a "little lamb." For some refugee children, their militarized childhood has been transformed into an embodied "habit-memory," a memory that has been unconsciously incorporated into their very bodies (Connerton 1989, 88). One refugee child said that she still marches down the streets of Thessaloniki like a soldier, even though now she is a committed pacifist and "hates uniforms." The militarized movements of her body are at odds with her present ideological convictions.

"We were like Janissaries" is another experiential trope refugee children who grew up in Eastern Europe often use to emphasize the fact that as children they were indoctrinated with political ideologies that they did not fully understand, that they should not be held responsible for, and that they disavow now as adults. One refugee child remembered with some amusement marching through the streets of a Czech village with his friends carrying portraits of Stalin and Tito, only to be told by a Czech that they should not be carrying Tito's portrait since he had recently fallen out of favor with Stalin. "We were educated to be faithful to the Greek Communist Party," he said. "That was the bad thing about it. And we didn't have our parents to teach us to question things. In that sense, you could say that we were Janissaries."

The use of the term "Janissaries," especially in the narratives of refugee children whose political perspectives are, broadly speaking, on the left, may seem surprising. In 1948, the Greek government had focused its propaganda effort on this same "Janissary" image, claiming that Greek children had been abducted in order to be transformed into "Slavocommunists" and enemies of their country. The majority of refugee children adamantly deny that they were transformed into "Slavs" and taught to "hate Greece." They readily admit, however, that they were thoroughly indoctrinated in communist ideology. In this context, the Janissary trope has nothing to do with Greek government propaganda. Refugee children use this trope to contrast this early period in their lives with a later period in which they emancipated themselves from the political influence of the Communist Party and began to construct their own identities as independent adults. These examples illustrate the way in which individual memories may "confiscate" master narratives and use them to a different end.

### Empowerment

In sharp contrast to these expressions of powerlessness, other episodes of the life histories of refugee children stress the many ways in which they tried, often successfully, to gain control of their own lives. One of the tropes that convey the theme of empowerment is the "escape story." In many narratives these "escape stories" play an important part in the memories refugee children have of the two long journeys that took them from their villages to Eastern Europe and then back again many years later. A few children, whose parents refused to let them leave home, defied them and ran away to join the column of children heading north across the Yugoslav and Albanian borders. Others attempted to escape early in their journey to Eastern Europe in an effort to return to their villages. A number of children, often driven by hunger, set out from Albania or from the infamous refugee settlement of Brailovo in southern Yugoslavia to return to their homes. Still other children tried to return to their villages in 1949 from Călimăneşti, a home in Romania where conditions were extremely difficult.

Other escape stories involve efforts to break free from the rigid rules of total institutions. Children in Eastern Europe ran away from their "homes" to watch football matches, swim in Lake Balaton, or meet girlfriends for dates. Yet another category of escape story is linked to the process of repatriation. Some children jumped off the trains that were taking them back to Greece so that they could return to Eastern Europe. After their repatriation, some refugee children tried unsuccessfully to return from Greece to Eastern Europe; others successfully "escaped" the isolated mountain villages of their birth by emigrating to Canada or Australia. Some children who were sent to a paidopoli also remember attempting to escape. Their stories either locate their escape attempt during the first few months after their arrival at a paidopoli and attribute it to feelings of homesickness, or else they situate it later in their lives when, as adolescents, they felt that a prolonged stay in a total institution conflicted with the lives they had set out for themselves.

Unlike the better-known Cold War narratives about escapes across the Iron Curtain from East to West, the escape stories of refugee children of the Greek Civil War are not heroic tales that serve the ideological purposes of a politicized master narrative.[9] Instead, they are usually told in a rather matter-of-fact way. In the overall economy of life-history narratives, these escape stories can be seen as an irruption of what Bakhtin (1981, 90–95) has called "adventure time" into the "routinized time" of highly regimented lives. As is the case in "adventure time," the success or failure of the escape is attributed entirely to chance. In most cases, the children were caught and brought back to the life courses set out for them by the adults in their lives. In a certain sense, therefore, these stories can be seen as confirmation of the powerlessness of refugee children. The main function of escape stories in these life-history narratives, however, is a different one. Adults represent their childhood selves not as helpless victims moved passively about by adult authority figures, but as agents of their own destiny, actively engaged in trying to assert control over their own lives.

Escape stories do play a part in the master narratives of both the right and the left, but there they serve an explicitly political purpose. Right-wing authors have used stories of attempted escapes from Eastern Europe (Manoukas 1961, 19–20) for the same purposes as left-wing authors have used stories of attempted escapes from paidopoleis (Servos 2001, 170)—to construct a coherent narrative that legitimates their own political ideology. In these politicized master narratives, these escapes are presented as a direct result of the fact that the children had been "abducted" against their will and placed in total institutions where conditions were particularly harsh. The rigid structures of these polarized master narratives, however, are contradicted at many points by the first-person accounts of the refugee children themselves.

These personal accounts show that escape stories exist on both sides of the political divide and that children tried to escape from both the children's homes in Eastern Europe and the paidopoleis in Greece. They reveal that children who were evacuated to Eastern Europe did not try to escape in just one direction—from Eastern Europe back to Greece. They also tried to escape in the opposite direction—from Greece back to Eastern Europe. Finally, the narratives of children in Eastern Europe and in the paidopoleis show that the decision to escape was often motivated by personal, rather than political, reasons, and that officials on each side of the conflict were unable to control "their" children. These aspects of the children's escape stories clearly undermine the coherence of the politicized master narratives of both right and left and are, therefore, passed over in silence by both sides. In the personal narratives of the refugee children themselves, however, these escape stories emerge as eloquent testimony to the spirit of independence and resistance of children who wanted to return to their homes or to start new lives in a different world of their own choice.

The life-history narratives of refugee children of the Greek Civil War also contain themes of disobedience and rebellion: breaking rules, talking back to teachers, and questioning the authority of those in charge. "Rebellious child" stories often provide insight into the formation of the narrators' political identities. In some cases, rebelliousness is presented as a response to a stigmatized identity—having the "wrong" name, the "wrong" family history, or the "wrong" national identity.

Fanis Tzikas, a Greek refugee child, spent many years in the paidopoli at Ziro. His father had fought with the partisans and been killed by the Greek

Army. Fanis' life story is structured in its entirety around a constant tension between confinement and stigmatization, on the one hand, and acts of rebellion and attempts to escape, on the other. Describing some of his more painful experiences, Fanis said:

> When someone says to a young child, "The partisans killed your parents," and the other children start saying, "Fanis' father was one of them," won't that child start hating me? It was terrible. I'll remember these things forever; they were driven into my mind like nails. In '58, we had some problems. We were seventeen, eighteen years old, and they didn't let us out at all. So one day, fifteen of us revolted. There was nothing else we could do.
>
> "Either let us out or send us home for good!" I said.
>
> "No!" they said. "You'll do what we say."
>
> So fifteen of us just left. We put our bags over our shoulders and went down to the main road. We knew places where we could get through the barbed wire. Each of us was going home. But they brought us back and gave us a good beating.

In Eastern Europe another "rebellious child" was born because of his name, Yiannis Papadopoulos.[10] In spite of the fact that his father, a partisan, had been killed in battle on Mount Vitsi, communist officials running the home where he lived associated his last name with that of a wealthy capitalist and founder of a large supermarket chain in Greece. They kept questioning him about his relationship to this famous man, who they suspected was his close relative. With a mixture of pride, irony, and bitterness, Yiannis explained that because of this frequent harassment he lost interest in school and began to run away from the home for short periods of time. As a result of his unruly behavior, he earned the nickname "deserter" (*lipotaktis*) and the admiration of his schoolmates.

The rebellious behavior of adolescent refugee children in Eastern Europe was part of a broader process of empowering young people that was taking place throughout the region. Alternative youth cultures, largely inspired by Western models, were spreading through Eastern Europe in the late 1950s and 1960s as young people reacted against the ideal of the "new socialist man" promoted by communist officials. Stylish clothes, long hair, rock-and-roll, sexual liberation, and a desire to travel abroad played an important part in these youth movements, which many refugees became involved in when they left the children's homes and became full members of their host societies. Such behavior was denounced by both Greek and local communist leaders as deplorable manifestations of "hooliganism" and generated much conflict between young refugees and the leadership of the Greek Communist Party. One Macedonian refugee child referred to this process of emancipation as "*dedogmatizacija.*"

The most important form of empowerment that emerges from the life-history narratives of the refugee children is linked to a process of social, rather than political, emancipation. In both sets of narratives, the notion of empowerment is constructed around a rural/urban dichotomy and an opposition between nature and culture. Looking back at their early childhood from the perspective of urban, educated adults, they have reimagined their once familiar village homes as poor, backward, and "uncivilized." Their narratives of empowerment make use of a process Maria Todorova (1997) has called "balkanization": the construction in political discourse of Balkan cultures as backward and primitive. Individual narrators have "balkanized" the villages of their birth and "debalkanized" themselves by portraying themselves as adults who have escaped the rigid confines of village life to become "citizens of the world." When Yianna Liourou described her arrival in Hungary at the age of eleven, she said, "Back in the village we were savages (*agrianthropoi*); we lived day in and day out with the animals. After we received our new clothes, we looked like little dolls; we felt really proud. At home we didn't know what nice clothes were."

Refugee children taken to Eastern Europe and to paidopoleis expressed their sense of empowerment by contrasting their "backward," rural childhoods with the "civilized," urban lives they had planned for their future. They realized that their forced departure from home, in spite of all the pain it caused them, had opened a path to social mobility and the promise of a better life; they realized that education was the means by which they could achieve this goal. On a deeper level, the journeys through time and space recounted in the life-history narratives of refugee children from the Greek Civil War are what Bakhtin (1986, 21–23) has called stories of "human emergence." Forced by circumstances beyond their control to leave isolated mountain villages in northern Greece, these children embarked on journeys of change and growth. By the end of these journeys—in Athens, Skopje, Budapest, or Toronto—they had become different people inhabiting different worlds. This is what refugee children mean when they say, as they often do at the conclusion of their life stories, "We became human beings (*anthropoi*); we became people of the twentieth century." And in Greek culture, the essential quality of human beings is the ability to take responsibility for their own actions, defy their destiny, and change the course of their own lives.[11]

## Children's Homes in Eastern Europe
## and the Paidopoleis: A Comparison

The rhetoric of the Greek Communist Party and the Greek government re-
garding the fate of the refugee children was inspired by the opposed political ideologies struggling for hegemony throughout the Cold War. Each
side portrayed Greece during the Civil War as a closed, polarized world in
which a moral battle was being fought between innocent victims and evil
victimizers; each presented a static and sedentarized view of the world that
portrayed their enemies as having been engulfed by an evil and absolute
political system, "Slavocommunism" or "monarchofascism." For this reason, each side regarded the children evacuated by the other side as "lost to
the nation."

The individual narratives of experience analyzed in the preceding pages
present even more striking similarities than do the master narratives of
the organizations that carried out the evacuation programs. The narrative
themes and experiential tropes through which refugee children reflect on
the meaning of their lives often reveal parallel cultural responses to similar situations: the ability to cope with personal trauma through the formation of bonds of solidarity with peers, the independent sense of identity
acquired through education, and the break with their rural past brought
about by the processes of migration, urbanization, and modernization.
There are, however, two important differences between these two sets of
narratives. First, in life stories of children of the paidopoleis, feelings of estrangement from parents and the notion of a "lost childhood" play a much
less significant role than they do in the stories of refugee children taken to
Eastern Europe. This difference can be attributed to the fact that most children living in paidopoleis were separated from their families for a much
shorter period of time.

Second, although both groups consider education the crucial factor that
determined the degree of social mobility they enjoyed in their lives, for the
children of the paidopoleis this mobility was more a dream than a reality,
a dream they transmitted to their children that would be realized only in
the next generation. In Eastern Europe, most refugee children received a
good education and were able to earn a decent living as skilled laborers or
professionals. In the homes of Queen Frederica, however, most children
were trained as cobblers, carpenters, or seamstresses, trades that did not fit
in with the life projects they had set out for themselves. This is the major
complaint of children who grew up in paidopoleis, independent of their

present political views. Efterpi Tsiou stated it clearly: "At the paidopoli I wanted to study. It's not that I didn't like sewing and weaving, but I wanted to study. I wanted to become an educated person."

The fact that these two groups of children use similar tropes to construct themselves as meaningful subjects undermines the monolithic dichotomy of the Cold War master narratives of both the Greek Communist Party and the Greek government. Yet the relationship between these master narratives and the narratives of experience of specific individuals is considerably more complex. Some themes found in personal narratives replicate those that dominate master narratives, such as the notion of victimhood. At other points, personal narratives "borrow" or "confiscate" themes in order to give them a different meaning. For example, adult refugee children use the term "Janissaries," the dominant image in Greek nationalist discourse about the *paidomazoma*, to refer ironically to themselves when they were younger, more naïve, and more susceptible to the influence of communist propaganda. Finally, personal narratives may completely transform or refute important themes of these master narratives. Accounts of attempted escapes from the paidopoleis or from Greece to Eastern Europe, for example, undermine the right-wing master narrative, while escape stories of children who attempted to return to Greece from Eastern Europe undermine the public discourse of the left.

At a more fundamental level, however, the personal narratives of shared experiences—which become part of collective narratives because of the repeated occurrence of common themes—contradict the two master narratives at their most essential points. Both the Greek Communist Party and the Greek government went to great efforts to keep "their" children under their control. They each had plans for the construction of a new society, and they hoped that "their" children would play a central role in these two diametrically opposed political projects. Early in their lives, refugee children accepted these roles to some extent, but, as their personal accounts of agency, empowerment, and emancipation demonstrate, in the end many of them developed their own plans for the future. They had their own ideas about the roles they would play in the narratives of their lives.

It is clear, then, that despite the fact that refugee children of the Greek Civil War endured tragic years of separation from their homes and families, both evacuation schemes succeeded in their humanitarian efforts by providing safe haven to the children under their care. It is equally clear, however, that they failed in their political projects, since the individual life-history narratives of children do not conform neatly to the two opposing master narratives of the period. They are uniquely complex, personal accounts that bear the unmistakable mark of their individual narrators. But they also form part of a shared history, a collective narrative of experience, through which the refugee children of the Greek Civil War have successfully created meaningful lives from the difficult experiences through which they lived.

# EIGHT

# The Politics of Memory: Creating a Meaningful Past

Forgetting, I would even go as far as to say historical error, is a crucial factor in the creation of a nation, which is why progress in historical studies often constitutes a danger for [the principle of] nationality.

—Ernest Renan ([1882] 1990, 11)

When a past marked by deep collective trauma is transformed into history, memories of the past continue to haunt the present through the politics of memory and the politics of forgetting. The groups involved in these processes—which we have called political communities of memory—seek to control the memories of this contested past by constructing and promoting coherent public narratives that serve specific ideological goals, the most important of which is to legitimate the present political, ethnic, and national identities of the members of these communities. Public narratives present their audiences with sanitized versions of the past, in which all the inner contradictions that characterize the private memories of specific individuals are smoothed over or edited out. The politics of the present, therefore, plays a much more significant role in shaping these master narratives than do the experiences of the past that were actually shared by the people who constitute the communities of memory.

The "memory boom" that has swept through Western European and American cultures since the 1980s has produced an impressive body of academic research on the "politics of memory."[1] It has also affected the broader public in a variety of ways: through anniversary celebrations, museum exhibitions, television documentaries, heritage tours, and more recently through websites, electronic discussion lists, and blogs. A major component of this explosion of interest in the politics of memory is specifically concerned with the politics of war memories. Until recently, academic debates on this topic have been dominated either by a top-down approach, focusing on the way states construct their own official master narratives of the past in order to legitimize their authority, or by a bottom-up approach, using life stories of participants in the historical events and focusing on the psychological effects of trauma on individuals and local communities. In both approaches, the "politics of memory" is examined primarily within a national context, while the increasingly important transnational dimensions of the subject are largely ignored.

In *Commemorating War: The Politics of Memory*, Ashplant, Dawson, and Roper (2000, 12) suggest moving beyond a polarized dichotomy between a top-down and a bottom-up approach by focusing on the interaction between these two levels. We can also observe the workings of the politics of memory in the intermediate space between the public sphere of the state and the private sphere of the individual, a space that can be broadly defined as "civil society."[2] From this perspective, the politics of war memories is "the struggle of different groups to give public articulation to, and hence gain recognition for, certain memories and the narratives within which they are structured" (16). Ashplant, Dawson, and Roper further suggest examining what they call "arenas," the sociopolitical spaces within which social actors advance claims for the recognition of their memories, and "agencies," the institutions through which these demands for recognition are channeled (16–17). Finally, they stress the need to take into account the effects of globalization on the ways in which war memories are articulated and contested in what are often now transnational arenas (70–72).

These insights contribute in important ways to our understanding of the processes by which the propaganda war of the mid-twentieth century over the evacuation of children from northern Greece has been transformed into a war of memory in the twenty-first century. At first glance, the terms in which the debate is carried out ("kidnapped" versus "saved") may seem similar, but the political issues at stake, the global cultural resources from which master narratives draw their arguments, and the arenas and agencies through which social actors seek recognition for their versions of events have all changed in significant ways. At both the national and the transnational level, this transformation was triggered by major developments in the 1990s that led to a new post–Cold War order at the beginning of the twenty-first century.[3]

In the early years of the Cold War, the propaganda war over the *paidomazoma* was mainly waged at the highest levels of authority. The agencies that produced the two competing master narratives of the Greek Civil War were the Greek government and the Greek Communist Party (which had state-like authority over the refugee population in Eastern Europe), while international organizations such as the United Nations and the International Red Cross constituted the arenas in which the two agencies confronted each other, each claiming public recognition of its own "truth."

Since the late 1980s, however, the Greek government has disappeared from the scene in this dispute. In 1989, Greek political forces made a decisive move to break with the bitter and polarizing legacy of the Civil War by voting into power a government of national unity, which included representatives of both the right and the left. Although short-lived, this government symbolically "buried the past" by burning millions of police files on supporters of the left, passing a law on the "lifting of the consequences of the Civil War," and imposing an official policy of reconciliation. Partly as a result of this process, the right-wing New Democracy Party abandoned its anticommunist rhetoric (Andoniou 2007, 182–84). For all subsequent governments, right or left, the *paidomazoma* ceased to be an official issue.[4] Ironically, this officially sanctioned policy of reconciliation and forgetting has sparked renewed public debate on some of the most sensitive and controversial aspects of the Civil War, such as the *paidomazoma* and the issue of political violence (Kalyvas 2006). In the process, the arenas and agencies most centrally involved in the politics of memory have shifted significantly, moving down from the state level to occupy a broad range of intermediate sociocultural spaces and institutions including, among others, literature, the media, academic organizations, and nonprofit associations.

In contrast to the events taking place in Greece, where the national government has moved to the background in the dispute over how to interpret the Civil War past, developments in neighboring Yugoslavia during the 1990s led to the emergence of another government as a new actor on the scene. As long as Macedonia was part of the Federal Republic of Yugoslavia, the Macedonian government had only limited power. When Macedonia gained its independence in 1991, however, the plight of Macedonian refugee children became part of the "constitutive narrative" of the Macedonian nation and, therefore, the Macedonian state (Bellah et al. 1985, 153). Even in this case, nonstate agencies that constitute civil society in the Republic of Macedonia, such as the transnational Association of Refugee Children from Aegean Macedonia, have played a more important role than the state itself in shaping public discourse (Brown 2002, 72).

The political communities of memory involved in the dispute over the *paidomazoma*, include members of the Civil War generation, whose memories were based on firsthand experiences of the war itself, as well as people who were born after 1949 and have no living memory of the war. The agencies through which these communities of memory seek recognition include Greek and Macedonian associations of refugee children, village and regional associations in Greece and the diaspora, political organizations associated either with the communist left or with the more extreme right, and academic organizations like the Network for the Study of Civil Wars based in Greece and the Modern Greek Studies Association based in the United States.

The arenas in which these agencies confront one another are also different now than they were during the Cold War. Then, the politics of memory was mainly contested in newspapers and on radio and television; today, new media are available in which a wider public can also participate: electronic discussion lists, websites, academic conferences, commemorations, and reunions. Because of their more open character, these new arenas are particularly suitable for the expression of marginalized opinions and for the expansion of notions of "cultural intimacy" (Herzfeld 2005) into a global "diasporic public sphere" (Appadurai 1996). As a result of the physical dispersion of the initial communities of experience, these political communities of memory have been transformed into transnational communities participating in what Appadurai (1996) has called "global cultural flows." An important aspect of these diasporic cultural politics is the process through which new ideologies of the post–Cold War era, such as the transnational discourses on trauma, victimhood, and human rights, are now being incorporated into old national narratives (Ashplant, Dawson, and Roper 2000, 25).

Here we examine the workings of the politics of memory in contemporary settings by analyzing four ethnographic examples. The first two involve political communities of memory properly speaking: the Association of Refugee Children from Aegean Macedonia and the Pan-Macedonian Association USA, Inc. The third focuses on a prominent member of the Greek American community of memory, Nicholas Gage, and his book *Eleni*. And the fourth explores the transformation of the village of Lia, the birthplace of Nicholas Gage, into a site of memory and the multiple ways in which its inhabitants have attempted to cope with their painful and still bitterly contested past.

## The Association of Refugee Children from Aegean Macedonia

The Association of Refugee Children from Aegean Macedonia (*Združenie na decata begalci od Egejskiot del na Makedonija*) is a transnational umbrella organization that brings together refugee children from all over the world who identify themselves as Macedonians. It is headquartered in Skopje and has branches in Romania, Hungary, Poland, the Czech Republic, Canada, and Australia. It also has close ties with other organizations of the Macedonian diaspora (Brown 2002).

This association plays an important role in the lives of its members by establishing transnational networks of communication among individuals who are now scattered around the world, but who have been marked forever by their shared experiences of war and exile. The primary goals of the association are political: to keep alive the memory of its members' refugee past and to gain international recognition for its version of history. The political goals of the association are clearly expressed in its title. It is made up of people who continue to define themselves as children (*deca*) and refugees (*begalci*), although in strictly chronological and legal terms they are neither. By identifying themselves as "refugee children" members of the association emphasize the politically and morally loaded themes of lost childhood, moral innocence, collective trauma, and "impossible return" that have played major roles in both the association's master narrative and in the personal narratives of the individual Macedonian refugee children who are its members.

The association was established in the mid-1980s at the initiative of Macedonian refugee children in Toronto. It is probably no coincidence that individuals who had emigrated to Canada from Poland, where they had taken part in an early Macedonian "revival movement," played a leading role in the establishment of the association (Van Boeschoten 2003b). After their arrival in their new homeland, this group of refugees began publishing a newsletter, *Makedonski Glas* (Macedonian Voice), and in 1978 organized the first reunion of refugee children living in Canada. At this point, the organizers of the reunion decided to establish an association that would bring together Macedonian refugee children from all over the world. The important role of memory in the activities of the association is illustrated by the title of its newsletter, which has been published (in Macedonian) since 1993: *Nezaborav* ("Against Forgetting"; Brown 2002, 64). This newsletter presents articles about the history of the Greek Civil War, the experiences of the refugee children during and after the war, and the human rights issues facing the Macedonian minority of northern Greece.

The most significant activity of the association has been the organization of international reunions of Macedonian refugee children, the first two of which were held in Skopje in 1988 and 1998, the fortieth and fiftieth anniversaries, respectively, of their departure from Greece. These two events constitute the main arena through which the association has sought recognition for its master narrative of the evacuation of its members from northern Greece. Between the first and the second reunions, however, important political developments took place that led to changes in the broader meaning of this narrative. We now know that the reunion of 1988 took place on the eve of the breakup of Yugoslavia and the bloody civil war that followed, a war from which only Macedonia, of all six Yugoslav republics, was spared. At the time of the reunion, the Socialist Republic of Macedonia was still one of the federated states of Yugoslavia, and communism still the official ideology of the state. Yugoslav authorities in Belgrade were extremely reluctant to allow the reunion to take place, both because the main organizers, a group of refugee children living in Canada, were residents of a foreign, capitalist country and because they feared that the open expression of Macedonian nationalism might pose a threat to the unity of Yugoslavia. Yugoslav authorities were also afraid that any acknowledgment of the existence of a Macedonian minority in Greece might endanger Yugoslavia's efforts to improve its relationships with its southern neighbor.[5] Belgrade finally agreed to allow the reunion to take place on the condition that it would maintain a humanitarian focus and stress both the defense of human rights and respect for the territorial integrity of neighboring countries.

At the opening ceremony, attended by about three thousand participants, speakers stressed the "communist tradition of the Macedonian people" and the ideal of "Brotherhood and Unity" that held together Yugoslavia's constituent nationalities. The reunion, however, was primarily a deeply human event. Relatives and friends were reunited after forty years of separation. They shared memories of the past and cried together as they looked at images of their evacuation and their "homes" in Eastern Europe; they reflected together upon the meanings of their "lost childhoods." The reunion provided Macedonian refugee children an opportunity to express strong personal emotions. At the same time the reunion also made a powerful political statement.

As a public performance of shared victimhood, the reunion contributed to the construction of a "community of suffering" among Macedonian refugee children. As an act of commemoration, it contributed to the construction of a master narrative of the events that had permanently marked their lives. A photographic exhibit at the old Skopje railway station and documentary films shown at the reunion presented dramatic images of the children's departure from their homes and their lives in Eastern Europe. A theatrical performance at the end of the opening ceremony, which deeply moved the audience, depicted the Civil War's disruption of traditional Macedonian village life and presented a dramatic reenactment of their departure, their journey across the border, and their desire to return to their homes. The play was accompanied by old newsreel footage of the Civil War, pictures of destroyed and now abandoned villages, and videotaped interviews with village women who attempted to describe the pain they felt when they were separated from their children.

Speakers at the opening ceremony completely ignored the controversy surrounding the children's departure in Greek public discourse—whether they were "kidnapped" or "saved." Instead, they reconstructed the event as a story of persecution and sacrifice. The children's fate was presented as an odyssey, an escape from hell. Through the use of the biblical term "Exodus," the departure of the children was symbolically linked to the divinely sanctioned flight of the Israelites from Egypt, where they had been enslaved, and their arrival in the promised land after forty years of wandering in the desert. In the discourse of the Association of Refugee Children from Aegean Macedonia, the refugee children were not "kidnapped" by the Greek Communist Party; they were "saved" from a Greek state that had persecuted them relentlessly because of their ethnicity. In addition, the term "Exodus" implicitly linked the notion of persecution with the political demand for the right to return home after forty years of exile. Another religious image used in official speeches to stress the suffering of the innocent Macedonian refugee children was that of Golgotha, the hill on which Christ was crucified.

In spite of official instructions from Belgrade to the contrary, the 1988 reunion also contained many explicit expressions of Macedonian nationalism. Most significantly, the reunion served to incorporate the fate of the refugee children into a *national* narrative of suffering. The Macedonian president described the children's "odyssey," which led them from northern Greece to Eastern Europe, as "a great moment in the tragic destiny of the Macedonian people in the first half of the twentieth century, a moment marked by genocide, exodus, and forced migration, whose goal was the destruction of the very name of Macedonia."

Several acts of commemoration that featured prominently in the reunion program served to integrate even more forcefully the experience of the Macedonian refugee children into the national narrative of suffering of the Macedonian people. A member of each of the national associations of refugee children represented at the reunion (Polish, Czech, Canadian,

Australian, etc.) visited various "memory sites" commemorating crucial events in Macedonian history, such as the 1903 Ilinden Uprising against Ottoman rule, which Macedonian postwar historiography considers the country's first, albeit unsuccessful, effort to obtain national independence (Brown 2003).

The construction of this national master narrative culminated in the erection of a monument in the center of Skopje to honor the memory of the "mothers," the Macedonian women who accompanied the refugee children during their evacuation from northern Greece to their final destinations in Eastern Europe (see fig. 10). This monument, created by Nasio Bekiarovski, a refugee child and well-known artist living in Skopje, was placed in a park celebrating the "woman warrior" (žena borec). The monument depicts a "mother" carrying an infant with two young children following close behind her. The inscription beneath the sculpture reads: "Homeland—the yearning of the persecuted/expelled" (Tatkovinata—Kopnež na Progonetite).[6]

This monument incorporates the experiences of the refugee children into the canon of Macedonian national history. In the process, it equates the suffering of the refugee children with the suffering of the entire nation. Public memory of the children's evacuation is transformed into what Volkan and Itzkowitz (2000, 232) have called a "chosen trauma":

> The mental presentation (a cohesive image) of an event that caused a large group of people (i.e., an ethnic group) to feel victimized, humiliated by another group, and to suffer losses, especially that of self-esteem. While a group does not choose to be victimized, it does "choose," consciously as well as unconsciously, to psychologize and mythologize what has occurred and define its identity by referring to the event.

While this reinterpretation of the refugee children's experiences as part of a national master narrative seems to conform well to traditional patterns of Balkan nationalism, delegates from Canada and Australia offered a different, more modern version of Macedonian nationalism. In their speeches, they combined the affirmation of a Macedonian national identity and political demands for the respect of Macedonians' cultural and political rights with a universal, cosmopolitan, antiwar message. They incorporated into the narratives of their experiences notions of pacifism and multiculturalism, which they brought from their new homes, as well as elements of an emergent transnational discourse on victimhood, trauma, and human rights.

This perspective was fully reflected in the final declaration of the 1988

10. The monument erected in 1988 in the park of the "woman warrior" in central Skopje to honor the Macedonian women who accompanied the refugee children from northern Greece to new "homes" in Eastern Europe. The inscription reads, "The Yearning of the Persecuted/Expelled." Photograph by Loring Danforth.

reunion, which was addressed to the international community and approved by the audience:

Through this gathering we express our commitment to the ideals of liberty, democracy, and peace, as well as our desire to create a world free from chains, free from hatred, and free from discrimination. . . . We who passed through the hell of war, trauma, and exile are well aware of the personal and collective tragedies people have experienced. . . . We do not want any other children in the world to suffer our destiny. . . . In the name of basic human rights and freedoms, we former refugee children from Aegean Macedonia, now citizens of many countries in the world, . . . demand the revocation of the prohibition by which we Macedonians are deprived of the right to return to Greece because we are not Greeks by birth. . . . We appeal to you to respect all the rights of the Macedonian national minority: the right to equality before the law, the right to the protection of Macedonian national and intellectual integrity, and the right to learn our mother tongue. . . . The national minorities that live in the Balkans have a historic chance to live together and build a strong foundation for brotherly cooperation and a more humane future. We believe that the future of the Balkans should be settled by cooperation, open communication, and free democratic development.[7]

The second world reunion of Refugee Children from Aegean Macedonia, held in 1998, was influenced in crucial ways by the emergence of the Republic of Macedonia in 1991 as a newly independent state, and by the ethnic cleansing that had taken place during the Yugoslav wars, which many refugee children had watched in horror as it unfolded before them on their television screens. While the structure of the 1998 reunion was similar to that of 1988 and while the rhetoric of victimhood and sacrifice was fully preserved, the meanings attributed to the refugee children's fate as part of a national master narrative were quite different.

By 1998, the refugee children's fate had become part of an "invented tradition" (Hobsbawm and Ranger 1983) that served to legitimate the ideology of the new nation-state. An example of this was the use of the "exodus" trope as the subject of a new commemorative stamp issued by the Macedonian postal service. It featured a painting by Kole Manev, a former refugee child and an artist with an international reputation. Manev's painting, entitled *Flight* (*Zbeg*), depicts an exhausted column of "mothers" and children ascending a rocky, mist-shrouded mountain path on their way to the Greek-Yugoslav border.

The most important indication of the new political context in which the 1998 reunion took place, however, was the opening speech given by Kiro Gligorov, the first president of the newly independent Republic of Macedonia. In his opening address, Gligorov reproduced the imagery of a "community of suffering" through the key symbols of the "exodus" and "Golgotha." At the same time, however, he equated the suffering of the refugee children with that of the new nation-state, promising that "Just as you over-

came your Golgotha, the Republic of Macedonia will overcome its own."
Gligorov welcomed the participants to "free Macedonia," which many, he
said, were visiting for the first time. He hoped they would feel they were "in
their homeland." President Gligorov also linked the evacuation of refugee
children from northern Greece to the more recent events that had occurred
during the breakup of the former Yugoslavia. He called for people throughout the world to say "never again to war, terror, ethnic cleansing, and the
destruction of human rights." Finally, he issued a plea for a peaceful solution to the Macedonian conflict: "Macedonia wants peace, understanding,
and open borders. It wants to join the European Union as a European nation." In this way, the fate of the refugee children was linked not only to
the history of the Macedonian nation, as in 1988, but to the future of the
new Macedonian state as well.

The master narrative that the Association of Refugee Children from
Aegean Macedonia has constructed is a narrative of collective trauma in
which refugee children are presented as helpless and innocent victims of
war. It is also an account of an intentional campaign of ethnic cleansing
and genocide carried out by the Greek government. In a special issue of
*Nezaborav* that appeared during the 1998 reunion, the Association of Refugee Children asserted that "Aegean Macedonians were victims of the Greek
government's policies of denationalization and assimilation, including all
the elements of *genocide*" (emphasis added). This rhetoric of victimization
facilitates the transformation of this master narrative into a national narrative. It does so both through its construction of a "community of suffering"
and through its focus on a mythologized "chosen trauma"—the evacuation
of Macedonian refugee children from northern Greece—as a powerful symbol of the suffering nation.

This nationalist version of the past as a "chosen trauma" serves two political goals. First, it offers public recognition of the pain and loss the refugee children have experienced. It holds out hope for some kind of compensation for all the injustices, past and present, that they have suffered.
Ideally this compensation would include the right to return to the land of
their birth (*roden kraj*), the restoration of their citizenship rights in Greece,
and the restitution of their property rights in the villages of their birth. This
goal was widely shared by the refugee children we interviewed, although
many were no longer interested in a permanent return to their homes or
in regaining title to their properties. Second, this nationalist version of the
past calls for the international recognition of the Macedonian state, the
Macedonian nation, and the Macedonian minority of Greece. This political
agenda is shared by the Association of Refugee Children and transnational

Macedonian human rights organizations, but not necessarily by all refugee children of Macedonian origin. Some have lost interest in this agenda, some have adopted the national identities of the countries where they have lived most of their adult lives, and some fear the political consequences that participation in Macedonian organizations would have for themselves and for their relatives in Greece.

The politics of memory deployed by the Association of Refugee Children from Aegean Macedonia implies the elimination, through a process of "editing out" or "forgetting," of certain facts that do not fit neatly into this national master narrative but that do figure prominently in the personal narratives of Macedonian refugee children and are documented by historical evidence. For example, Macedonian nationalist discourse on ethnic cleansing and genocide is contradicted by the historical record, which clearly shows that the Greek Army did not specifically target Macedonian villages with the aim of driving their inhabitants out of Greek territory.[8] It is also contradicted by common sense: Macedonian refugee children were not driven out of Greece by the Greek government; they were evacuated by the Communist Party, which had promised the Macedonians of northern Greece equal rights after the war and guaranteed their education in the Macedonian language. Finally, this discourse is contradicted by the life stories of the refugee children themselves, who recount in great detail the terrible consequences of the war that led them to flee the country.

In the master narrative of the Association of Refugee Children, the discourse of ethnic cleansing and genocide is part of a moral history of the Macedonian minority of Greece, demonstrating that the Greek government has been, and still is, guilty of "denationalizing" the members of this group. In this discourse, the evacuation of children from northern Greece, like the entire Civil War, is transformed from a political into an ethnonational conflict. This new interpretation is consistent with the rewriting of Macedonian history in a nationalist key after the breakdown of socialist Yugoslavia.[9] By focusing exclusively on the fate of Macedonian refugee children, the authors of this historical narrative "forget" that approximately half the children evacuated to Eastern Europe were Greek and that both Macedonian and Greek children were victims of the violence of the Civil War. They also disregard the fact that in most cases the parents of refugee children, whether they were Greek or Macedonian, supported the partisans' cause. Finally, they ignore the communist ideology that pervaded the refugee children's education in Eastern Europe. This discourse depoliticizes and "nationalizes" a conflict in which the ethnicity of the Macedonian minority in Greece played a significant role, but which was essentially a political conflict between two opposing ideologies. It is also contradicted by the life stories of the refugee children themselves, which reserve an important place for the political beliefs of their parents, the personal relationships they developed with Greek children during their years of exile, and the influence of communist ideology on their daily lives.

The personal narratives of refugee children contradict a second theme in the association's master narrative, the refugee children as helpless and innocent victims. As we have shown in the previous chapter, refugee children legitimately assert their political innocence on the grounds that they were in fact very young at the time of their evacuation. But they certainly were not helpless victims. In the master narrative of suffering victims, all evidence of agency, choice, and will, which plays such a prominent part in the refugee children's private narratives, disappears completely.

A third contrast emerges in the portion of the public master narrative that presents the Republic of Macedonia as the national "homeland" of the refugee children. In their personal narratives, many Macedonian refugee children complained about the discrimination they experienced when they first settled in the republic in the 1950s, and they present their lost villages in northern Greece as their true homeland. It is the trauma of an "impossible return" to this homeland that has marked their present identities. The master narrative as articulated at the reunions of the association is a sedentarized narrative of the nation, which privileges the view of refugees as individuals with a single national identity who have been "uprooted" from a fixed and stable homeland. In the personal narratives of the refugee children, however, the experience of being a refugee is presented both as an experience of pain and loss and as a journey into a cosmopolitan world of open horizons and multiple identities.

In spite of these marked differences between the single, coherent national master narrative of the Association of Refugee Children of Aegean Macedonia and the multiple, often contradictory, life-history narratives of the refugee children themselves, there are also many similarities between the two. In both narratives, the horror of war, the pain of separation and exile, and the loss of childhood innocence are vividly conveyed. Both also exhibit a commitment to peace, freedom, and respect for human rights, including the right of the refugee children to return to the villages of their birth.

## The Pan-Macedonian Association USA, Inc.

The Pan-Macedonian Association USA, Inc., lies at the heart of the large transnational Greek Macedonian diaspora. It has sister organizations in

Australia, Canada, South Africa, and Greece itself. In each country the association has numerous local chapters, as well as many member organizations made up of emigrants from specific villages and towns in Greek Macedonia. Worldwide, the national Pan-Macedonian associations are organized into a federation that holds a world convention in Greece every year.

Over the last two decades the Pan-Macedonian Association has devoted itself to promoting the Greek position on the Macedonian issue. In this campaign of political mobilization, the politics of memory has played a crucial role. Members of the association have been extremely active organizing rallies, demonstrations, and letter-writing campaigns as part of their lobbying efforts to persuade government officials in their host countries to support "the Greekness of Macedonia." According to its website, the primary goals of the association are "to protect the Hellenic origin of the name, history, and culture of Macedonia and to counter falsifications and distortions of history."[10]

Since 1991 the top priority on the agenda of the Pan-Macedonian Association has been to prevent the Republic of Macedonia from being internationally recognized by its constitutional name, the Republic of Macedonia. The Pan-Macedonian Association and the Greek government strongly object to this usage and have insisted that international organizations such as the United Nations and the European Union refer to the Republic of Macedonia by the temporary designation "the Former Yugoslav Republic of Macedonia," or FYROM. According to this view, the name "Macedonia" belongs exclusively to Greece, and the controversy over the name is "a matter of identity that cannot be negotiated, an issue of heritage that cannot be disputed."[11] More recently, the Pan-Macedonian Association has staged campaigns to obtain international support for recognizing the compulsory exchange of populations under the Lausanne Treaty (1923) as an act of "genocide" perpetrated against the Greek Orthodox population of Turkey. In the meantime, it has not forgotten other important historical events that marked the early years of its existence. Among these events, the *paidomazoma* occupies a prominent place.

The Pan-Macedonian Association USA, Inc., was established in 1947, at a crucial point in the Greek Civil War, just after the adoption of the Truman Doctrine and the beginning of American involvement in the armed conflict. According to the association's homepage, American aid "saved Greek Macedonia from the Communist threat."[12] At a critical moment of the Greek Civil War, this new organization played a crucial role in turning American public opinion in favor of the Greek government—a particularly important job since a significant segment of American and Greek American public opinion had supported the Greek left as a result of its contribution to the defeat of Nazi Germany (Georgakas 1987, 11; Yavis [1944] 1987). The *paidomazoma* was a central mobilizing issue in this campaign. Greek Americans dressed in Greek national costume paraded through New York City to demand "the return of our 28,000 children." Famous Americans, including President Truman himself, condemned the removal of children from their homes and advocated their immediate return (Royal Greek Embassy 1950, 19–32). During the following decades, the issue of the refugee children receded into the background, but anticommunism remained high on the American political agenda. Cold War policies and McCarthyism deeply affected the Greek American community. As a result, immigrant organizations that had previously been apolitical or held more liberal views became politically active on the right (Georgakas 1987).

The Pan-Macedonian Association has long played a leading role in the larger transnational political community of memory concerned with defending the once dominant, state-sponsored, anticommunist master narrative of the Civil War. According to this narrative, "Slavocommunists" staged an insurrection against the legitimate government of Greece, sought to betray the Greek nation to its foreign neighbors to the north, and, in an act of genocide, kidnapped the "children of Greece" and sent them behind the Iron Curtain to be dehellenized and raised as Slavs and communists. For conservative Greeks on both sides of the Atlantic, the memory of the *paidomazoma* functioned as a "chosen trauma," just as it did in a very different way for the community of Macedonian refugee children.

The main core of this transnational political community of memory is composed of right-wing, nationalist Greek Macedonians, who are united both by the shared political views they hold in the present and by the shared traumas they suffered in the past. They are bitter because they feel that the Greek state no longer recognizes the sacrifice they made in defense of the nation and because they feel that "their" victims (victims of left-wing violence) have been forgotten by mainstream Greek society. Like members of the Association of Refugee Children from Aegean Macedonia, members of the Pan-Macedonian Association also constitute a "community of suffering" committed to fighting "Against Forgetting." The difference is that while the Association of Refugee Children from Aegean Macedonia is devoted to nurturing memories of the violence of the Greek state and the right-wing paramilitary groups that supported it, the Pan-Macedonian Association is devoted to keeping alive memories of the violence of the Greek Communist Party.

In Greece, there are two ways in which this right-wing political community of memory makes its voice heard in the public arena. The first involves acts of commemoration that celebrate the defeat of communism at the end of the Civil War and honor the memory of Greek soldiers killed by the partisans. The most famous celebration of this sort is held every year on Mount Vitsi on August 29, the day on which the Democratic Army was defeated in 1949. Before 1982, it was a national holiday, but it was discontinued as an official celebration as a result of the "politics of oblivion" inaugurated by the socialist PASOK government. In recent years, these celebrations have attracted not only members of the original community of experience, but also organizations on the extreme right, whose members are generally too young to have actually participated in the Civil War (Andoniou 2007, 158–91).

This community also seeks to control the memory of the Civil War by intervening in arenas where historical knowledge is produced and circulated. Part of its effort is channeled through newspapers, television programs, and websites controlled by the populist right. In recent years, however, academic lectures and conferences have been increasingly targeted. The principle aim of this war of memory is to defend the "correct," anticommunist, Greek nationalist version of history inherited from the Cold War era against the left-wing historiography that has come to dominate both academic and public discourse in Greece since the 1980s.

The seminar at Princeton University described at the beginning of this book was part of this campaign. In the weeks before the seminar, the Pan-Macedonian Association exerted heavy pressure on Princeton's Hellenic Studies Program to cancel the event. In spite of this pressure, our presentation took place as scheduled on May 10, 2005. The large audience for what was generally a very small and sedate seminar included several officials of the Pan-Macedonian Association and representatives of the Greek American press from New York City. The best-known member of the audience was Nicholas Gage, the author of *Eleni*. Also in attendance were members of the educated elite of the Greek American community: university professors, high-school teachers, and businessmen. Many had arrived in the United States in the 1950s or 1960s and had been marked in their childhood by personal and family memories of left-wing violence during the Civil War. One member of the audience was a former general who had served in the Greek Army; others had members of their families forcefully recruited or executed by the partisans. For this group, participation in this political community of memory was primarily based on their own personal experiences. Others, however, belonged to the post–Civil War generation and had settled in the United States more recently. They were linked to this community of memory less by personal experience than by a shared political interpretation of the history of the Greek Civil War.

The main goal of our presentation was to demonstrate that the master narratives with which *both* the Greek government *and* the Greek Communist Party have described the evacuation program are based on a similar essentialist discourse of the nation in which "home" is a fixed, territorialized locus of belonging. We contrasted this notion with a different concept of "home," which we found evidence for in our interview material, a "moveable concept" of home with multiple meanings and overlapping attachments to different people and places. Our argument fell on deaf ears because most people in the audience were interested in only one point: Would we confirm or attempt to deny that the Greek Communist Party had taken the children from their villages to Eastern Europe by force? We refuted the widespread notion that the evacuation program had been a mass "kidnapping," but we did state clearly that some children had been taken by force and that many other acts of violence had been carried out by the partisans against the civilian population of northern Greece.

Our main concern was to break through the rigidity of discourse inherited from an era in which there was no room for ambiguity or doubt. We presented ethnographic details from the life-history narratives of refugee children themselves to show that their experiences were considerably more complex than the monolithic master narratives of the Cold War suggest. These personal life stories, we concluded, confirm Liisa Malkki's view that "displacement may enable a different and sometimes subversive reshuffling of nationalist verities" (Malkki 1995b, 15). It was probably this "reshuffling of nationalist verities" that most upset our critics. In their view, there was one and only one "truth": the *paidomazoma* had been an unprecedented atrocity perpetrated by the communists against "the children of Greece" (Pan-Macedonian Association USA, Inc. 2005a).

During the discussion that followed, we realized that the controversy our presentation had provoked was at the heart of the topic we were investigating. We decided, therefore, to make the Pan-Macedonian Association's claim to "the truth" an object of our analysis in its own right. In fact, it is through the construction of just such exclusive truths and attempts to gain public recognition for specific versions of the past that political communities of memory are formed (Ashplant, Dawson, and Roper 2000, 16, Ballinger 2003, 268). The debate at the Princeton seminar, the texts published by the Pan-Macedonian Association in reaction to our presentation, and the email messages we subsequently exchanged with members of the audience offer valuable insights into the processes through which this particular community of memory produces its own truth.

In its first reaction to the Princeton seminar, the Pan-Macedonian Association defined the *paidomazoma* as "the most horrid crime of humanity" (Pan-Macedonian Association USA, Inc. 2005a). This claim is an excellent example of what has been called Greek exceptionalism, an approach to Greek history focusing on its singularity that refuses to situate historical events in a broader comparative framework (Beaton 2009, 6; Conway 2004; Gallant 1997). As we have shown in chapter 1, the organized separation of children from their parents in wartime is by no means a phenomenon unique to the Greek Civil War; it has been documented for most of the armed conflicts that have taken place in Europe during the twentieth century. In all these cases, the consequences for both children and their families were more than tragic. Only in one case, however, can we truly speak of a "crime against humanity": the so-called Lebensborn project carried out by the Nazis, in which "racially valuable" children were kidnapped mostly from Eastern Europe and placed for adoption with German families in order to strengthen the "master race."

Against this background, the claim that the *paidomazoma* was "the most horrid crime of humanity" can be read as a narrative device used by the Pan-Macedonian Association to stress the uniqueness of the suffering of the Greek nation. By portraying the removal of children from their homes by the partisans as an act of aggression by an alien "other" toward a noble "self," the Pan-Macedonian Association has defined itself as a community of suffering and transformed a conflict over the interpretation of a complex historical event into an oversimplified moral issue understood as a battle between good and evil. This "moralizing impulse," as Hayden White (1981) has called it, was more than evident both during the Princeton seminar and in the Pan-Macedonian Association's response. Through this process, the political community of memory to which the Pan-Macedonian Association belongs was constructing itself as a moral community.

One of the cornerstones of this moral community is the exclusive claim to victimhood. Nicholas Gage claimed that the children being evacuated by the communists could not be considered "refugees," that they could only be seen as "victims" of a terrible crime. The real refugees were people like himself, he argued, people who tried to escape the violence of the partisans (N. Gage 2004, 2). Other members of the audience agreed and argued that "hostages" was the only appropriate term to use to refer to the children who were evacuated to Eastern Europe.

Although in a few cases children who were taken to Eastern Europe may legitimately be called "hostages,"[13] the extension of this label to *all* refugee children from the Greek Civil War is a gross exaggeration that is convincingly contradicted by our own research and by other authoritative sources, such as the reports of UNSCOB and the International Red Cross. Gage's claim ignores the fact that the repatriation of the refugee children was made difficult by *both* the communist authorities in Eastern Europe *and* the Greek government (Hradecny 2005; Lagani 1996). It also ignores the fact that in the mid-fifties a substantial number of refugee children *were* allowed to return to their families in Greece, but many refused to do so. In this polarized account, which places all the victims on one side, the difficult process through which children and their families decided whether to return to Greece is glossed over in a reductionistic master narrative of victimhood. From our perspective, Gage is just as much a refugee child as the children who are the subject of this book, since he too was forced to leave his home and country of origin because of a "well-founded fear of persecution" (Article 1 of the Geneva Convention Relating to the Status of Refugees).

Another aspect of the "moralizing impulse" of this community of memory is its focus on an essentialized, ahistorical image of the "Greek mother." In the statement it published after the seminar, the Pan-Macedonian Association quoted a passage from Gage's book *Eleni*, in which a woman from his village defiantly refused to give up her children to the *paidomazoma*: "She gave the answer that every Greek mother would give, even though she knew the answer was death: 'NONE of us will give you our children'" (Pan-Macedonian Association 2005a, N. Gage 1983, 260). The implication is that women who *did* consent to the departure of their children were "bad mothers" who did not possess the essential virtue of the ideal Greek mother, maternal love. Other mothers, however, who loved their children just as much, believed that the only way to save them was to send them away from their homes and what they perceived as mortal danger.

Members of the audience at the Princeton seminar also claimed that we painted "too rosy a picture" of the lives led by the refugee children in Eastern Europe. In its response to our presentation, the Pan-Macedonian Association cited another passage from *Eleni*, in which Gage recounted the memories of two of his covillagers who were taken to Eastern Europe in which they vividly depict the awful conditions they experienced during the first period of their exile: "In the barracks in Albania, they survived mostly on soup made of leeks and on raw dandelion greens, which they scavenged from nearby fields" (Pan-Macedonian Association USA, Inc. 2005a;

N. Gage 1983, 262). Many of the "modern, well-dressed teenagers" (Pan-Macedonian Association USA, Inc. 2005a), whose photographs we showed at the Princeton seminar had passed through precisely the same experiences of utter deprivation in 1948, as the life-history narratives we present in this book clearly show. From the perspective of the Pan-Macedonian Association, however, the positive image we presented of the refugee children's lives in Eastern Europe was unacceptable because it contradicted their own right-wing master narrative of the *paidomazoma*.

While members of the Pan-Macedonian Association were angered by our presentation primarily because of what they perceived to be its procommunist bias, they were also very troubled by our use of the term "Macedonian" to refer to children who, from their perspective, were really "Greeks," or more specifically, "Slavic-speaking Greeks." Although our presentation focused on the experiences of refugee children regardless of their ethnic identity, our use of this term alone was interpreted as evidence of our support for recognizing the Republic of Macedonia under its constitutional name and for recognizing the existence of a Macedonian minority in Greece.

From a Greek nationalist perspective, the issue of the refugee children is linked to the Macedonian Question in several important ways. Although the Greek Civil War was a conflict between right and left, in the eyes of the Greek right, communists were by definition Slavs, not Greeks (Gounaris 2002, 65). According to this view, the refugee children were abducted on purpose so that they could be turned into "Slavocommunists." The fact that half of the refugee children were native speakers of Macedonian and came from families who defined themselves as "Macedonians" before they left Greece is ignored. The Greek right presents these Macedonian-speaking children as "Greek" children who were "Slavicized" *after* they were taken to Eastern Europe.

Greek nationalists are also appalled by the fact that the Greek Communist Party in exile explicitly recognized the identity of these Slavic-speaking children as *Macedonians* and referred to them as "Macedonian children" (*Makedonopoula*).[14] In light of the contemporary controversy over the name under which the Republic of Macedonia should be internationally recognized, the frequent use of this term more than fifty years ago by the Greek Communist Party in Eastern Europe, amply documented by historical evidence, undermines many of the arguments used by Greek nationalists to prevent the Republic of Macedonia from being recognized under its constitutional name. This is why members of the Pan-Macedonian Association suggested that we had doctored the photograph we showed at the Princeton seminar that depicted a group of children at a summer camp in Poland in 1950 standing under a sign identifying them as "expatriate Greek and Macedonian children" (*ekpatrismena Ellinopoula kai Makedonopoula*; see fig. 11).

Finally, the present conflict over the *paidomazoma* is also linked to the Macedonian conflict because Macedonian refugee children have sought the right to return to the villages of their birth in Greece, a right many of them do not enjoy at present under Greek law. This "right of return" is anathema to Greek nationalists, both because they consider these former refugee children to be enemies of the nation and because they fear "the creation" of a Macedonian minority in northern Greece (Kofos 2003).

11. Young refugee children at a summer camp in Poland in 1951. The sign hanging above their heads identifies them as "expatriate Greek and Macedonian children." The term "Macedonian children" (*Makedonopoula*) was commonly used by the Greek Communist Party both during and after the Civil War. Photograph courtesy of Riki Van Boeschoten.

An important component of the public discourse deployed by the Pan-Macedonian Association is the claim that the *paidomazoma* constituted an act of genocide. In an online publication that followed the Princeton seminar, Pan-Macedonian Association vice president Nina Gatzouli claimed that in 1948 the UN Special Committee on the Balkans had characterized the evacuation of the children by the Greek Communist Party as an act of genocide against the Greek race (Pan-Macedonian Association USA, Inc. 2005b). In fact, this statement was actually the *charge* leveled against the communists by the Greek representative to the United Nations (United Nations 1948a, 29), not the *conclusion* reached by UNSCOB. The Pan-Macedonian Association USA, Inc., falsely attributed the charge of genocide to a prestigious international organization rather than to a representative of the Greek government in a desperate attempt to legitimate the right-wing Greek nationalist master narrative of the *paidomazoma*.

If, to some extent, the Greek charge before the United Nations that the *paidomazoma* was an act of "genocide" can be explained by the climate of "moral panic" that pervaded Greek society in March 1948, the contemporary use of the term "genocide" in relation to the *paidomazoma* by the Pan-Macedonian Association is much more difficult to justify. Today we know that the great majority of these children not only survived but preserved their mother tongue, their culture, and their national identity just as well as, if not better than, most Greek Americans. Article 3, paragraph e of the 1948 UN Convention on Genocide refers to the forcible transfer of children from one ethnic or national group to another with the explicit aim of destroying their original culture. Even today, this paragraph is still invoked by officers of the Pan-Macedonian Association to justify defining the *paidomazoma* as an act genocide. Whether or not they were abducted, the refugee children of the Greek Civil War, both Greeks and Macedonians, were removed by members of their own ethnic groups and raised in institutions also run primarily by members of their own ethnic groups.

The evacuation of children from their villages in 1948, therefore, clearly does not meet the criteria for genocide laid down in the UN Convention. Nor does it meet the essential criterion that inspired this legal instrument: there must be a deliberate *intention* to *physically* destroy a national group. The Pan-Macedonian Association's charge that the *paidomazoma* was an act of genocide can only be understood in reference to its ethnic nationalist conception of the Greek nation. Because communists must be "Slavs" and not "Greeks," the "children of Greece" raised in homes in Eastern Europe controlled by communists *must* have been dehellenized and unlawfully transformed into members of an alien nation.

On the other side of the national divide, the Association of Refugee Children from Aegean Macedonia has made a parallel claim of genocide a centerpiece of its own politics of memory. While the Pan-Macedonian Association claims that the *paidomazoma* was an act of genocide carried out by the Greek Communist Party against the Greek nation, the Association of Macedonian Refugee Children claims that it was an act of genocide carried out by the Greek government against the Macedonian nation. These two opposing claims are directly related to the issue of the national identity of the refugee children who were evacuated to Eastern Europe. For this reason they are also closely linked to the Macedonian conflict more generally. Both in the discourse of the Association of Refugee Children from Aegean Macedonia and in the discourse of the Pan-Macedonian Association, the definition of the *paidomazoma* as an act of genocide is factually wrong. It serves, however, as a crucial building block in the creation of two national master narratives in which each nation is constructed as a "community of suffering." In both master narratives, the refugee children were unlawfully removed from their homes, "expelled" because of their Macedonian national identity in the Macedonian case, and "abducted" in order to be stripped of their Greek national identity in the Greek case.

The Pan-Macedonian Association's master narrative of the *paidomazoma* seeks the recognition of an absolute historical truth, a truth that members of the association consider to be a national truth. In many respects, this master narrative reproduces the arguments advanced by members of this political community of memory in Greece, but there is one important difference: In addition to being members of the Greek national community, Greek Americans are simultaneously members of the American national community, and a transnational diaspora. The views of Greek Americans about what happened to the children evacuated from their villages during the Greek Civil War fifty years ago have been heavily influenced by the processes through which they negotiate these three interwoven identities—Greek, American, and Greek American.

In our third example, we analyze these processes by examining the politics of memory from a different perspective, that of Nicholas Gage, a prominent member of the Greek American political community of memory. We explore his book *Eleni* as an influential and highly politicized account of the *paidomazoma* against the backdrop of the specific social and political circumstances that shaped the lives of postwar Greek immigrants to the United States.[15]

## Nicholas Gage, *Eleni*, and the Greek American Community

The political community of memory to which the members of the Pan-Macedonian Association belong is to a large extent a "textual community." Their representations of the past, in other words, are less based on their personal experiences or memories than they are on a limited number of texts, which they use as resources to construct and legitimate their identities.[16] Among these works, Nicholas Gage's *Eleni* approaches the status of "sacred text," not so much because of the "facts" recounted in the book, but because of its moral and political message. As a powerful emotional story, *Eleni* supports all the claims made by this political community of memory: the unambiguousness of their status as victims, the uniqueness of their suffering, and the exquisite virtues of a Greek mother's love. For these reasons, *Eleni* has become a constitutive narrative of the *paidomazoma* for the community of memory made up of right wing Greek nationalists at home and in the diaspora.

*Eleni* is, first of all, the moving story of a deeply traumatized child and the events leading up to his mother's death. For Gage, writing this memoir has undoubtedly helped him come to terms psychologically with this tragic event. At the same time, however, *Eleni* is a profoundly political book, offering a one-sided account of the Greek Civil War in which the communists are unrelentingly portrayed as cruel torturers and unscrupulous murderers. After its publication in 1983, *Eleni* enjoyed astounding success. Reviews in the American press described it enthusiastically as "a Greek tragedy so overwhelming that the reader will feel as if his heart is being torn out, page by page."[17] It achieved "best seller" status selling over three million copies worldwide, received numerous awards, and was made into a Hollywood film (Mitsotakis 2004, xxi).

In *Eleni*, Gage describes the devastating consequences of the Greek Civil War on the village of Lia, where he was born, in the mountains of Epirus just south of the Albanian border. Eleni's husband (Gage's father) had emigrated to America, the "land of opportunity," many years earlier. For that reason Eleni was known in the village as the *"Amerikana."* During World War II most of the villagers of Lia sympathized with the communist-led resistance to the Axis occupation. Lia, therefore, acquired the nickname "Little Moscow." It was burned to the ground by German troops.

With the onset of the Civil War, a climate of fear and suspicion gradually spread through the village. Many villagers continued to support the partisans, but a significant number of men with royalist sympathies fled to the neighboring town of Filiates. Eleni's father, a prosperous miller, and her brother-in-law were the leaders of this royalist group, and the partisans considered them traitors to their cause. It was at this moment, long before leaders of the Democratic Army began to plan the evacuation of children from the war zone, that Eleni made a first unsuccessful attempt to send her children away in the hope they would eventually be able to join their father in the United States.

During one of the major military confrontations of the Civil War, the village of Lia was captured by the partisans. The harsh constraints imposed on individual households and in particular the forced recruitment of young girls to join the Democratic Army slowly eroded what had remained of the villagers' support for the communist cause. Local partisan leaders, in turn, began to see "traitors" everywhere. Some villagers took advantage of the situation to settle old scores with their neighbors by denouncing them to the partisans' security police. Real or imagined traitors were jailed, tortured, and executed. Terrified by this general climate of fear, and more specifically by rumors of the communist plan to evacuate the children of the village to Eastern Europe, on April 20, 1948, Eleni organized the escape of her children and twenty other villagers to government-controlled territory. This time she was successful.

Leaders of the Democratic Army considered this mass escape an act of treason. They were afraid that anyone who fled the village and escaped to the government side would provide the Greek Army with valuable information about the positions and the morale of the partisan forces. Their fear was not entirely unfounded. Partisan leaders, therefore, decided to set an example. Eleni and six other villagers were arrested, and after a show trial in the village square, five of them were found guilty and sentenced to death. Eleni was the chief suspect, not only because she had organized the escape, but also because she was the wife of an "American capitalist" and the daughter of a well-known royalist. Despite the fact that several villagers, including some known communists, bravely spoke out in their defense, Eleni and four others were executed on August 28, 1948. Their bodies were dumped in a ravine in the hills above the village.

In a *New York Times* article that appeared shortly after the book's publication, Gage wrote that *Eleni* was "a true story," told "without a political axe to grind" (N. Gage 1984, 22). In a "note from the author" at the end of the book, Gage attempted to establish his authority even more convincingly by stressing that "all the names, places, and dates" in the book were "real" and that every incident in it that he did not personally witness was described to him by at least two people in independent, tape-recorded interviews (N. Gage 1983, 471). In the same note, however, Gage also acknowledged that "following the example of Thucydides" he had put words in the mouths of people he had spoken with and had attributed thoughts, feelings, and actions to them as he thought appropriate.

Although the basic "facts" of his mother's death, as outlined above, are undoubtedly accurate, Gage has written an account that skillfully integrates actual historical events, on the one hand, and unsupported reconstructions, unreliable memories, and rumors, on the other, in order to create a plot that clearly serves a specific political purpose. Characterizing the end of the twentieth century as the "era of testimony," Felman and Laub (1992, 5) have argued that as a rule testimony is "composed of bits and pieces of a memory that has been overwhelmed by occurrences that have not settled into understanding or remembrance." Such testimony, they continue, does not offer "a completed statement, a totalizable account" of past events. In *Eleni*, Gage has woven together individual testimonies and his own biased interpretations in an attempt to produce this kind of totalizable account in order to show that Greek communists were inherently evil.

In spite of Gage's repeated claims that his book is completely apolitical, it obviously supports a right-wing political agenda. Gage admits that when he arrived in Greece in 1977 he was shocked to see what he described as a "renaissance of Communist power" in which "the best talents of Greece were busy rewriting the history of the [Civil] war" by denying communist atrocities, such as the execution of civilians and the abduction of children to Eastern Europe (N. Gage 1983, 7–8). Since its publication in 1983, *Eleni* has been used throughout the world as a tool of anticommunist propaganda. In a nationally televised speech delivered in 1987, for example, Ronald Reagan cited the story of Eleni as an inspiration for his efforts to win the Cold War, describing the film based on Gage's book as the "true story" of a mother who was "tried, tortured, and shot by the Greek Communists" because she "smuggled her children out to safety . . . to America."[18]

On the back cover, *Eleni* is advertised as a book about the abduction of innocent children by evil communists and a heroic mother who paid for her resistance with her life. The arguments advanced by Gage and members of the Pan-Macedonian Association at the Princeton seminar replicate this description precisely. Yet the actual account of events in Lia presented by Gage himself tells a very different story. When he describes the *paidoma-zoma* for the first time, Gage acknowledges that the program was initially a voluntary one (1983, 246). In April 1948, in the midst of fierce fighting between the two opposing armies, parents were asked to sign a document stating that they agreed to send their children to Eastern Europe in order to save the children's lives. Initially, only two women volunteered to send their children, but eventually some twenty children were evacuated from the village with the consent of their parents (1983, 259–61, 282).

A second group of twenty children left for Eastern Europe during Eleni's trial at the end of August. This group was not taken by force, either; their parents were loyal to the partisan cause and feared for their children's lives after the heavy shelling of the village two days earlier (382–83). A third group of children left for Albania shortly after the trial and a few days before the entire village was forcibly evacuated by the partisans under heavy bombardment by government artillery. Gage does not specify whether this group was taken by force, but he mentions the case of Dina Veneti, who was simply told to prepare her son for departure (417). Veneti, whose husband had fought in the government army, stood trial together with Eleni but was acquitted. When we interviewed her in Lia in June 2006, Dina Veneti told us that her son had in fact been taken against her will but that she had been too afraid to object.

Consequently, according to Gage's own account, there is no conclusive evidence to support the claim that all the children who left Lia between March and August 1948 were forcibly abducted. Gage also states that the partisans allowed many children to stay behind in the village after the others had been evacuated. In addition, it is clear that Eleni's decision to organize her children's escape was *not* directly motivated by *actual* cases of abduction. Eleni had first conceived her plan at the beginning of the Civil War; she had been inspired both by her desire to reunite her family in America and by her fear of the partisans. The actual escape was motivated by rumors that the forced abduction of village children was imminent. Young Nicholas had contributed to these rumors when he ran home in panic to tell his mother that he had overheard two partisans on horseback discussing this possibility. Given the devastating consequences it had for his mother, for Gage himself, and for all the members of his family, this incident must have haunted Gage for the rest of his life. As Gage put it in his own words: "The conversation overheard by an eight-year-old boy hidden in a bean field on an April afternoon in 1948 would change the lives of everyone in the Gatzoyiannis family forever" (269).

Historical research has shown that during violent conflicts, fear and rumor are often the driving force behind historical events. In the life stories collected for this book, fear frequently emerges as a powerful factor influencing the decision parents on both sides were forced to make about evacuating their children from their villages. *Fear of abduction*, however, is not the same thing as *abduction itself*.

In the discourse of the right-wing political community of memory, the execution of Eleni presents irrefutable evidence that women who refused to hand over their children to the communist forces for evacuation to Eastern Europe were punished by death. Again, the account offered by Gage does not confirm this claim. Although many women openly resisted the idea of volunteering their children for the evacuation program, none of them was punished except Eleni. At the trial, none of the other four villagers who were executed together with Eleni faced charges related to the *paidomazoma*. Although this charge *was* brought against Eleni, the main reason for her conviction, according to Gage, was that the judge had found her guilty of "fascist leanings and disloyalty to the cause" (379).

The events surrounding the evacuation of the children of Lia to Eastern Europe, therefore, not only fail to support, but actually contradict, Gage's claims and the master narrative of the Pan-Macedonian Association itself. For Gage and the Pan-Macedonian Association, however, it is not the history of these events that is of primary concern; it is their meaning. These events are used to tell a moral story, a story of bravery and cowardice, sacrifice and cruelty, good and evil. It is the story of Eleni, the quintessential Greek mother, who made the ultimate sacrifice for the sake of her children. The main purpose of Gage's book is to justify and give meaning to his mother's death.

As Gage put it at the beginning of *Eleni*, "No one doubted that she died so I could live" (4). This comment carries a heavily loaded ideological message. According to Gage, being evacuated by the communists to Eastern Europe was the equivalent of being sentenced to death. Similarly, when his sister Glykeria, who had been forcefully recruited by the partisans, boarded a ship bound for Eastern Europe, Gage described the journey as a "ride to Hades on Charon's raft" (428). Gage's argument resonates tellingly with the "genocide" trope used by the Pan-Macedonian Association and the image of the children slaughtered by King Herod that was part of the Greek government's discourse on the *paidomazoma*.

The representation of Eastern Europe as a "dystopian nightmare" (Kalogeras 1993, 84), in contrast to the utopian dream of America as a land of freedom and opportunity, serves simultaneously a very personal purpose and an explicitly political one. The most powerful evidence of the personal significance this representation has for Gage is the dramatic rhetorical question he put to us in an angry email he sent us after the Princeton seminar. If the children had been "evacuated" for their own safety, he asked, if life in Eastern Europe had been as "rosy" as we had portrayed it, why would his mother have sacrificed her life to prevent her children from being saved from harm?

From Gage's perspective, the evil communist regimes in Eastern Europe and his own family's success in the United States, where the streets "really did seem to be made of gold" (N. Gage 2004, 328), justified his mother's sacrifice and proved she did not die in vain. From our perspective, however, the excruciating dilemma Eleni confronted epitomizes the tragedy of the Greek Civil War, where politics tore apart families, villages, and the entire Greek nation. Because Eleni belonged to a right-wing family and because her husband lived in America, the only choice she thought she had was to send her children south to government-controlled territory in order to save them from forces she perceived as her enemy.

What is omitted from Gage's politically motivated narrative, however, and what prevents it from serving as an accurate account of the evacuation program of the Greek Communist Party, is that many other mothers in northern Greece whose families sympathized with the partisans made exactly the opposite choice. They sent their children north to Eastern Europe for the same reason Eleni sent her children south to government-controlled territory—to save them from forces they perceived as their enemy. Gage's account also ignores the fact that people who supported the partisans and lived in villages controlled by the Greek Army faced the same kind of terror and violence that Eleni did, but carried out by the opposite side. Finally, the contrast Gage draws between life behind the Iron Curtain and life in America ignores the fact that many of the refugee children who settled in Eastern Europe, despite all the hardships and pain they endured, *were* able to build meaningful lives for themselves and now have fond memories of that difficult period in their lives. Some of the experiences these refugee children lived through during their "odyssey" to Eastern Europe were actually quite similar to Gage's own "odyssey," as he characterized his journey to America in the subtitle of his autobiography (N. Gage 2004).

Like refugee children evacuated to Eastern Europe, Gage, endured an extremely painful separation from his family and the war-torn village of his birth and a difficult journey to safety in the United States. Like many of them, he was traumatized by the loss of a parent and by the terrible scenes he witnessed as a child during the Civil War. Setting out on his long journey, Gage, like other refugee children, took with him cherished objects that reminded him of home (N. Gage 2004, 7), but he also found an exciting new world where he had his first encounters with the amenities of "modern" life. Gage, along with many of the children who grew up in Eastern Europe, found new opportunities in his host country and a path to upward social mobility through education. Having built new lives for themselves, Gage and other refugee children felt they had become "people of the twentieth century," and when they returned to their homes as adults, they were dismayed by the backwardness and isolation of village life, a life that had once seemed so familiar to them.

For both Gage and the refugee children who are the subject of this book, return visits to their villages were ambivalent emotional experiences. Their homes were no longer their homes; as returning visitors they were both natives and strangers. In this sense, Gage's narrative of his journey to America and the narratives of refugee children who were evacuated to Eastern Europe are remarkably similar. Gage and the people whose lives we examine here are all members of the same generation. They are all refugee children of the Greek Civil War.[19]

## Lia, a Memorial Village

The village of Lia, located high in the Mourgana range, has changed dramatically since 1948, when some sixty children crossed the mountains into Albanian territory on their way to Eastern Europe and Eleni Gatzoyiannis was executed by the communists. A new asphalt road takes visitors from Ioannina to Lia in less than an hour. In 1954, the first refugee children repatriated from Hungary had to take a long bus ride and then walk for hours to reach "home," a village in ruins, with no running water, electricity, or any of the other amenities they had grown used to in Eastern Europe. Most of these children left Lia again to work in Athens or to begin new lives abroad. In 1940 the village had 787 inhabitants; today there are only 50 permanent residents, most of them elderly, but during the summer the population swells to over 300. The combined effects of Civil War violence, poverty, and isolation have led the inhabitants of Lia to emigrate in search of better futures. Among these migrants, Lia lives on as an imagined community through its two brotherhoods, one based in Athens, the other in Worcester, Massachusetts.

At first sight, Lia looks like any of the other "traditional" villages that dot the mountains of Epirus. With its one- and two-story houses of rough gray stone, it appears to casual visitors as a "perfect example of picturesque, rugged peasant life," as it is described in a colorful tourist brochure available at the village guesthouse. Yet, according to the same brochure, Lia is unique: it is a "village marked by history," made famous by Gage through his best-selling account of the death of his mother, Eleni. In fact, Lia has become a "memorial village," a pilgrimage site for visitors from all walks of life who have been inspired by Eleni's story. This peculiar form of heritage tourism has opened up the village to the world. It has brought significant economic advantages to the people of Lia, but it has also imposed a heavy burden on them. It has made it difficult for them to move beyond their painful past and focus their attention on the future.

Lia also differs from neighboring villages because of what could be called its "American connection." A few sumptuous whitewashed villas stand out among the more traditional gray stone village houses, "antique" iron lampposts light the path to the village spring, and at the entrance to the village, a new luxury-class guesthouse constructed in "traditional village style" welcomes visitors to Lia. Last but not least, Gage's daughter Eleni has recently restored her grandmother's house, which now serves as a major attraction for visiting tourists (E. Gage 2004). Much of this new and expensive work has been paid for with American money donated by Nicholas Gage, the John Kostas Brotherhood of Lia in Worcester, and other Greek American benefactors. Heritage tourism and Greek American investment are clearly linked and have both profoundly influenced social relationships among villagers and their memories of the Civil War.

Nowhere else in Greece has the local memory of the evacuation of children during the Civil War been so deeply influenced by public debate. The villagers of Lia are still to this day struggling to come to terms not only with their own memories, but also with the effects of the publicity their community has received as a result of Gage's book. The case of Lia is also exceptional because, as a result of this publicity, experiential and political communities of memory openly confront each other in one and the same arena, the public space of village life. In this process the politics of memory are contested by four different groups of people: permanent residents of Lia, members of the Athens Brotherhood, members of the Worcester Brotherhood, and heritage tourists.

We conducted fieldwork in Lia in June 2006 with several goals in mind. Our first aim was to understand the conditions under which children had been removed from the village and sent to Eastern Europe in 1948. We were also interested in learning how repatriated refugee children, as well as the other inhabitants of Lia, have come to terms with such a difficult and haunting past almost sixty years after the tragic events themselves had taken place. In addition, we were eager to explore the impact of Gage's book (and the heritage tourism it has generated) on the social life of Lia. Finally, we were committed to doing everything we could to include in our book narratives of people who had been "kidnapped" from their homes to ensure that our treatment of the evacuation program was as fair and balanced as possible. We felt obligated to accept the challenge Gage presented us after the Princeton seminar: to come to Lia, where, he promised, we would find "dozens" of people whose experiences had not been as "rosy" as those we had described at the seminar.

During our fieldwork in Lia, we interviewed six villagers who had been involved in different ways in the evacuation program, and we spoke more informally to many more. Some of these people had been recommended to us by Gage; others we found ourselves. We took great care to ensure that the people we spoke with represented a variety of political perspectives and personal experiences. We were particularly concerned to find people who we thought could offer us an account of the *paidomazoma* as a violent act of kidnapping. In spite of all our efforts, however, we learned of only one child who had been taken away to Eastern Europe against his mother's will: Dina Veneti's son, whose case was described in *Eleni*.

While memories of the evacuation of children from Lia in 1948 vary widely, there is, nevertheless, considerable agreement across the political divide with regard to the main events that took place. A small number of left-wing families escaped to Albania to avoid being caught by the Greek Army long before the evacuation program of the Communist Party was carried out. In April 1948, when the partisans asked parents to volunteer their children for evacuation, some families, mostly supporters of the left, agreed, but many others did not.

The family of Agni Andoniou tried to maintain a neutral stance in the civil war threatening to destroy her village.[20] Although she is closely related to the Gage family, Agni told us that she did not accept some of the main arguments of Gage's book. Invoking God—"who sees all things"—as her witness, she insisted that the refugee children were well cared for in Romania and that none of them had been taken from the village by force. Agni's mother had agreed to send her two sons with the partisans, but she refused to let her daughter go with them. After a few months of heavy fighting, though, she changed her mind and allowed Agni, who was seven at the time, to join the second group of children leaving for Albania. While Agni's mother finally decided to send all her children away, other families volunteered one child and kept the others at home. In many cases, families refused to give up any of their children at all.

Since his parents were working for the partisans, thirteen-year-old Nikos Marangos was being cared for by his grandparents. He said that many parents had agreed to send their children away because they had nothing to feed them. Nikos' grandparents, however, refused to let him go; he was their only grandchild, their only hope for the future. The partisans challenged their decision, asking: "Why are you keeping him here? He's hungry!" "We are two old tree trunks," Nikos' grandfather replied, "and he is our young sapling." Eventually Nikos was forced to leave Lia with his mother and grandmother in September 1948. They spent three months in a refugee camp in Albania, where they suffered from hunger and lice, before they were sent to Hungary.

Almost everyone in the village we spoke with confirmed that the partisans had evacuated the whole village of Lia by force in September 1948 and that, once in Albania, many children had been forcefully separated from their relatives. Yet these same people also stated that the organized evacuation program of the Communist Party had not been conducted by force. Acknowledging that in some cases parents who volunteered their children were more motivated by fear of the partisans than by fear of government shelling, people also insisted that many parents had refused to give up their children and that none of them except Eleni Gatzoyianni had been punished by the partisans as a result.

Niki Samara, a slim, lively woman in her seventies, had good reason to hate the partisans. They had killed several members of her family and threatened to execute her because she had refused an order to work for them. In spite of her hatred of the communists, Niki described bonds of solidarity that crossed political lines: her own brother and his wife had been saved from execution by the timely intervention of a left-wing friend. These local networks of solidarity reveal some of the ways in which the people of Lia and other villages in northern Greece tried to maintain the social ties they had forged in the past in order to help them live together again in the future (Loizos 1981; Van Boeschoten 1997, 160–65). The preservation of such memories in Niki's otherwise quite politicized account undermines polarized versions of history that have reconfigured the Greek Civil War as an unambiguous conflict between good and evil.

When asked about the *paidomazoma*, Niki immediately said that everyone had been taken by force. It soon became clear, though, that she was referring to the forced evacuation of the entire village by the partisans in September 1948. The partisans had threatened to kill her on the spot if she refused to leave. The journey to Albania was an ordeal: she had no milk to feed her baby, and she later suffered from pneumonia and lost a lung. Niki could *not*, however, confirm that any children had been separated forcefully from their parents earlier that summer during the organized evacuation program carried out by the Communist Party.

Like Niki Samara, Dina Veneti made no secret of her political beliefs. In the village, her home is known as "the military house." On the wall next to her front door is a bronze plaque with a picture of her late husband in uniform; during the Civil War he was an officer in the Greek Army. According to Dina, this was the main reason why she had been arrested and put on trial together with Eleni Gatzoyianni. Now in her eighties, Dina told her story in a brisk and angry voice, full of colorful phrases and ominous dreams. "My soul is black," she told us, "because when the partisans came—like wolves—and occupied the village, we went through hell. They stole our food, and we had nothing to eat. Then I was forced to spend six years in exile in Hungary." When Dina stood trial in August 1948, she had a son of six and two younger children. Shortly after she was acquitted and released from jail, a partisan told her to prepare her son for departure. After all the suffering Dina had been through, she was too afraid to refuse. "For me," she said, "it was as if they had executed me after all. What mother wants to be separated from her child?" A few days later, she, too, was forced to leave Lia with her other two children and the rest of the villagers.

Niki Samara and Dina Veneti have been deeply marked by the left-wing violence they suffered during the Civil War. Yet, in spite of the anticommunist tenor of their accounts, they did not claim that the children of Lia had been abducted by the partisans. Instead, they confirmed the stories we had heard from other villagers. Although Dina Veneti's son was obviously taken against her will, she saw this as an act of reprisal for her "uncooperative" attitude toward the partisans rather than as part of a more generalized communist-inspired abduction scheme.

Each of these four life histories is told from a different political perspective; each presents different individual experiences, different subjective truths. Yet taken together, they also reveal local memories of the *paidomazoma* in Lia that are largely shared, local memories in which, with only one exception we are aware of, force was not involved in the organized program in which the partisans evacuated children from the village and took them to Eastern Europe. The inhabitants of Lia, however, were severely distressed by the forced mobilization of young men and women to serve in the Democratic Army, the forced evacuation of the entire village, the appalling conditions in the refugee camps in Albania, and the forced separation of family members that took place there and that lasted for years, even decades, afterward.

Local memories of the *paidomazoma* in Lia support the analysis of the experiences of refugee children we have presented in this book and undermine the validity of claims that the evacuation program of the Greek Communist Party had been a mass abduction scheme. The important new insights we gained from our research in Lia concern the multiple meanings attributed to the term *paidomazoma* in right-wing public discourse. While the Greek government originally coined this term to refer to the organized evacuation program conducted by the Communist Party, today right-wing Greek nationalists use the term in a much broader sense, according to which all forms of partisan violence—forced mobilization, forced evacuation of entire villages, as well as the organized evacuation of unaccompanied children—are conflated into one category.

Our research in Lia also revealed that even the most virulent anticommunist memories, to the extent that they refer to individuals' *own* experiences, frequently contradict the master narratives developed by the Greek government, the Pan-Macedonian Association, and Gage himself. These insights demonstrate that concrete memories of experience and the political interpretation of these experiences often conflict with one another. Finally, the life history narratives of villagers across the political spectrum show that, in spite of its status as an international best seller, *Eleni* has not become the official story of the *paidomazoma* in the village of Lia. In fact, as we soon discovered, villagers hold a wide range of views on Gage's controversial book.

When investigative reporter Vasilis Kavvathas visited Lia in 1984 to find material for *The Other Eleni*, his angry rebuttal to Gage's book from the perspective of the left, he found very few villagers willing to discuss the events described in *Eleni*; most in fact said that they had not even read the book (Kavvathas 1985, 136–37, 192). Had he been more sensitive to the role of silence in social memory, Kavvathas might have understood that listening to such silences, and the conflicts and traumas they conceal, is as important as listening to memories that are actually expressed in words (Laub 1992; Passerini 2003). By 2006, the heated controversy provoked in Greece by the publication of *Eleni* had subsided, as had the tensions that constituted the painful legacy of the Civil War and the Cold War that followed. Instead of silence, we heard testimony that many villagers were trying to mend the damaged social relations of the past and had reconsidered their earlier views of Gage's book.

Some supporters of the left told us that the book was "full of lies," while others on the right maintained that it was too mild in its denunciation of the communists' crimes. Many other villagers, however, were ready to recognize that Gage had written his book "because of his pain" and were therefore willing to condone some of the inaccuracies they thought the book contained. Overall, the villagers' attitudes toward the book and its author remained deeply ambivalent. While many saw Gage as a benefactor who had contributed significantly to the economic development of the village, many also said that *Eleni* had perpetuated the political tensions dividing the village at precisely the moment when people were ready to move beyond the painful legacy of the past.

Much of this resentment was focused on the way Gage reinterpreted the events leading up to his mother's execution and the nature of the social relations that existed within the village at the time. Many villagers said that Gage's book focused exclusively on the suffering of the right: "We have our pain, too," villagers said, reclaiming the right of other voices to be heard. "Gage wasn't the only person whose mother died. Our family could have written a book, too." Regardless of their political views, many villagers objected to Gage's frequent use of village gossip to make his story more appealing to a foreign audience. By attributing adultery, greed, jealousy, and cowardice to named individuals, they argued, Gage violated the principle of what Michael Herzfeld has aptly called "cultural intimacy" (2005, 142) by exposing in an international public space what is only appropriate for private discussion among insiders.

Many villagers also objected to the way Gage "balkanized" (Todorova 1997) Lia, by describing "primitive customs," such as drinking wine from a dead woman's skull, which they say have never been practiced in the village. In addition, by attributing much of the responsibility for his mother's execution to the jealousy of her fellow villagers, Gage has made the process of reconciliation within the village much more difficult. Most of all, however, villagers objected to the way Gage's book has come to control the memory of events that occurred in Lia during the Civil War, especially the *paidomazoma*.

Gage's book *Eleni* is an example of the multiple ways in which the local and the global are intertwined in this conflict over memory. Based on local stories told by a "native," who is also a "global citizen," and interpreted to serve a global political discourse, Gage's book was repatriated to Lia as an international best seller. It not only confronted local actors with a "globalized" version of their own history, but it also attracted tourists from around the world who followed in its tracks. In addition, the "local" actors who were directly involved in this memory war are, to a significant extent, themselves "global citizens." Although now they live once again in the village where they were born, they spent much of their lives elsewhere—in the United States, Hungary, Romania, or Athens. Their experiences in other countries, as well as their contacts with foreign visitors, have strongly influenced the ways they have come to understand the history of their native village.

The guesthouse (*xenonas*) of Lia is a central locus of this conflict over memory. It forces us to reconceptualize received ideas about place as the natural site of bounded cultures rooted in specific territories.[21] Built as a memorial to Eleni Gatzoyianni, the guesthouse of Lia has become a political arena in which forces of local, national, and global power are engaged in a bitter struggle over the meaning of the *paidomazoma*. Here the past is commodified and packaged for the tourist gaze (Urry 1990).

Upon entering the dining room of the guesthouse, which is nicely decorated with traditional village handicrafts, visitors are immediately confronted with a "theatre of memory" (Samuel 1994). Books by Nicholas Gage and his daughter Eleni, *Eleni*, *A Place for Us*, and *North of Ithaca*, as well as a DVD documenting the activities of the Worcester-based Brotherhood of Lia, are conveniently spread out on a wooden table in the foyer. On the walls hang pictures and press clippings publicizing the visits of important celebrities, such as Constantine Mitsotakis, then prime minister of Greece, whom Gage brought to Lia by helicopter to speak at the opening of the guesthouse in 1990. An aerial photograph of the village shows the location of all the places mentioned in *Eleni*, places that have now become memory sites. At the reception desk, maps are available for visitors who are interested in taking a tour of the village, retracing Eleni's footsteps during the last days of her life.

A new road sign, the only one in the village, leads visitors from the guesthouse along Eleni Gatzoyianni Street to the first stop on their memory tour: the newly rebuilt house of Eleni Gatzoyianni herself. From there, visitors can make their way up the hill behind the village to the site of Eleni's execution. Ironically, the only person recent visitors are likely to find there to serve as their guide is Fotis Makris, a cowherd and former refugee child, whose communist uncles are blamed by right-wing villagers for all the evil that befell them during the Civil War. In 1984, the role of guide was played by Lambros, a developmentally disabled man, who, for a small fee, would lead tourists to the execution site of Eleni Gatzoyianni, the woman he referred to as the "Amerikana who brings money" (Kavvathas 1985, 141).

The commodification of the past and the focus on just one of the many victims of the Civil War has deeply divided the community of Lia. As a symbol of this one-sided memorialization of the village, the guesthouse itself has been transformed into a contested memory site. In this arena, two opposed poles of political power confront one another: the village council and the Greek Brotherhood of Lia, on the one hand, and Nicholas Gage and the American Brotherhood of Lia, on the other. This division is also reflected in the topography of the village. The guesthouse is reserved for tourists and guests and is rarely visited by local residents, except for supporters of the American Brotherhood of Lia and Gage's network of friends and allies, known as "the American boys." Villagers generally socialize at Lia's only coffeehouse, where members of both political factions often sit and drink together. These two different modes of sociability recall the distinction drawn by Herzfeld (1991) between "monumental time," which dominates the guesthouse, and "social time," which governs the life of the coffeehouse.

The political significance of the guesthouse is nowhere more obvious than in the entries left in the guest books kept at the front desk. These texts reveal another global dimension of the politics of memory in Lia: the perspectives of tourists and visitors from around the world. Nearly all the comments in the guest books focus on *Eleni* and the political message of Gage's book. Many of them are addressed personally to Nicholas Gage, who is clearly seen as the driving force behind the construction of the guesthouse as a monument to his mother.

At the time of our research, the guest books covered the period from 1989 to 2005. Many different categories of people have left comments over the years: foreign tourists, right-wing Greek nationalists, government officials, schoolteachers and their students, and finally, members of the Greek diaspora, some of them originally from Lia. These guest book entries offer unique insights into the process through which public memory is constructed around the events leading up to Eleni's death.

The precise nature of these public memories varies according to the social, political, and national identities of the visitors; it also varies according to the date of their visit. For several years after the official inauguration of the guest house by Prime Minister Constantine Mitsotakis in July 1990, most comments left by Greeks were written by right-wing nationalists, former army officers, war veterans, and politicians. The majority of these, written in virulently anticommunist language, link Eleni's sacrifice directly to the defense of the Greek race, the Greek nation, and the Greek state against the threat of communism. Some comments express support for the Greek nationalist position on the Macedonian conflict; others call for the territorial expansion of Greece.

In the following years, however, new comments transformed Eleni from a right-wing hero and "victim of communism" into a *national* hero, an ideal Greek mother as a gendered symbol of the Greek nation. In 1993, for example, two Greek schoolgirls hailed Eleni as "the mother of us all," a woman "who with great courage and bravery fought for the honor of our nation." In this role Eleni can be compared with Queen Frederica, the "mother of all Greek children," who also personified the Greek nation as a loving mother. In this way, a united national memory is constructed out of an extremely divisive moment in Greek history. One visitor implicitly acknowledged the discrepancy of these two discourses in 1990, when he first characterized Lia as a place of "national pilgrimage" and "national memory," and then added almost as an afterthought: ". . . and a place of national reconciliation."

Foreign visitors, on the contrary, have interpreted *Eleni* and their visit to Lia in a more universal manner, emphasizing their opposition to war and other forms of violence. An Austrian couple visiting Lia in 1993 stressed the need to restore the house of Eleni Gatzoyianni as a monument against "fanaticism and war crimes, such as those being committed now in Yugoslavia." Foreign visitors were also more prone to express a critical view of Gage's book and of the memorialization of Lia. A German visitor began his comment with a reference to *For Whom the Bell Tolls*, Hemingway's famous novel about the Spanish Civil War. He wrote that "the death of a person touches me deeply," but then added that "histories have two sides and other versions are possible." It is noteworthy that critical comments and messages with more universal values become more frequent—from Greeks as well as foreigners—with the passage of time. In 1995, a Greek visitor wrote, "Each coin has two sides. That is all I want to say."

Members of the Greek diaspora traveling in Greece in search of their "roots" are often less interested in the political message of *Eleni*, but the comments of former refugee children and their children are particularly interesting. In what Marianne Hirsch calls "post-memories" (the relationships a second generation has to powerful, often traumatic experiences lived by their parents' generation) former refugee children draw on their own personal memories and their own family histories to refute Gage's version of the *paidomazoma* or to reflect on the meaning of their own life stories. A young woman who came to Lia in an attempt to learn more about the life of her grandfather was obviously under great emotional stress when, at 6:30 one morning, she described the Civil War as the most painful period in Greek history:

> It's very hard to live in a village knowing that somebody on the "other side" killed your mother. It's also very hard to be a descendant of people who brought death to your village, to carry the sins of your parents on your shoulders. And it's hard to be a child of the paidomazoma and to return from "another homeland" to your birthplace, which you always believed was paradise, but which turned out to be worse than hell.

While this comment is dominated by feelings of pain and guilt, other comments left by former refugee children from Lia contrasted the version of public memory they read in Gage's book with their own family memories: "Lia is not only the village of Eleni, but the village of many other Elenis on the other side. . . . We heard a very different version of Eleni's story from our grandmother, who lived and grew up with her in this very place."

Throughout the guest books, more critical and reflexive comments like these are in the minority. They form a counter-discourse to the dominant public memory emerging from these texts in which Eleni remains a symbol for the right-wing master narrative in the memory politics of the present. The very presence of these comments inscribed in counterpoint to mainstream narratives suggests that the end of the Cold War has created a new discursive space for alternative readings of *Eleni* in which more universal values have found a prominent place.

The village of Lia is a traumatized community. A violent Civil War history, conflict over the meaning of the past, and the glare of international attention as a result of the work of Nicholas Gage have all combined to damage the basic fabric of village social life. The *paidomazoma* continues to play a central role in the tensions that poison social relations in Lia. Smoldering under a surface of apparent goodwill, feelings of resentment, anger, and guilt hamper villagers' efforts to come to terms with their past. On occasion, these feelings erupt into bitter arguments.

On July 1, 2006, our last day of fieldwork in Lia, we returned to the village after visiting a controversial Civil War monument in the neighboring village of Tsamandas. We sat down at the village coffeehouse where a group of men were quietly playing cards. When we mentioned our visit to the monument in Tsamandas, Dimitris, a rightist born in another village, remembered how at the age of eight he had gone into hiding to avoid being taken by the partisans and sent to Eastern Europe. His older brother, who had worked for the Greek government, had been saved from the partisans by a left-wing friend. In gratitude, Dimitris added, his brother later saved his left-wing friend from being executed by the Greek government. Dimitris concluded his story by stressing how much both sides had suffered during the Civil War.

Thanos, a leftist, agreed, adding, "We need reconciliation; we need to forget all this hatred." Then he described how he had been forced by the partisans to leave the village with his grandmother in September 1948, but he insisted that he had been well treated growing up in a children's home in Hungary. Suddenly Dimitris accused Thanos of having been brainwashed in Hungary, having become a Janissary, and having betrayed his own country. Thanos objected strenuously. He had always remained a Greek; it had been the Greek state that had treated him badly after his return from Eastern Europe. In spite of the fact that he had spent time in a paidopoli after his repatriation, he had never been able to find a good job. People just said he was a communist from behind the Iron Curtain.

At this point Dimitris treated Thanos and the other men playing cards to a beer. Then the argument continued. Dimitris charged that for the past thirty years all the books about the "bandit war" had been written by the left; the voice of the right had been silenced. That immediately sparked angry comments about Nicholas Gage and *Eleni*. One man said the book was a one-sided attempt to vindicate the position of the right. Another said that the book was pure fiction. A third said it would have been better if Gage had never written the book at all; then Lia would be peaceful and quiet now. In the end, they all agreed that the old hatreds were gradually disappearing as members of the generation of the Civil War grew old and died. Twenty years ago, they said, leftists and rightists never sat together at the village coffeehouse the way they do now.

This incident illustrates the fact that the people of Lia attempt to mend village social relations by recognizing the need for reconciliation. By buying a beer for these left-wing men, Dimitris expressed his desire to overcome the hatreds of the past and create reciprocity and goodwill in village social relationships in the present. Many villagers, but primarily those on the left, stress that an essential precondition for this reconciliation is the public recognition that *both* sides suffered during the Civil War. As a material sign of such recognition, the Athens Brotherhood of Lia suggested the erection of a monument in the village celebrating the memory of *all* Civil War victims. So far, no consensus on this idea has been reached.

Efforts at reconciliation have been seriously hampered by the extremely divisive annual ceremony that takes place in the neighboring village of Tsamandas located ten kilometers from Lia in a valley surrounded by the Mourgana Mountains set up against the Albanian border. In 1981, at the initiative of a private association called Friends of the [Greek] Army, a monument was erected to commemorate the deaths of 120 soldiers of the Greek Army who had been ambushed, executed, and buried in a mass grave by the partisans late in the Civil War. The monument is an obelisk of white marble blocks standing on a plaza of cement tiles set on top of a hill at the entrance to the village. Many years after its erection, the names of other Greek soldiers and civilians who died at the hands of the "alien-inspired" (*xenokinitoi*) communist forces were inscribed on two large plaques set at the base of the monument. One of these names is that of Eleni Gatzoyianni.

Every year on the last Sunday in September, a memorial service is held at the monument in Tsamandas. In 1989, the Greek government adopted a politics of reconciliation and oblivion and moved to transform "ceremonies of hatred" that had commemorated victories of the Greek Army over the partisans into ceremonies honoring all victims of the Civil War. Since then, the monument in Tsamandas has become yet another "contested memory site," where the victorious right continues to assert the validity of its own master narrative and tries to silence the counter-narrative of the left. In the process, the many private individual narratives that confound the one-sided master narratives of both the right and the left are also ignored.

Most of the people of Lia attempt to cope with the past and build a new future by retreating into silence. As the mayor of Lia told us, "in order to overcome the hatred of the past, each one of us has to keep his own truth to himself." This self-imposed silence is one of the ways the people of Lia resist the publicity that Nicholas Gage's book has inflicted on them; it enables them to avert the gaze of both tourists and ethnographers. This silence does not mean that they have forgotten the past; it means, instead, that they "remember the past without rancor," as the ancient Athenians swore to do with the oath that stands as the epigraph to the last chapter of this book.

In the words of Luisa Passerini, the inhabitants of Lia lay their memories of the Greek Civil War to rest somewhere "between silence and oblivion." This is an appropriate, even necessary, stance to adopt in "communities where there is still a perception of a common good to be saved or restored." In such communities, "silence has the function of making it possible to distance oneself from the past—not necessarily to forget—in certain areas of public life, while in others the remembering goes on" (Passerini 2003, 247). To the villagers of Lia whom we may have disturbed with our presence, we apologize. We regret that we interrupted the silence with which they have sought to distance themselves from their difficult and painful past.

# Epilogue

*Mi mnisikakein.* (Remember the past without rancor.)

—Ancient Athenian oath

The dialectical relationship between remembering and forgetting is one of the most significant features of the politics of memory. Political communities of memory use "the imperative to remember" as an antidote "against forgetting" and as a quintessential element in the construction of "constitutive narratives" of the nation, as our analysis of the Association of Refugee Children from Aegean Macedonia and the Pan-Macedonian Association USA, Inc., both reveal. At the same time, the use of memory to construct a moral community of suffering means that certain elements of the community's historical experience must be forgotten. The political use of *Eleni* and the guesthouse of Lia as memorials to Eleni Gatzoyianni imply the erasure of the memory of other victims of the Civil War, particularly those on the left.

Forgetting, however, is also an option consciously chosen by members of local communities in order to overcome divisions inherited from the past. Some of the residents of Lia have sought this option, but they have been unable to block out all the traumatic memories from the past that continue to haunt their lives. "Post-memories," either in the form of memories transmitted through family networks or shaped in reaction to public debates, continue to haunt the lives of later generations of villagers who did not live through the Civil War.

This tension between remembering and forgetting is also obvious in the social and political messages conveyed by the various monuments that shape collective memories of the Greek Civil War. In their introduction to

*The Art of Forgetting,* Forty and Küchler argue that it is an "inevitable feature of memorials . . . [that] they permit only certain things to be remembered, and by exclusion cause others to be forgotten" (1999, 9). In conducting the research for this book, we have encountered three monuments associated with the evacuation of refugee children from their homes during the Civil War: the monument to the Macedonian "mothers" and the refugee children they cared for in Skopje, the statue of Queen Frederica in Konitsa, and the monument to the soldiers in the Greek Army killed by the partisans in Tsamandas (see figs. 6 and 10 above).

The monument to the Macedonian "mothers" and their refugee "children" "remembers" the fate of these refugees and incorporates them into the master narrative of Macedonian national history. It "forgets," however, that there were many *Greek* "mothers" and *Greek* children who traveled the same route into exile and who lived in the same children's homes in Eastern Europe. By presenting this evacuation as an "expulsion" of Macedonian children from their homeland carried out by the Greek state, rather than as an evacuation of Macedonian and Greek children carried out by the Greek Communist Party, this monument also "forgets" that the Greek Civil War was not a struggle between Macedonians and Greeks, but a struggle between left and right. It transforms what was fundamentally a political conflict into an ethnic or national one.

The statue of Queen Frederica, erected in 1953 in the central square of Konitsa in Epirus, honored the queen's role as "mother of all Greek children" and more specifically as "mother of the Orphans," the mother of all the children raised in paidopoleis. This statue was removed from its place of honor in the town square after the 1973 referendum abolishing the monarchy. The fact that the statue of Queen Frederica continues to lie "forgotten" in a storehouse stands as testament to the politics of oblivion inaugurated by the Greek government in 1989. The fate of this statue also demonstrates that those who were victorious in the Civil War and in the war of memory that followed have finally been defeated, at least in this particular battle. The old right-wing Greek nationalist perspective, like the statue of Queen Frederica, has been relegated to the storehouse of discredited ideologies that will, we hope, prove less potent in the world of the early twenty-first century than they have in the past.

Finally, the controversy surrounding the monument of Tsamandas can be read as a conflict between the official politics of oblivion of the Greek government and efforts to vindicate right-wing memories of the Civil War initiated by a private association of Greek Army veterans. Although this memorial was initially built to honor only Greek soldiers killed by the partisans, the inscription of Eleni Gatzoyianni's name on the monument has expanded the scope of its significance to include support for right-wing discourse on the *paidomazoma* as articulated by Nicholas Gage in *Eleni*, by the Pan-Macedonian Association in its recent political activity, and by both Gage and the officers of the Pan-Macedonian Association in the positions they took at the Princeton University seminar with which we opened this book. The three monuments considered here stand as architectural evidence of three attempts to memorialize different master narratives of the evacuation of children from northern Greece by the Communist Party in 1948.

One crucial question, however, remains. Why is this evacuation program still relevant in contemporary Greek political discourse? Why is the *paidomazoma* still such a controversial issue today, sixty years after the end of the Greek Civil War, and twenty years after the end of the Cold War? We conclude by suggesting some tentative answers to this difficult question. These answers involve broad issues that extend well beyond the scope of this book: the treatment of refugees driven from their homes in military conflicts, the impact of globalization on political discourse at the state and national level, and finally the role of memory in "working through" collective trauma during the process of postconflict reconciliation.

The contemporary issue that lies at the heart of the ongoing controversy over the *paidomazoma*, an issue that constitutes the "unfinished business" of the Greek Civil War, is the Macedonian conflict, a dispute that has figured prominently in Greek foreign policy since the 1980s. A crucial element of this conflict is the "impossible return" of former refugee children from northern Greece who have a Macedonian national identity. As noted in chapter 2, while the Greek government initially demanded the return of *all* the refugee children "kidnapped" from northern Greece, in 1982, when the mass repatriation of political refugees from Eastern Europe was well under way, the newly elected socialist government restricted the right of return to refugees who were "Greeks by birth." This decision opened new wounds for former refugee children who identified themselves as Macedonians, since it effectively prevented them from returning to the villages of their birth in northern Greece.

At the same time, this situation has created considerable political tension between Greece and the Republic of Macedonia, where the majority of Macedonian refugee children live. While the Macedonian government has placed the right of Macedonian refugees to return to Greece high on its political agenda, the Greek government fears the radicalization of its own Macedonian minority, whose existence it continues to deny (Danforth 1995; Kofos 2003). For decades, this issue, together with the related question of restoring the property rights of Macedonian refugees, troubled diplomatic relations between Greece and Yugoslavia. It was rarely brought into the open, however, in an attempt to avoid disturbing what had been (since the late 1950s) the good relationship between the two countries. This situation changed dramatically in 1991, when the Republic of Macedonia became independent and Macedonian politicians began to place this issue, as well as that of the Macedonian minority in Greece, on the negotiating table. In this way, the Macedonian refugee children from the Greek Civil War have become a significant source of tension in the broader Macedonian conflict.

The political dispute over the fate of Macedonian refugee children has taken on a new dimension for another reason. Increased globalization and the end of the Cold War have created new anxieties and new global political discourses, which have changed the ways in which nation-states and transnational national communities have come to deal with both minorities and refugees. In his *Fear of Small Numbers*, Arjun Appadurai (2006, 23) refers to a new emotional Cold War between those who identify with the losers and those who identify with the winners in the new world order. Appadurai has also revised his earlier, somewhat premature, views on the imminent death of the nation-state (1996), arguing that the loss of sovereignty that nation-states have experienced has changed the nature of nationalism in important ways. In an era of globalization, he writes, "some essential principles and procedures of the modern nation-state—the idea of a sovereign and stable territory, the idea of a containable and countable population, the idea of a reliable census, and the idea of stable and transparent categories—have come unglued" (2006, 6).

On the one hand, these new developments may create an increased cosmopolitanism, often expressed in the language of human rights and multiculturalism; on the other hand, they may lead to increased ethnic and national conflict. Appadurai attributes these new developments to the fact that "the nation-state has been steadily reduced to the fiction of its ethnos as the last cultural resource over which it may exercise full dominion" (2006, 23). In this context, minorities—even the smallest and least powerful—may present an even greater threat than they did in the past. They may also be turned into scapegoats and blamed for the perceived dangers posed by an increasingly globalized world. According to Appadurai, therefore, "minorities in a globalizing world are a constant reminder of the incompleteness of national purity" (2006, 84).

Both these new anxieties and the new political discourse on human rights, victimhood, and genocide help us understand why the memory of the *paidomazoma* continues to be such a controversial issue at the beginning of the twenty-first century. We suggest that the seemingly anachronistic replay of Cold War scenarios by Nicholas Gage and the Pan-Macedonian Association, public fear in Greece of a mass repatriation of Macedonian political refugees, the essentialist discourse of Greek and Macedonian nationalisms, and the discourse on "diaspora Hellenism" (*apodimos ellinismos*) deployed by the Greek government should all be seen as novel responses to new situations, not simply as the products of the mechanical reproduction of old ideologies.

The Pan-Macedonian Association's characterization of the *paidomazoma* as an act of "genocide" committed by the Greek Communist Party and the Association of Refugee Children from Aegean Macedonia's characterization of it as an act of "genocide" committed by the Greek government have both been at least partially influenced by the new currency of the discourse on human rights and victimhood in the global media today. In its more cosmopolitan version, this same discourse on human rights and multiculturalism has provided new legitimacy to the battles waged by the Association of Refugee Children from Aegean Macedonia (especially by its diaspora organizations in Canada and Australia) on behalf of the human rights of the Macedonian minority of northern Greece.

Recent developments in Spain illustrate an alternative way of domesticating the ghosts of the past in a society deeply affected by a bloody civil war. After Franco's death, the politics of oblivion seemed the only way to guarantee a peaceful transition to democracy (Aguilar 2001). In recent years, however, there has been increasing public pressure to break this "pact of silence." In response to this pressure, in 2007 the Spanish government passed the Law on the Recovery of Historical Memory, intended to compensate and rehabilitate the victims of the Spanish Civil War. In 2008, it granted Spanish citizenship to 500,000 former political refugees and their descendants who now live scattered around the world.[1] Although not all Spaniards support this effort, the official recognition of the suffering of people on both sides of the Civil War and the final settlement of the lingering refugee problem seem to promise a way to treat the unhealed wounds of the past. With this approach, Spaniards are encouraged, not to "forget" the past, but rather, as the ancient Athenian oath exhorts, to remember it without rancor.

In the Greek case, the persistence of unassimilated trauma from the Civil War is another important reason why the *paidomazoma* is still a source of such bitter conflict today. For individual refugee children, this trauma is primarily associated with acts of war, separation from parents, loss of childhood, and feelings of estrangement after being repatriated or reunited with family. There are also collective traumas, often related to the process of remembering itself, that affect political communities of memory such as the village of Lia and Greek society as a whole.

The end of the Cold War has reawakened all the specters of the past; people believe they have been treated unjustly and seek recognition of their suffering in the public arena. In the 1980s, the suffering of the left was widely acknowledged. In the process, however, the suffering of the right, which had been fully acknowledged in the 1950s and 1960s, was temporarily "forgotten." Now the right seeks public recognition of its suffering again. This demand for recognition is an essential component of the process of "working through" the trauma of the past. Just as it may be therapeutic for individuals to recall tragic experiences of the past because it helps them to reexternalize the trauma (Laub 1992, 69), it may also be beneficial for entire communities to do the same. Enforced "forgetting," or "the politics of oblivion," may produce short-term positive effects, but in the long run it may be counterproductive (as in Spain), or it may actually lead to renewed violence (as in Yugoslavia).

These insights have led many conflict-ridden communities throughout the world to the realization that reconciliation with the past is only possible through the public recognition of collective trauma and of its devastating effects on everyone involved. The establishment of the Truth and Reconciliation Commission in postapartheid South Africa and similar attempts in Rwanda after the widespread massacres of 1994 were based on these premises. Other societies that adopted a policy of "reconciliation from above," such as Northern Ireland in 1994 (Dawson 1999) and Greece in the 1980s, soon discovered that past trauma cannot be so easily forgotten. In such cases, the lack of social recognition of the injustices of the past can lead to the development of a "politics of suffering" and the creation of public narratives of the past, which focus exclusively on the victims on one side of the conflict while ignoring those on the other.

This is precisely the type of one-sided narrative of suffering and victimhood that we encountered at the world reunions of Refugee Children from Aegean Macedonia in Skopje, in the publications of the Pan-Macedonian Association USA, Inc., and in Nicholas Gage's *Eleni*. The question remains: how can the politics of memory contribute in a positive way to the process of reconciliation and healing, rather than in a negative way to the process of factionalization and division? We agree with the villagers of Lia and the refugee children who believe that a genuine reconciliation with the past is only possible through the public recognition of the suffering of people on both sides of the conflict.

The suffering of Nicholas Gage and his mother Eleni at the hands of the Greek Communist Party has its counterpart in the suffering of other children and "other Elenis" (as Kavvathas calls them) at the hands of the Greek government. If we can hear more clearly the voices of all the refugee children of the Greek Civil War—Greeks and Macedonians, rightists and leftists, those raised in children's homes in Eastern Europe and those raised in the paidopoleis of Queen Frederica—only then will we come to realize that many of the experiences of the refugee children of the Greek Civil War were shared independently of their political affiliation, their national identity, and their place of exile. This realization will, in turn, make possible the mutual recognition of both the old suffering and the new challenges that these two groups of refugee children have confronted over the course of their lives.

We hope this book will contribute to the process of healing and reconciliation for the individuals and communities that have suffered the traumatic experiences of the Greek Civil War. We also hope that this book will offer a deeper understanding of the complex lives of refugee children of the Greek Civil War and of all the other children who are refugees from other wars in other parts of the world.

It is only appropriate to conclude with the voices of two of the refugee children whose life stories have contributed so much to this book. Both children who went to Eastern Europe and children who went to the paidopoleis of Queen Frederica have reflected deeply on the meanings of their lives. They themselves have suggested ways in which this process of healing and reconciliation can be furthered. The following statements convey effectively and forcefully the message that many refugee children of the Greek Civil War would like to leave for their children and grandchildren. They are powerful examples of the impossibility of forgetting, the destructiveness of remembering with rancor, as Nicholas Gage has done, and the value, the virtue, of remembering without rancor.

Mary Rosova, a Macedonian refugee child raised in Czechoslovakia and living now in Toronto, concluded her life story with a wish for a future of peace and understanding.

> I remember when we went to our reunion in Skopje in 1988, our declaration was, "Let no child experience what we did. Let no parents long for their children as ours did." . . . If we can find a common language, we'll find we have a lot more in common than things that divide us. We don't hate anybody. We

have to learn from the past so we can have a better future for our children
and for generations to come.

Kostas Dimou is a Greek refugee child who was raised in paidopoleis
in Greece and lives now in Ioannina. His father was killed by a soldier in
the Greek Army. After describing a haunting scene he remembered from
his childhood—a group of women singing a lament over the body of an
unknown soldier that had been dug up by wolves—Kostas tried to convey
the impact this memory had on him for many years afterward.

> From 1948 to 1992, I had the same nightmare every night. I dreamt I was
> there at the spring. Every time I knelt down to drink, I woke up. In 1992, I
> happened to visit the same place during an excursion with some friends. I
> immediately remembered the whole scene—the body, the women, the la-
> ment. After that, the nightmare stopped. I made a vow to hold a memorial
> service at the spring, to honor the souls of all the people who died in the
> Civil War. All the people, on both sides of the war.

On August 30, 2009, in a small ceremony surrounded by family and
friends, Kostas Dimou fulfilled his vow.

# ENDNOTES

INTRODUCTION

1.  This is a more accurate number than the one cited in the announcement of the Princeton seminar. For a detailed discussion of this issue see chapter 2.
2.  For an anticommunist, Greek nationalist perspective, see Bougas (2006), N. Gage (1983), Karavasilis (2006), and Paliouras (2003); for a Macedonian nationalist perspective, see Naumoff (2003) and Stojanovik-Lafazanovska and Lafazanovski (2002); and for a Greek communist perspective, see Gritzonas (1998) and Servos (2001).
3.  Other people from Macedonia use "Macedonian" as a term of self-ascription in an *ethnic* or *regional* sense; that is, they have a Greek national identity and a Macedonian ethnic or regional identity. These people often call themselves "Greek Macedonians" (*Ellino-Makedones*). When referring more generally to Slavic-speaking inhabitants of Greek Macedonia during the 1930s and 1940s, we use the term "Slavic speakers."

CHAPTER ONE

1.  See http://www2.ohchr.org/english/law/refugees.htm.
2.  See http://www2.ohchr.org/english/law/crc.htm.
3.  On the interdisciplinary, cross-cultural study of childhood, see Ariès (1962), Hawkes and Hiner (1991), James and Prout (1997), Jenks (1996), Stephens, (1995), and Zelizer (1985). For a more recent discussion of the anthropology of childhood, see the special issues of the *American Anthropologist* (109, no. 2 [2007]: 241–306) and of *Anthropology News* (49, no. 4 [2008]).
4.  See Labajos-Pérez and Vitoria-Garcia (1997), Legarreta (1984), and Vigil et al. (1999).
5.  See Baumel (1990), Fox and Abraham-Podietz (1999), Harris and Oppenheimer (2000), and Whiteman (1993).
6.  Estimates of the number of children who were abducted by the Nazis range from a high of 500,000 (Clay and Leapman 1995, 128) to a low of 50,000 (Heinemann 2004).
7.  This account is based on Clay and Leapman (1995), Heinemann (2004), and Sereny (2001, 25–52). For more information, see Hrabar, Tokarz, and Wilczur (1981) and Macardle (1949).

8. For a long time, the Civil War was a taboo subject in Greece. More recently, however, it has generated a vast scholarly literature. Valuable sources in English include Baerentzen, Iatrides, and Smith (1987), Carabott and Sfikas (2004), Clogg (1979, 133–65), Close (1993, 1995), Collard (1990), Iatrides (1981a, 1981b), Iatrides and Wrigley (1995), Kalyvas (2006), Loulis (1982), Mazower (1993, 2000), Panourgiá (2009), Voglis (2002), and Vlavianos (1992). For valuable sources in Greek, see Fleischer (2003), Iliou (2004), Koutsoukis and Sakkas (2000), Margaritis (2000, 2001), Nikolakopoulos, Rigos, and Psallidas (2002), Van Boeschoten (1997), Van Boeschoten et al. (2008), and Voutira et al. (2005).

9. See Hirschon (1998, 2003), Ladas (1932), and Pentzopoulos (1962).

10. See Carabott (1997, 2003), Karakasidou (1993), Kostopoulos (2000), and Varda (1993).

11. Greek government, *Official Journal* [in Greek] 2, no. 1 (Jan. 5, 1983). The word "*yenos*" has a wide range of meanings that includes birth, blood, descent (especially in the male line), race, species, and nation (Herzfeld 2005, 76–77). The phrase "*Ellines to yenos*" conveys an essentialized notion of national identity based on biological ties of birth and blood (Just 1989.)

12. On the role of the Macedonian Question in the Greek Civil War, see Carabott (2003), Kofos (1964, 1989, 1995), Minehan (2004), and Rossos (1997). On the Macedonian Question generally and the Macedonian minority of northern Greece more specifically, see Carabott (1997, 2003), Cowan (2000), Danforth (1995, 2001, 2003), Gounaris (1994), Human Rights Watch/Helsinki (1994), Karakasidou (1997), Kostopoulos (2000), Mackridge and Yannakakis (1997), Roudometoff (2000 and 2002), and Varda (1993).

13. Union of Professional Women of the Dodecanese, *Mother Greece and Her Children*, Athens (1949), p. 7, Modern Greek Archive/League for Democracy in Greece, King's College, London (hereafter MGA), PM 66/9.

14. See Hourmouzios (1972, 224), *New York Times*, Dec. 30, 1949, 8, and *Time Magazine*, Jan. 9, 1950.

CHAPTER TWO

1. Cable from "Andronikos" to "Spyros" (Petros Roussos), January 29, 1948, Arheia Sinhronis Koinonikis Istorias (hereafter ASKI), box 153, file 7/40/19.

2. Cable from the Yugoslav Communist Party to the Greek Communist Party, February 9, 1948 (Kondis and Sfetas 1999, 116).

3. News bulletins of the Democratic Army (Deltio tou dimokratikou stratou Elladas), March 3 and 4, 1948. Reprinted in *Documents of the Greek Progressive Movement* (Dokoumenda tou Ellinikou Proodeftikou Kinimatos) (1978).

4. Representative of the Greek Government to UNSCOB, letter, February 27, 1948, United Nations Office at Geneva (hereafter UNOG), file A/AC.16/149.

5. Announcement by the Provisional Democratic Government, March 7, 1948 (Baerentzen 1987, 130–31).

6. Cable from Markos Vafiadis, February 20, 1948, ASKI, box 153, file 7/40/31.

7. Cable from "Andronikos" to Ioannidis, March 15, 1948, ASKI, box 153, file 7/40/51.

8. Other Greek communist sources cited similar numbers when referring to children cared for in institutions. See EVOP (1950, 3), Gangoulias (2004, 64), and Martinova-Buckova (1998, 33).

9. ASKI box 153, file 7/40/74 and Ristović (2000, 24).

10. For other cases, see Ristović (2000, 31–34).

11. UNSCOB report on the second special report of Observation Group 1 (August 19–24, 1948), National Archives, London (hereafter NA), FO 371/72234/R11243.

12. UNSCOB report on the twentieth report of Observation Group 1 (October 1–15, and November 12, 1948, Konitsa area), NA FO 371/72235/R13136, Annex A.

13. See Nachmani (1990) for a detailed discussion of the role UNSCOB played in the Greek Civil War.

14. UNSCOB instructions, March 25, 1948, NA FO 371/7225/R3880.

15. Forty-fifth UNSCOB meeting, March 4, 1948, NA FO 371/72224/R3365.

16. Foreign Office to Washington, D.C., confidential telegram, May 30, 1948, NA FO 370/72230/R6260.

17. Diary of Sofia Couleva, entry dated March 4, 1949, Archiv na Makedonija (hereafter AM), Skopje, file 997.1.75/147–187.

18. In March and April 1949, Paskal Mitrovski (Pashalis Mitropoulos), the only Macedonian minister of the Provisional Democratic Government, sent two warning letters to the Politbureau of the Greek Communist Party demanding the immediate cessation of all efforts to recruit children in Eastern Europe (Kirijazovski and Martinova-Buckova 1983, 118–20 and 211–13).

19. In 1950, 35 percent of all refugees in Eastern Europe, except for Yugoslavia, were Macedonians (Kirijazovski 1989, 53–56), but this percentage increases to nearly 60 percent, if the 30,000 Macedonian refugees living in Yugoslavia (Kofos 1964, 168) are included. Data on the ethnicity of refugee *children* are less precise. Macedonian children made up 51 percent of all refugee children in Romania and 85 percent in Yugoslavia (AM, file 997.1.76/281 and 997.12/3–4). There were no Macedonian-speaking children in Eastern Germany or Bulgaria, and the data from other countries have not been preserved. Combining these statistics with those from other sources on individual countries, we estimate the number of Macedonian-speaking children in Eastern Europe as a whole at 50 percent (Gritzonas 1998, 187; Lagani 1996, 66; Van Boeschoten 2003b).

20. ASKI, box 29, file 2/1:9.

21. EVOP, memorandum, August 20, 1951, p. 4, MGA/PM 119, published in Budapest.

22. See Decree M of 1948 and Laws 2536/1953 and 3781/54 on the resettlement of border areas and the confiscation of properties, Decree LZ of 1947 on the deprivation of citizenship, and Decree 4234 of 1962 on security issues (Comité des refugiés politiques grecs (1963), p. 17, MGA/PM 70/2). See also Kirijazovski (1989, 137–43) and Panhellenic Union of Repatriated Political Refugees (1996, 111–13). According to Kirijazovski, under this legislation nearly half a million acres of land were confiscated, and more than 20,000 political refugees were deprived of their citizenship.

23. EVOP, memorandum, August 20, 1951.

24. Comité des refugiés politiques grecs (1963), p. 20, MGA/PM 70/2, a pamphlet on the refugee children published by the Committee of Greek Political Refugees in Eastern Europe.

CHAPTER THREE

1. This account of Queen Frederica's trip to Konitsa is based on Barber (1948), Papanicolaou (1994, 155), Queen Frederica of the Hellenes (1971, 107–11), Sulzberger (1948), and Ward (1992, 269).

2. Hourmouzios (1972, 197), and Union of Professional Women of the Dodecanese, *Mother Greece and Her Children*, Athens (1949), p. 13, MGA/PM 66/9.

3. Alexandra Mela, *To hroniko tis vasilikis pronoias* (n.d.; cited henceforth as Mela n.d.), Elliniko Logotehniko kai Istoriko Arheio (ELIA [Greek Literary and Historical Archive]), Athens. This unpublished typewritten manuscript, probably written about 1967 and available at the ELIA Archive in Athens, is an important source for the history of the paidopoleis. See also Brouskou (1989).

4. Summary Report on the Activities of H.M. the Queen's Fund Organization "Relief for the Northern Provinces of Greece," July 1947 to June 1949, p. 2, MGA/PM 75/38.

5. Mrs. O. Marcy, wife of the second secretary of the US Embassy in Athens, memo to the US State Department entitled "Refugee Children Cared for by the Queen's Fund," December 12, 1948, p. 2, NA FO 371/78361/1789. See also UNESCO (1949).

6. Hourmouzios (1972, 197), and Mela (n.d., 54).

7. Meeting of the Fund-raising Executive Committee, August 7 and 13, 1947, cited in Vervenioti (1999, 3).

8. Greek liaison officer Alexander Dalietos, communication to UNSCOB, April 22, 1948, NA FO 371/72229/R5118.

9. Ibid.

10. Summary Report, p. 3, MGA/PM 75/38.

11. *Mother Greece and Her Children*, p. 11 (emphasis added).

12. *Mother Greece and Her Children*, p. 17.

13. Memorandum, March 1948, NA FO371/78361/1789, p. 4.

14. Queen's Fund, Summary Report, MGA/PM 75/38, p. 4.

15. National Welfare Organization, "Sindomi anafora stin idrisi kai tis drastiriotites tou ethnikou organismou pronoias 1947–1977" (Brief Report on the Founding and the Activities of the National Welfare Organization, 1947–1977), typed manuscript, Athens, 1977, ELIA/Archive Kalliga/Vasiliki Pronoia, p. 17. See also Gritzonas (1998, 122), and Vasiliki Pronoia (1957, 52).

16. Memorandum, March 1948, FO371/78361/1789, p. 7.

17. *Mother Greece and Her Children*, p. 20.

18. Lady Norton, reports on the village adoption scheme and on the Royal Technical School of Leros, NA FO 371/87776/RG/1711/9, March 31, 1950.

19. *ELIA/Archive Kalliga/Vasiliki Pronoia/National Welfare Organization 1977*, 10–12, a report on the activities of the National Welfare Organization from 1947 to 1977.

20. On Greek nationalism during this period, see Gounaris (2002), Hasiotis (2009), and Karakasidou (2000).

21. Summary Report, MGA/PM 75/38, pp. 4–5.

22. These ideas are developed further in Brouskou (1989, 1993).

23. *Mother Greece and Her Children*, p. 29.

CHAPTER FOUR

1. Interview with Kostas Tsimoudis, May 10, 2001, Alexandroupolis, Greece. Translated from the Greek.

2. Interview with Evropi Marinova, June 19, 1999 and May 10, 2003, Budapest, Hungary. Translated from the Greek.

3. Interview with Stefanos Gikas [pseud.], April 1, 2001, Athens, Greece. Translated from the Greek.

4. Interview with Maria Bundovska Rosova, August 12, 2000, Toronto, Canada. In the original English.

CHAPTER FIVE

1. Interview with Efterpi Tsiou, June 11, 2001, Likorahi, Greece. Translated from the Greek.
2. Interview with Traian Dimitriou, August 13, 2000 and October 20, 2003, Toronto, Canada. In the original English.
3. Interview with Kostas Dimou, June 14, 2001, Ioannina, Greece. Translated from the Greek.

CHAPTER SIX

1. See, for example, Marrus (1985), Miserez (1988), and Stein (1981).
2. See Bammer (1992), Bhabha (1992, 1994), Blu (1996), S. Hall (1990, 1993), Kondo (1996), and Massey (1991, 1992).
3. See Brown (2003), Gounaris (1989), Hill (1989), Mandatzis (1996), and Petroff (1995).
4. On the relationship between living in a foreign land and death, see Danforth (1982, 90–95).
5. *Anagnostiko yia tin triti taxi* (Politikes kai Logotehnikes Ekdoseis, 1961), p. 23.
6. This account is reminiscent of scenes in the *Odyssey* where Odysseus establishes his identity by revealing a scar on his foot (19. 391, 21. 217, and 24. 329). Compare also the scene in modern Greek folk songs where a wife tells her husband, who has been away for many years, to prove who he is by describing a mole she has on her breast (Ioannou 1970, 80).
7. Each of these terms denotes a different level of intimacy, from the diminutive "mamáka," the most intimate, to "mitera," the most formal.
8. For additional material on the position of Macedonians from Greece in the Republic of Macedonia, see Brown (2003), Kolbe (1999), and Monova (2001, 2007).
9. Examples include Dimitri (2000), Donevski (1996), Kičevski (1998), and Pop-Janevski (1996). See also Simovski (1998), a massive three-volume encyclopedia and atlas documenting all "the inhabited places of Aegean Macedonia." Slyomovics (1998, 3) describes a similar encyclopedia of Palestinian villages occupied by Israelis as "a memorial book on a grand scale," whose goal is to "represent a destroyed, common national past for future generations."
10. Kallithea is a pseudonym.
11. *Mitria Patrida* (*Stepmother Fatherland*) is the title of a 1981 novel by Mihalis Ganas, a former refugee child (cited in Apostolidou 2010, 92).
12. Their situation was similar to that of Macedonian refugee children who had "returned" to the Republic of Macedonia discussed above.
13. As John Acton noted, "Exile is the nursery of nationality" (1967, 146, cited in Anderson 1994, 315).
14. See Danforth (1995, 227) for a similar contrast between Greece as a biological mother and Greece as an adoptive mother.

CHAPTER SEVEN

1. *Petrina Hronia* (Years of Stone) is the title of a well-known film (1985) by Pandelis Voulgaris. This metaphor is widely used to convey the harsh climate of repression that the Greek left experienced for three decades after the Civil War.
2. Novels by Boutos (2000) and Skroumbelos (2005) focus on rapes that allegedly took place in the paidopoleis. On a television program that aired in February 2006, former residents of the paidopoleis described their childhood experiences there.

Some of the participants later complained that the television program was biased and that their accounts had been taken out of context (Theoloyis 2006).

3. Some representative works in this debate include Antze and Lambek (1996), Ashplant, Dawson, and Roper (2000), LaCapra (2001), Langer (1991), Winter (1995, 2006), Winter and Sivan (1999), and Young (1993). These studies on war memories are rarely based on ethnographic fieldwork or on oral testimony. For important exceptions, see Cappelletto (2005) and Thomson (1994).

4. See Mannheim ([1928] 1952), Olick and Robbins (1998, 14), and Winter (1999, 40).

5. For examples of this localized approach, see Cappelletto (2005), Van Boeschoten (2005, 2007), and Winter (1999).

6. Michael Herzfeld (1987, 34) has observed that in Greek culture the right to resist the workings of fate is considered a quintessential quality of being human. This attitude is very different from the commonsense notion of "fatalism," in which people are powerless to change future events that have been divinely ordained.

7. About one fourth of the refugee children we interviewed had lost at least one parent during the Civil War.

8. See, for example, Kostas Tsimoudis' life story in part 2.

9. Stories of escapes from behind the Iron Curtain are prominent in post-communist public memory. The new museum at the site of Checkpoint Charlie, the famous crossing point between East and West Berlin, devotes much of its exhibit space to famous escapes to the West.

10. On the importance of having the right or wrong surname during the Metaxas regime, see Panourgiá (2009, 46).

11. See Herzfeld (1987, 34, 171, 195) and Panourgiá (2009, 220).

CHAPTER EIGHT

1. The French historian Pierre Nora (1989) first pointed to the pervasiveness of memory in contemporary societies. Important work on the "politics of memory" includes Aguilar (2001), Ashplant, Dawson, and Roper (2000), Gillis (1994), Hodgkin and Radstone (2003), Lebow et al. (2006), Rappaport (1998), Watson (1994), Winter (2006), and Wood (1999).

2. For a discussion of the concept of civil society, see Cohen and Arato (1995), Gellner (1994), J. Hall (1995), and Hann and Dunn (1996).

3. See Anderson (1992), Appadurai (2006), and Bauman (2007).

4. The Greek government, however, has continued to play a major role in all issues related to the return to Greece of refugee children who have a Macedonian national identity and to the Macedonian conflict more generally.

5. The official position of the Greek government at that time was, and still is, that there is no "Macedonian minority" in Greece and that the northern provinces of the country are inhabited by "Slavophone" or "bilingual" Greeks. (See Danforth 1995, 108–41.)

6. The verb *progoni* can be translated as both "to persecute" and "to expel." The underlying meaning is to "drive out." We thank Victor Friedman for this insight.

7. The speech was recorded in Macedonian by Van Boeschoten; the English translation is ours.

8. Although at the local level Greek right-wing paramilitary bands did single out members of ethnic minorities and tried to force them to leave their villages by burning

their houses or raping their women, this "ethnic cleansing" was not a practice supported by official government policy (Van Boeschoten 2003a, 44).

9.   Brown (2003, 211, 244) and Brunnbauer (2004).

10.  See http://www.panmacedonian.info.

11.  See "The Need and Creation of the Pan-Macedonian Association," a text signed by Nina Gatzouli, supreme secretary of the association (http://www.panmacedonian .info/about.htm). For more detailed information on the "name issue," see Brown (2003, 34–36), Cowan (2000, xiii–xvi), Cowan and Brown (2000, 1–14), Danforth (1995, 142–85; 2010, 591–94), and Sutton (1997).

12.  "The Need and Creation of the Pan-Macedonian Association." (See note 11.)

13.  See, for example, the account of Eirini Damopoulou presented in Bougas (2006).

14.  See the Greek documents prepared by EVOP, the institution responsible for the children's education in Eastern Europe (Archive of Macedonia, Skopje, docs. 997.1.76/281 and 997.12/3–4).

15.  For a more extensive analysis of this issue, see Arapoglou (2005), Danforth (2008), and Kalogeras (1993).

16.  On the concept of "textual communities" see Brown (2003, 51), Rappaport (1998), and Wertsch (2002, 13).

17.  San Diego Union, mentioned on the cover page of the paperback edition of *Eleni* (N. Gage 1983).

18.  Reagan's speech is available at http://reagan2020.us/speeches/Forward_For_Freedom .asp.

19.  Unlike most refugee children, however, Gage was not raised in an institution. Upon his arrival in the United States, he was immediately reunited with his father and lived with him and other members of his family in Worcester, Massachusetts.

20.  We have used pseudonyms for all the inhabitants of Lia we interviewed except for those whose real names appear in the work of Nicholas Gage (1983, 2004) and his daughter Eleni (2004).

21.  See Feld and Basso (1996), Gupta and Ferguson (1997), and Low and Zuniga (2003).

EPILOGUE

1.   On the Law on the Recovery of Historical Memory, see the BBC report published on July 18, 2006, available at http://news.bbc.co.uk/go/pr/fr/-/2/hi/europe/5192228 .stm. On the measure granting Spanish citizenship, see the report of December 27, 2008 available at http://news.bbc.co.uk/go/pr/fr/-/2/hi/europe/7735267.stm. (Both sites accessed on December 27, 2008.) Finally, on the experiences of "war children" in Franco's Spain, see Richards (2005).

# REFERENCES

## ARCHIVES
### Greece
Arheia Sinhronis Koinonikis Istorias (ASKI [Archives of Contemporary Social History]), Athens.

  Archive of the Greek Communist Party (KKE), 1942–1968. Boxes 130–131, 153, 367, 373–375, 377, 3127.

  Archive of the radio station "Free Greece," 1947–1968. Box 29.

Elliniko Logotehniko kai Istoriko Arheio (ELIA [Greek Literary and Historical Archive]), Athens.

  Kalliga Archive/Vasiliki Pronoia.

### Republic of Macedonia
Archiv na Makedonija (AM), Skopje, Collection 997 (Macedonian emigration to Eastern Europe). Box 1.

### United Kingdom
Modern Greek Archive/League for Democracy in Greece (MGA), King's College, London.

  CHRON 1 Evacuated Children 1948–55.

  PM Printed Materials: PM66 Case of the Greek Children, PM70. Repatriation of Greek Refugees, PM75 Civil War Pamphlets, PM110, 117–119, 127 EVOP.

The National Archives, London (NA), Public Record Office (Kew), Series 371 (General Correspondence (Political).

  FO 371/72218–72235, 87652, 87703–5 UNSCOB 1948–50.

  FO 371/78361 Evacuated Children 1948–49.

  FO 371/78370–5 Refugees from Bandit-controlled Areas 1948–49.

  FO 371/87776–8 Relief Work in Greece 1949–50.

### Switzerland
United Nations Office at Geneva (UNOG). Series A/AC-16 UNSCOB Archive, 1948–49.

### United States
Firestone Library, Rare Books Collection, Princeton.

  CO881 Nancy Crawshaw collection 1944–49.

  CO815 Norman Gilbertson collection 1945–53.

PUBLISHED PRIMARY SOURCES

Greek government. 1983. *Efimeris tis kiverniseos tis ellinikis dimokratias* (Official journal) 2, no. 1, Jan. 5.

International Committee of the Red Cross, Joint Reports on the Repatriation of Greek Children (1949–51).

UNSCOB reports (1948–49).

United Nations yearbook (1948–49).


SECONDARY SOURCES

Acton, John E. E. D. A. 1967. *Essays in the Liberal Interpretation of History; Selected Papers, by Lord Acton.* Chicago: University of Chicago Press.

Aguilar, Paloma. 2001. *Memory and Amnesia: The Role of the Spanish Civil War in the Transition to Democracy.* Oxford: Berghahn Books.

Amindas, Kosmas. n.d. *Ethniki andistasi, emfilios polemos. Anamniseis enos kapetaniou.* Thessaloniki: Bibis.

Anastasiadis, Yiannis. 1993. *Mnimes apo ti drasi tou aristerou kinimatos tou aiyiptioti elllinismou.* Athens.

Anderson, Benedict.1991. *Imagined Communities: Reflections on the Origins and Spread of Nationalism.* Rev. ed. London: Verso Press.

———. 1992. The New World Disorder. *New Left Review* 193:3–13.

———. 1994. Exodus. *Critical Inquiry* 20:314–27.

Andoniou, Yorgos. 2007. The Memory and History of the Greek Forties. Ph.D. diss., European University Institute.

Antze, Paul, and Michael Lambek, eds. 1996. *Tense Past: Cultural Essays in Trauma and Memory.* London: Routledge.

Apostolidou, Venetia. 2010. *Travma kai mnimi: I pezografia ton politikon prosfigon.* Athens: Polis.

Appadurai, Arjun. 1996. *Modernity at Large: Cultural Dimensions of Globalization.* Minneapolis: University of Minnesota Press.

———. 2006. *Fear of Small Numbers: An Essay on the Geography of Anger.* Durham, NC: Duke University Press.

Araidi, Na'im. 1985. *Back to the Village* [in Hebrew]. Tel Aviv: 'Am 'Oved.

Arapoglou, Eleftheria. 2005. Identity Configuration and Ideological Manipulation in Nicholas Gage's *A Place for Us. Melus* 30 (3):71–93.

Ariès, Philippe. 1962. *Centuries of Childhood: A Social History of Family Life.* New York: Knopf.

Ashplant, Timothy G., Graham Dawson, and Michael Roper. 2000. The Politics of Memory and Commemoration: Contexts, Structures and Dynamics. In *Commemorating War: The Politics of Memory,* edited by Ashplant, Dawson, and Roper, 9–85. London: Routledge.

Athanasiadis, Georgios. 1951. I morfosi ton paidion mas. *Neos Kosmos* 8:29–38.

Baerentzen, Lars. 1987. The "Paidomazoma" and the Queen's Camps. In *Studies in the History of the Greek Civil War, 1945–49,* edited by Lars Baerentzen, John O. Iatrides, and Ole L. Smith, 127–57. Copenhagen: Museum Tusculanum Press.

Baerentzen, Lars, John O. Iatrides, and Ole L. Smith, eds. 1987. *Studies in the History of the Greek Civil War, 1945–49.* Copenhagen: Museum Tusculanum Press.

Bailey, Anthony. 1980. *America, Lost and Found.* New York: Random House.

Bakhtin, Mikhail. 1981. *The Dialogic Imagination: Four Essays.* Austin: University of Texas Press.

———. 1986. *Speech Genres and Other Essays*. Austin: University of Texas Press.

Ballinger, Pamela. 2003. *History in Exile: Memory and Identity at the Borders of the Balkans*. Princeton, NJ: Princeton University Press.

Bammer, Angelika. 1992. Editorial. In "The Question of 'Home.'" Special issue, *New Formations* 17:vii–xi.

Barber, Mary. 1948. Greece. *Time Magazine*, January 19, 1948.

Barth, Fredrik. 1969. Introduction. In *Ethnic Groups and Boundaries*, edited by Barth, 9–38. Boston: Little Brown.

Basch, Linda, Nina Schiller, and Christina Szanton Blanc. 1994. *Nations Unbound: Transnational Projects, Postcolonial Predicaments, and Deterritorialized Nation-States*. New York: Gordon and Breach.

Bastide, Roger. 1970. Mémoire collective et sociologie du bricolage. *L'Année Sociologique* 21:65–108.

Bauman, Zygmunt. 2007. *Liquid Time: Living in an Age of Uncertainty*. Cambridge: Polity Press.

Baumel, Judith Tydor. 1990. *Unfulfilled Promise: Rescue and Settlement of Jewish Refugee Children in the United States, 1934–1945*. Juneau, AL: Denali Press.

Beaton, Roderick. 2009. Introduction. In *The Making of Modern Greece: Nationalism, Romanticism and the Uses of the Past (1797–1896)*, edited by Roderick Beaton and David Ricks, 1–11. London: Ashgate.

Bellah, Robert, R. Madsen, W. Sullivan, A. Swidler, and S. Tipton. 1985. *Habits of the Heart: Individualism and Commitment in American Life*. Berkeley: University of California Press.

Bhabha, Homi. 1992. The World and the Home. *Social Text* 31/32:141–53.

———. 1994. *Location of Culture*. London: Routledge.

Blu, Karen I. 1996. Where Do You Stay At? Homeplace and Community among the Lumbee. In *Senses of Place*, edited by Steven Feld and Keith Basso, 197–228. Santa Fe, NM: School of American Research Press.

Bondila, Maria. 2003. "*Polihronos na zeis, megale Stalin*": *I ekpaidefsi ton paidion ton Ellinon politikon prosfigon sta anatolika krati (1950–1964)*. Athens: Metaihmio.

Borneman, John. 1992. *Belonging in the Two Berlins: Kin, State, Nation*. Cambridge: Cambridge University Press.

Bougas, Ioannis. 2006. *I foni tis Eirinis. I martiria tis Eirinis Damopoulou apo to paidomazoma*. Thessaloniki: Erodios.

Boutos, Vasilis. 2000. *Ta dakria tis vasilissas*. Athens: Nefeli.

Boyden, Jo. 1997. Childhood and the Policy Makers: A Comparative Perspective on the Globalization of Childhood. In *Constructing and Reconstructing Childhood: Contemporary Issues in the Sociological Study of Childhood*, edited by Allison James and Alan Prout, 190–229. 2nd ed. London: Routledge Falmer.

Boyden, Jo, and Joanna de Berry. 2004. Introduction. In *Children and Youth on the Front Line: Ethnography, Armed Conflict and Displacement*, edited by Boyden and de Berry, 11–17. Oxford and New York: Berghahn Books.

Breckenridge, Carol, and Arjun Appadurai. 1989. Editors' Comment: On Moving Targets. *Public Culture* 2 (1):i.

Breckenridge, Carol A., Sheldong Pollock, Homi K. Bhabha, and Dipesh Chakrabarty, eds. 2002. *Cosmopolitanism*. Durham, NC: Duke University Press.

Brouskou, Aigli. 1989. Vos parents ne sont plus vos parents. *Nouvelle Revue d'Ethnopsychiatrie* 14:71–82.

———. 1993. Stratiyikes tis pronoias yia to paidi ton 20o aiona. In *Oikoyeneia-paidiki prostasia-koinoniki politiki,* edited by Eleni Agathonos-Georgopoulou, 68–72. Athens: Instituto Iyeias tou Paidiou.

Brown, Keith. 2002. *Macedonia's Child-Grandfathers: The Transnational Politics of Memory, Exile, and Return, 1948–1998.* Donald W. Treadgold Papers in Russian, East European, and Central Asian Studies, 38. Seattle: University of Washington Press.

———. 2003. *The Past in Question: Modern Macedonia and the Uncertainties of Nation.* Princeton, NJ: Princeton University Press.

Brunnbauer, Ulf. 2004. Serving the Nation: Historiography in the Republic of Macedonia (FYROM) after Socialism. *Historein* 4:161–82.

Cappelletto, Francesca, ed. 2005. *Memory and World War II: An Ethnographic Approach.* Oxford: Berg.

Carabott, Philip. 1997. The Politics of Integration and Assimilation *vis-à-vis* the Slavo-Macedonian Minority of Inter-war Greece: From Parliamentary Inertia to Metaxist Repression. In *Ourselves and Others: The Development of a Greek Macedonian Cultural Identity since 1912,* edited by Peter Mackridge and Eleni Yannakakis, 59–78. Oxford: Berg.

———. 2003. The Politics of Constructing the Ethnic "Other": The Greek State and Its Slav Speaking Citizens, ca. 1912—ca. 1949. *Jahrbücher für Geschichte und Kultur Südostevropas/ History and Culture of South Eastern Europe* 5:141–59.

Carabott, Philip, and Thanasis D. Sfikas, eds. 2004. *The Greek Civil War: Essays on a Conflict of Exceptionalism and Silences.* Center for Hellenic Studies, King's College, London, Publication 6. Aldershot: Ashgate.

Clay, Catrine, and Michael Leapman. 1995. *Master Race: The Lebensborn Experiment in Nazi Germany.* London: Hodder and Stoughton.

Clifford, James. 1988. *The Predicament of Culture.* Cambridge, MA: Harvard University Press.

———. 1997. *Routes: Travel and Translation in the Late Twentieth Century.* Cambridge, MA: Harvard University Press.

Clogg, Richard. 1979. *Short History of Modern Greece.* Cambridge: Cambridge University Press.

Close, David H., ed. 1993. *The Greek Civil War, 1943–1950: Studies of Polarization.* London: Routledge.

———. 1995. *The Origins of the Greek Civil War.* Longman: New York.

Cohen, Jean, and Andrew Arato. 1995. *Civil Society and Political Theory.* Cambridge, MA: MIT Press.

Collard, Anna. 1990. The Experience of Civil War in the Mountain Villages of Central Greece. In *Background to Contemporary Greece,* edited by Marion Sarafis and Martin Eve, 223–54. London: Merlin.

Comité des refugiés politiques grecs. 1963. *Nous voulons rentrer dans notre Patrie!* MGA/ PM 70/2.

Connelly, John. 2000. *Captive University: The Sovietization of East German, Czech, and Polish Higher Education, 1945–1956.* Chapel Hill: University of North Carolina Press.

Connerton, Paul. 1989. *How Societies Remember.* Cambridge: Cambridge University Press.

Conway, Martin. 2004. The Greek Civil War: Greek Exceptionalism, or Mirror of a European Civil War? In *The Greek Civil War: Essays on a Conflict of Exceptionalism and Silences,* edited by Philip Carabott and Thanasis Sfikas, 17–40. Aldershot: Ashgate.

Coufoudakis, Van. 1981. The United States, the United Nations and the Greek Question, 1946–1952. In *Greece in the 1940s: A Nation in Crisis,* edited by John O. Iatrides, 275–96. Hanover, NH: University Press of New England.

Cowan, Jane K., ed. 2000. *Macedonia: The Politics of Identity and Difference*. London: Pluto Press.

Cowan, Jane, and Keith Brown. 2000. Introduction: Macedonian Inflections. In *Macedonia: The Politics of Identity and Difference*, edited by Jane Cowan, 1–27. London: Pluto Press.

Cowan, Jane, Marie-Bénédicte Dembour, and Richard Wilson, eds. 2001. *Culture and Rights: Anthropological Perspectives*. Cambridge: Cambridge University Press.

Dalianis-Karambatzakis, Mando. 1994. *Children in Turmoil during the Greek Civil War, 1946–49: Today's Adults*. Stockholm: Karolinska Institutet.

Danforth, Loring M. 1982. *The Death Rituals of Rural Greece*. Princeton, NJ: Princeton University Press.

———. 1995. *The Macedonian Conflict: Ethnic Nationalism in a Transnational World*. Princeton, NJ: Princeton University Press.

———. 2001. "We Are Macedonians! We Are Not Greeks!" The Macedonian Minority of Northern Greece. In *Endangered Peoples of Europe: Struggles to Survive and Thrive*, edited by Jean S. Forward, 85–99. London: Greenwood.

———. 2003. "We Crossed a Lot of Borders": Refugee Children of the Greek Civil War. *Diaspora* 12 (2):169–209.

———. 2008. I sillogiki mnimi kai i kataskevi taftotiton sta erga tou Nicholas Gage. In *Mnimi kai lithi tou ellinikou emfiliou polemou*, edited by Riki Van Boeschoten et al., 257–68. Thessaloniki: Epikendro.

———. 2011. Ancient Macedonia, Alexander the Great and the Star or Sun of Vergina: National Symbols and the Conflict between Greece and the Republic of Macedonia. In *A Companion to Macedonia*, edited by Joseph Roisman and Ian Worthington, 572–98. Oxford: Wiley-Blackwell.

Dawson, Graham. 1999. Trauma, Memory, Politics: The Irish Troubles. In *Trauma and Life Stories: International Perspectives*, edited by Kim Lacy Rogers, Selma Leydesdorff, and Graham Dawson, 180–204. London and New York: Routledge.

Dimitri, Michael A. 2000. *Nevolijani: Portrait of a Macedonian Village*. Fort Wayne, IN: Alexandra.

Donevski, Giorgi. 1996. *Bapčor*. Skopje.

Douglas, Mary. 1966. *Purity and Danger*. London: Routledge.

Dubinsky, Karen. 2007. Babies without Borders: Rescue, Kidnap and the Symbolic Child. *Journal of Women's History* 19 (1):142–50.

Elefandis, Angelos. 2000. 1947: Andartopliktoi, mia mera. *Arheiotaxio* 2:94–96.

EVOP (Greek Committee for Child Support). 1950. *If you really love us, bring peace to Greece*. MGA/PM 66/8.

———. 1951. Memorandum. MGA/PM 119.

Farakos, Grigoris. 2005. I thesi kai o rolos ton politikon prosfigon sto kommounistiko kinima kai tis politikes exelixeis tis horas mas. In *"Ta opla para poda": Oi politikoi prosfiyes tou ellinikou emfiliou polemou stin anatoliki Evropi*, edited by Eftihia Voutira et al., 17–27. Thessaloniki: Panepistimio Makedonias.

Featherstone, Mike. 1990. Global Culture: An Introduction. In *Global Culture: Nationalism, Globalization and Modernity*, edited by Featherstone, 1–14. London: Sage.

Fejtö, François. (1956) 1996. *La tragédie hongroise*. Paris: L'Harmattan.

Feld, Steven, and Keith Basso, eds. 1996. *Senses of Place*. Santa Fe, NM: School of American Research Press.

Felman, Shoshana, and Dori Laub. 1992. *Testimony: Crises of Witnessing in Literature, Psychoanalysis, and History*. New York: Routledge.

Fernandez, James. 1986. *Persuasions and Performances: The Play of Tropes in Culture*. Bloomington: Indiana University Press.

Fleischer, Hagen, ed. 2003. *I Ellada '36–'49. Apo ti diktatoria ston emfilio, tomes kai sineheies*. Athens: Kastanioti.

Forty, Adrian, and Susanne Küchler, eds. 1999. *The Art of Forgetting*. Oxford: Berg.

Foucault, Michel. 1979. *Discipline and Punish: The Birth of the Prison*. New York: Vintage Books.

Fox, Anne L., and Eva Abraham-Podietz. 1999. *Ten Thousand Children: True Stories Told by Children Who Escaped the Holocaust on the Kindertransport*. West Orange, NJ: Behrman House.

Gage, Eleni N. 2004. *North of Ithaca*. New York: St Martin's Griffin.

Gage, Nicholas. 1983. *Eleni*. New York: Ballantine Books.

———. 1984. My Mother's Murder: The Killer and Others Respond. *New York Times*, July 8,1984, 22.

———. 2004. *A Place for Us: A Greek Immigrant Boy's Odyssey to a New Country and an Unknown Father*. Worcester, MA: Chandler House Press.

Gallant, Thomas. 1997. Greek Exceptionalism and Contemporary Historiography: New Pitfalls and Old Debates. *Journal of Modern Greek Studies* 15 (2):209–16.

Gangoulias, Giorgos. 2004. *Paidomazoma: Ta paidia sti thiella tou emfiliou polemou kai meta*. Athens: Iolkos.

Geertz, Clifford. 1973. *The Interpretation of Cultures*. New York: Basic Books.

Gellner, Ernest. 1994. *Conditions of Liberty: Civil Society and Its Rivals*. London: Hamisch Hamilton.

Georgakas, Dan. 1987. The Greeks in America. *Journal of the Hellenic Diaspora* 14 (1–2): 5–54.

Georgitsa-Papadimitrakopoulou, Elli. 1997. *Paidopolis "Ayia Trias."* Thessaloniki.

Gillis, John, ed. 1994. *Commemorations: The Politics of National Identity*. Princeton, NJ: Princeton University Press.

Gionis, Dimitris. 2006. Paidomazoma, ena thema "taboo." *Eleftherotipia*, 15 July.

Goffman, Erving. 1962. *Asylums: Essays on the Social Situation of Mental Patients and Other Inmates*. Chicago: Aldine.

Gounaris, Vasilis (Basil). 1989. Emigration from Macedonia in the Early Twentieth Century. *Journal of Modern Greek Studies* 7 (1):133–51.

———. 1994. Slavofonoi tis Makedonias: I poreia tis ensomatosis sto elliniko kratos, 1870–40. *Makedonia* 29:209–37.

———. 2002. *Egnosmenon koinonikon fronimaton: Koinonikes kai alles opseis tou andikommounismou sti Makedonia tou emfiliou polemou*. Thessaloniki: Paratiritis.

Gousidis, Dimitris. 1975. *Opou zeis den patrizeis . . . (I nea prosfiyia, mia akoma elliniki tragodia)*. Athens: Exandas.

Green, Anna. 2004. Individual Remembering and Collective Memory: Theoretical Presuppositions and Contemporary Debates. *Oral History* 32 (2):35–44.

Gritzonas, Kostas. 1998. *Ta paidia tou emfiliou polemou*. Athens: Filistor.

Gupta, Akhil, and James Ferguson, eds. 1997. *Culture, Power, Place: Explorations in Critical Anthropology*. Durham, NC: Duke University Press.

Halbwachs, Maurice. 1992. *On Collective Memory*. Chicago: University of Chicago Press.

———. (1925) 1994. *Les cadres sociaux de la mémoire*. Paris: Albin Michel.

———. 1997. *La mémoire collective*. Paris: Albin Michel.

Hall, John A., ed. 1995. *Civil Society: Theory, History, Comparison*. Cambridge: Polity Press.

Hall, Stuart. 1990. Cultural Identity and Diaspora. In *Identity: Community, Culture, and Difference*, edited by Jonathan Rutherford, 222–37. London: Lawrence and Wishart.

———. 1993. Culture, Community and Nation. *Cultural Studies* 7 (3):349–63.

Hann, Chris, and Elizabeth Dunn, eds. 1996. *Civil Society: Challenging Western Models*. London: Routledge.

Harrell-Bond, Barbara E., and Eftihia Voutira. 1992. Anthropology and the Study of Refugees. *Anthropology Today* 8 (4):6–10.

Harris, Mark J., and Deborah Oppenheimer. 2000. *Into the Arms of Strangers*. New York: Bloomsbury Publishing.

Hasager, Ulla. 1997. Localizing the American Dream: Constructing Hawaiian Homelands. In *Siting Culture: The Shifting Anthropological Object*, edited by Karen Fog Olwig and Kirsten Hastrup, 165–92. London: Routledge.

Hasiotis, Loukianos. 2009. Ethnikofrosini kai andikommounismos sto neaniko tipo: I periptosi tou periodikou Paidopolis, 1950–51. *Istor* 15:277–305.

Hawkes, Joseph M., and N. Ray Hiner, eds. 1991. *Children in Historical and Comparative Perspective*. New York: Greenwood Press.

Heinemann, Isabel. 2004. "Until the Last Drop of Good Blood": The Kidnapping of "Racially Valuable" Children and Nazi Racial Policy in Occupied Eastern Europe. In *Genocide and Settler Society: Frontier Violence and Stolen Indigenous Children in Australian History*, edited by Dirk Moses, 244–66. Oxford: Berghahn Books.

Herzfeld, Michael. 1987. *Anthropology through the Looking Glass*. Cambridge: Cambridge University Press.

———. 1991. *A Place in History: Social and Monumental Time in a Cretan Town*. Princeton, NJ: Princeton University Press.

———. 2005. *Cultural Intimacy: Social Poetics in the Nation-State*. 2nd ed. London: Routledge.

Hill, Peter. 1989. *The Macedonians in Australia*. Carlisle, Western Australia: Hesperian Press.

Hinton, Alexander Laban, ed. 2002. *Annihilating Difference: The Anthropology of Genocide*. Berkeley: University of California Press.

Hirsch, Marianne. 1996. Past Lives: Postmemories in Exile. *Poetics Today* 17.

Hirschon, Renée. 1998. *Heirs of the Greek Catastrophe: The Social Life of Asia Minor Refugees in Piraeus*. Oxford: Berghahn Books.

———, ed. 2003. *Crossing the Aegean: An Appraisal of the 1923 Compulsory Population Exchange between Greece and Turkey*. Oxford: Berghahn Books.

Hobsbawm, Eric. 1994. *Age of Extremes: The Short Twentieth Century, 1914–1991*. Harmondsworth: Penguin Books.

Hobsbawm, Eric, and Terence Ranger, eds. 1983. *The Invention of Tradition*. Cambridge: Cambridge University Press.

Hodgkin, Katharine, and Susannah Radstone, eds. 2003. *Contested Pasts: The Politics of Memory*. New York: Routledge.

Hoensch, Jorg. 1996. *A History of Modern Hungary, 1867–1994*. 2nd ed. Harlow: Longman.

Honwana, Alcinda. 2006. *Child Soldiers in Africa*. Philadelphia: University of Pennsylvania Press.

Hourmouzios, Stelios. 1972. *No Ordinary Crown: A Biography of King Paul of the Hellenes*. London: Weidenfeld and Nicolson.

Hrabar, Roman, Zofia Tokarz, and Jacek E. Wilczur. 1981. *The Fate of the Polish Children during the Last War*. Warsaw: Interpress.

Hradecny, Pavel. 2005. Aniparktoi figades: Aihmalotoi Ellines stratiotes stin Tsechoslovakia (apo to 1949 mehri ta mesa tis dekaetias tou 50). In *"Ta opla para poda": Oi politikoi prosfiyes tou ellinikou emfiliou polemou stin anatoliki Evropi*, edited by Eftihia Voutira et al., 189–204. Thessaloniki: Panepistimio Makedonias.

Human Rights Watch/Helsinki. 1994. *Denying Ethnic Identity: The Macedonians of Greece.* New York.

Hwang, Philip C., Michael E. Lamb, and Irving E. Sigel, eds. 1996. *Images of Childhood.* Mahwah, NJ: Lawrence Erlbaum Associates.

Iatrides, John O., ed. 1981a. *Greece in the 1940s: A Nation in Crisis.* Hanover, NH: University Press of New England.

———, ed. 1981b. *Greece in the 1940s: A Bibliographic Companion.* Hanover, NH: University Press of New England.

Iatrides, John O., and Linda Wrigley, eds. 1995. *Greece at the Crossroads: The Civil War and Its Legacy.* University Park: Pennsylvania State University Press.

ICRC (International Committee of the Red Cross). 1949. *Repatriation of Greek Children.* First Joint Report by the International Committee of the Red Cross and the League of Red Cross Societies. A 85. Geneva.

———. 1950. *Repatriation of Greek Children.* Second Joint Report by the International Committee of the Red Cross and the League of Red Cross Societies. A 85. Geneva.

———. 1951. *Repatriation of Greek Children.* Third Joint Report by the International Committee of the Red Cross and the League of Red Cross Societies. A 85. Geneva.

Iliou, Filippas. 2004. *O ellinikos emfilios polemos: I embloki tou KKE.* Athens: Themelio.

Ioannou, Giorgos. 1970. *To dimotiko tragoudi: Paraloyes.* Athens: Ermis.

James, Allison, and Alan Prout. 1997. Introduction. In *Constructing and Reconstructing Childhood: Contemporary Issues in the Sociological Study of Childhood*, edited by James and Prout, 1–6. 2nd ed. London: Routledge Falmer.

Jenks, Chris. 1996. *Childhood.* London: Routledge.

Jones, Howard. 1985. The Diplomacy of Restraint: The United States' Efforts to Repatriate Greek Children Evacuated during the Civil War of 1946–49. *Journal of Modern Greek Studies* 3 (1):65–86.

———. 1989. *A New Kind of War: America's Global Strategy and the Truman Doctrine in Greece.* Oxford: Oxford University Press.

Just, Roger. 1989. Triumph of the Ethnos. In *History and Ethnicity*, edited by Elizabeth Tonkin, Malcolm Chapman, and Maryon McDonald, 71–78. Association of Social Anthropologists Monographs, 27. London: Routledge and Kegan Paul.

Kalogeras, Yorgos. 1993. Eleni: Hellenizing the Subject, Westernizing the Discourse. *Melus* 18 (2):77–89.

Kalyvas, Stathis. 2006. *The Logic of Violence in Civil War.* Cambridge: Cambridge University Press.

Karakasidou, Anastasia. 1993. Politicizing Culture: Negating Macedonian Identity in Northern Greece. *Journal of Modern Greek Studies* 11 (1):1–28.

———. 1997. *Fields of Wheat, Hills of Blood: Passages to Nationhood in Greek Macedonia, 1870–1990.* Chicago: University of Chicago Press.

———. 2000. Protocol and Pageantry: Celebrating the Nation in Northern Greece. In *After the War Was Over*, edited by Mark Mazower, 221–46. Princeton, NJ: Princeton University Press.

Karavasilis, Niki. 2006. *The Abducted Greek Children of the Communists: Paidomazoma.* Pittsburg: Rose Dog Books.

Kavvathas, Vasilis. 1985. *I alli Eleni.* Athens: Alkion.

Kenney, Padraic. 1997. *Rebuilding Poland: Workers and Communists, 1945–1950.* Ithaca: Cornell University Press.

Keskini, Apostolia. 2003. Caught in the Crossfire: The Experiences of Civil War Children from Western Thrace, 1947–1950. MA diss., King's College, London.

Kičevski, Nikola. 1998. *Trsje I Trsjani.* Skopje.

Kirijazovski, Risto. 1989. *Makedonskata politička emigracija od egejskiot del na Makedonija vo istočnoevropskite zemji po vtorata svetska vojna.* Skopje: Kultura.

Kirijazovski, Risto, and Fana Martinova-Buckova, eds. 1981. *Egejska Makedonija vo NOB.* Vol. 5 (1948). Skopje: Archiv na Makedonija.

———. 1983. *Egejska Makedonija vo NOB.* Vol. 6 (1949). Skopje: Archiv na Makedonija.

Kitromilides, Paschalis. 1989. Imagined Communities and the Origins of the National Question in the Balkans. *European History Quarterly* 19:149–94.

Kofos, Evangelos. 1964. *Nationalism and Communism in Macedonia.* Thessaloniki: Institute for Balkan Studies.

———. 1989. I valkaniki diastasi tou makedonikou zitimatos sta hronia tis katohis. In *I Ellada 1936–1944. Diktatoria, katohi, andistasi,* edited by Hagen Fleischer and Nikolaos Svoronos, 418–72. Athens: Morfotiko Idrima ATE.

———. 1995. The Impact of the Macedonian Question on Civil Conflict in Greece, 1943–1949. In *Greece at the Crossroads: The Civil War and Its Legacy,* edited by John O. Iatrides and Linda Wrigley, 274–318. University Park: Pennsylvania State University Press.

———. 2003. Unexpected Initiatives: Towards the Resettlement of a Slav-Macedonian Minority in Macedonia. *To Vima,* 25 June 2003. http://www.macedonian-heritage.gr/ Opinion/comm_20030710Kofos.html.

Kokkalis, Petros, Elli Alexiou, and Georgios Athanasiadis. 1954. Ta paidia mas stis laïkes dimokraties. *Neos Kosmos* 9:51–60.

Kolbe, Kica. 1999. *Egejci.* Skopje: Kultura.

Kondis, Vasilis, and Spiridon Sfetas, eds. 1999. *Emfilios polemos: Engrafa apo ta yiougoslavika kai voulgarika arheia.* Thessaloniki: Paratiritis.

Kondo, Dorinne. 1996. The Narrative Production of "Home," Community, and Political Identity in Asian American Theater. In *Displacement, Diaspora and Geographies of Identity,* edited by Smardar Lavie and Ted Swedenberg, 97–117. Durham, NC: Duke University Press.

Kostopoulos, Tasos. 2000. *I apagorevmeni glossa: Kratiki katastoli ton slavikon dialekton stin elliniki Makedonia.* Athens: Mavri Lista.

Koutsoukis, Kleomenis, and Ioannis Sakkas, eds. 2000. *Ptihes tou emfiliou polemou 1946–49.* Athens: Filistor.

Kürti, László. 2002. *Youth and the State in Hungary: Capitalism, Communism and Class.* London: Pluto Press.

Labajos-Pérez, Emilia, and Fernando Vitoria-Garcia. 1997. *Los niños españoles refugiados en Bélgica (1936–1939).* Namur: Asociación de los Niños de la Guerra.

LaCapra, Dominick. 2001. *Writing History, Writing Trauma.* Baltimore: John Hopkins University Press.

Ladas, Stephen. 1932. *The Exchange of Minorities: Bulgaria, Greece and Turkey.* New York: MacMillan.

Lagani, Eirini. 1996. *To "paidomazoma" kai oi ellinoyiougoslavikes sheseis (1949–1953): Mia kritiki prosengisi.* Athens: I. Sideris.

Laiou, Angeliki E. 1987. Population Movements in the Greek Countryside during the Greek Civil War. In *Studies in the History of the Greek Civil War, 1945–1949,* edited by

Lars Baerentzen, John O. Iatrides, and Ole L. Smith, 55–104. Copenhagen: Museum Tusculanum Press.

Langer, Lawrence. 1991. *Holocaust Testimonies: The Ruins of Memory*. London: Yale University Press.

Laub, Dori. 1992. Bearing Witness, or the Vicissitudes of Listening. In *Testimony: Crises of Witnessing in Literature, Psychoanalysis, and History*, edited by Shoshana Felman and Dori Laub, 57–74. New York: Routledge.

Lavie, Smardar, and Ted Swedenburg, eds. 1996. *Displacement, Diaspora, and Geographies of Identity*. Durham, NC: Duke University Press.

Lazaridou, Margarita. 2004. *Polemos kai aima*. Athens: Dioyenis.

League for Democracy in Greece. 1951. *The Case of the Greek Children*. Cardiff, Wales: Cymric Federation Press.

Lebow, Richard N., Wulf Kansteiner, and Claudio Fogu, eds. 2006. *The Politics of Memory in Postwar Europe*. Durham NC: Duke University Press.

Legarreta, Dorothy. 1984. *The Guernica Generation: Basque Refugee Children of the Spanish Civil War*. Reno: University of Nevada Press.

Loizos, Peter. 1981. *The Heart Grown Bitter: A Chronicle of Cypriot War Refugees*. Cambridge: Cambridge University Press.

Loulis, John C. 1982. *The Greek Communist Party: 1940–44*. London: Croom Helm.

Low, Setha M., and Denise Lawrence-Zúñiga, eds. 2003. *The Anthropology of Space and Place: Locating Culture*. Malden, MA: Blackwell.

Macardle, Dorothy. 1949. *Children of Europe: A Study of the Children of Liberated Countries, Their War-time Experiences, Their Reactions, and Their Needs, with a Note on Germany*. Boston: Beacon Press.

Mackridge, Peter, and Eleni Yannakakis, eds. 1997. *Ourselves and Others: The Development of a Greek Macedonian Cultural Identity since 1912*. Oxford: Berg.

Malkki, Liisa. 1992. National Geographic: The Rooting of Peoples and the Territorialization of National Identity among Scholars and Refugees. *Cultural Anthropology* 7 (1):24–44.

———. 1995a. Refugees and Exile. *Annual Review of Anthropology* 24:495–523.

———. 1995b. *Purity and Exile: Violence, Memory, and National Cosmology among Hutu Refugees in Tanzania*. Chicago: University of Chicago Press.

———. 1996. Speechless Emissaries: Refugees, Humanitarianism and Dehistoricization. *Cultural Anthropology* 11 (3):377–404.

Mandatzis, Hristo M. 1996. Emigration from the District of Kastoria, 1922–30. *Balkan Studies* 37 (1):107–31.

Mann, Gillian. 2004. Separated Children: Care and Support in Context. In *Children and Youth on the Front Line: Ethnography, Armed Conflict and Displacement*, edited by Jo Boyden and Joanna de Berry, 3–22. Oxford and New York: Berghahn Books.

Mannheim, Karl. (1928) 1952. The Problem of Generations. In *Essays in the Sociology of Culture*, 276–322. London: Routledge & Kegan Paul.

Manoukas, Georgios. 1961. *Paidomazoma: To megalo englima kata tis filis*. Athens: Sillogos Epanapatristhendon ek tou Parapetasmatos.

Marcus, George E. 1998. Ethnography in/of the World System: The Emergence of Multi-Sited Ethnography. In *Ethnography through Thick and Thin*, 79–104. Princeton, NJ: Princeton University Press.

Marcus, George E., and Michael M. J. Fischer. 1986. *Anthropology as Cultural Critique: An Experimental Moment in the Human Sciences*. Chicago: University of Chicago Press.

Margaritis, Giorgos. 2000. *Istoria tou ellinikou emfiliou 1946–49*. Vol. 1. Athens: Vivlio-rama.

———. 2001. *Istoria tou ellinikou emfiliou 1946–49*. Vol. 2. Athens: Vivliorama.

Marrus, Michael R. 1985. *The Unwanted: European Refugees in the Twentieth Century*. Oxford: Oxford University Press.

Martinova-Buckova, Fana. 1998. *I nie sme deca na majkata zemja*. Skopje: Združenie na decata-begalci od egejskiot del na Makedonija.

Massey, Doreen. 1991. Global Sense of Place. *Marxism Today* 35:24–9.

———. 1992. A Place Called Home. *New Frontiers* 17:3–15.

Matthaiou, Anna, and Popi Polemi. 2003a. O ideotipos tou neou kommounisti. *Arheiotaxio* 5:154–62.

———. 2003b. *I ekdotiki peripeteia ton Ellinon kommouniston: Apo to vouno stin iperoria, 1947–1968*. Athens: Vivliorama-ASKI.

Matthews, Kenneth. 1972. *Memories of a Mountain War: Greece, 1944–1949*. London: Longman.

Mazower, Mark. 1993. *Inside Hitler's Greece*. New Haven: Yale University Press.

———, ed. 2000. *After the War Was Over: Reconstructing the Family, Nation, and State in Greece, 1943–60*. Princeton, NJ: Princeton University Press.

Mela, Alexandra. n.d. *To hroniko tis vasilikis pronoias*. Elliniko Logotehniko kai Istoriko Arheio (ELIA [Greek Literary and Historical Archive]), Athens.

Minehan, Philip B. 2004. What Was the Problem? A Comparative and Contextual View of the National Problems in the Spanish, Yugoslav and Greek Civil Wars of 1936–49. In *The Greek Civil War*, edited by Philip Carabott and Thanasis Sfikas, 41–56. Center for Hellenic Studies, King's College, London, Publication 6. Aldershot: Ashgate.

Miserez, Diana, ed. 1988. *Refugees—the Trauma of Exile*. Dordrecht, The Netherlands: Martinus Nijhoff.

Mitsopoulos, Thanasis. 1979. *Meiname Ellines*. Athens: Odysseas.

Mitsotakis, Constantine. 2004. Preface. In Nicholas Gage, *Eleni*. 2nd Greek ed., 21–25. Translated by A. Kotzias. Athens: Kerkyra.

Monova, Miladina. 2001. De l'historicité à l'ethnicité: Les Égéens ou ces autres Macédoniens. In "Homelands in Question," edited by Keith Brown. Special issue, *Balkanologie* 5 (1–2):179–97.

———. 2007. What's in a Name? Labelling and Classifying Collective Identities in the Republic of Macedonia. In *Cahiers Parisiens / Parisian Notebooks*, edited by Robert Morrissey. University of Chicago Center in Paris 3:650–69.

Nachmani, Anikam. 1990. *International Intervention in the Greek Civil War: The United Nations Special Committee on the Balkans, 1947–1952*. New York: Praeger.

Nakovski, Petre. 1987. *Makedonski deca vo Polska*. Skopje: Mlad Borec.

Naumoff, Olga. 2003. *My Name Is Sotir: A Memoir of a Child Evacuee*. Dearborn, MI: Splendid Associates.

News Bulletins of the Democratic Army. 1948. Reprinted in Documents of the Greek Progressive Movement [in Greek]. No. 20. Athens.

*New York Times*. 1949. Greece's Lament Enfolds Children. Dec. 30, 8.

Nikolakopoulos, Ilias, Alkis Rigos, and Grigoris Psallidas, eds. 2002. *O emfilios polemos apo ti Varkiza sto Grammo, Fevrouarios 1945—Avgoustos 1949*. Athens: Themelio.

Nobel, Peter. 1988. Refugees and other Migrants Viewed with a Legal Eye—or How to Fight Confusion. In *Displaced Persons*, edited by Kirsten H. Peterson and Anna Rutherford, 18–31. Sydney: Dangaroo.

Nora, Pierre. 1989. Between Memory and History. *Representations* 26:7–24.

———. 1997. *Les Lieux de Mémoire*. Paris: Gallimard.

Olick, Jeffrey, and Joyce Robbins. 1998. Social Memory Studies: From Collective Memory to the Historical Sociology of Mnemonic Practices. *Annual Review of Sociology* 24:105–40.

Olwig, Karen Fog, and Kirsten Hastrup, eds. 1997. *Siting Culture: The Shifting Anthropological Object*. London: Routledge.

Ortner, Sherry. 2005. Subjectivity and Cultural Critique. *Anthropological Theory* 5 (1): 31–52.

Paerregaard, Karsten. 1997. Imagining a Place in the Andes: In the Borderland of Lived, Invented, and Analyzed Culture. In *Siting Culture: The Shifting Anthropological Object*, edited by Karen Olwig and Kirsten Hastrup, 39–58. London: Routledge.

Paliouras, Dimitris. 2003. *Sto deftero platani*. Thessaloniki: Erodios.

Panhellenic Union of Repatriated Political Refugees. 1996. *To hroniko tis politikis prosfiyias sti Roumania*. Athens.

Pan-Macedonian Association USA, Inc. 2005a. Provocative Distortion of History and Effort of "Beautification" of Paidomazoma in Princeton. http://www.panmacedonian .info/PAIDOMAZOMA.htm.

———. 2005b. I akadimaïki eleftheria stirizetai stin istoriki alitheia kai yegonota. www .panmacedonian.info/kazamias_answer.htm.

Panourgiá, Neni. 2009. *Dangerous Citizens: The Greek Left and the Terror of the State*. New York: Fordham University Press.

Panter-Brick, Catherine. 2000. Nobody's Children. In *Abandoned Children*, edited by Catherine Panter-Brick and Malcolm T. Smith, 1–26. Cambridge: Cambridge University Press .

Papadopoulos, Filippas. 2001. *San ta poulia. Omoloyies Ellinon Oungarias*. Budapest: Greek Community Wipest.

Papadopoulos, Lisimahos. 1998. *Paidia tis thiellas—deti boure*. Prague.

———. 1999. *Nostimon imar—den návratů*. Prague.

Papanicolaou, Lilika S. 1994. *Frederica, Queen of the Hellenes: Mission of a Modern Queen*. Malta: Publishers Enterprises Group, LTD.

Passerini, Luisa. 1987. *Fascism in Popular Memory: The Cultural Experience of the Turin Working Class*. Cambridge: Cambridge University Press.

———. 1988. *Storia e soggettività: Le fonti orali, la memoria*. Florence: La Nuova Italia.

———. 2003. Memories between Silence and Oblivion. In *Contested Pasts: The Politics of Memory*, edited by Katharine Hodgkin and Susanna Radstone, 238–54. London: Routledge.

Pentzopoulos, Dimitri. 1962. *The Balkan Exchange of Minorities and Its Impact upon Greece*. Paris: Mouton.

Petersen, Roger. 2005. Memory and Cultural Schema: Linking Memory to Political Action. In *Memory and World War II: An Ethnographic Approach*, edited by Francesca Cappelletto, 131–54. Oxford: Berg.

Petroff, Lillian. 1995. *Sojourners and Settlers: The Macedonian Community of Toronto to 1940*. Toronto: University of Toronto Press.

Polemi, Popi. 1997. I elliniki neolaia stis anatolikes hores, 1948–1968: Katagrafi tekmirion apo ta Arheia Sinhronis Koinonikis Istorias. *Ta Istorika* 14 (27):445–50.

Pop-Janevski, Lazo. 1996. *Kosturskoto Selo D'mbeni*. Skopje: Aurora.

Portelli, Alessandro. 1991. Uchronic Dreams: Working-Class Memory and Possible

Worlds. In Portelli, *The Death of Luigi Trastulli, and Other Stories: Form and Meaning in Oral History*, 99–116. Albany: State University of New York.

Queen Frederica of the Hellenes. 1971. *A Measure of Understanding*. London: St. Martin's Press.

Rappaport, Joanne. 1998. *The Politics of Memory: Native Historical Interpretation in the Colombian Andes*. Durham, NC: Duke University Press.

Raptis, Mihalis. 1996. Ena axiologo ekpaideftiko ergo. In *To hroniko tis politikis prosfiyias sti Roumania*, 181–211. Athens: Panhellenic Union of Repatriated Political Refugees.

———. 1999. *Tiheroi mesa stin atihia*. Athens.

Relph, E. C. 1976. *Place and Placelessness*. London: Pion.

Renan, Ernest. (1882) 1990. What Is a Nation? In *Nation and Narration*, edited by Homi Bhabha, 8–23. London and New York: Routledge.

Ressler, Everett M., Neil Boothby, and Daniel Steinboch. 1988. *Unaccompanied Children: Care and Protection in Wars, Natural Disasters and Refugee Movements*. New York: Oxford University Press.

Richards, Michael. 2005. Ideology and the Psychology of War Children in Franco's Spain, 1936–1945. In *Children of World War II: The Hidden Enemy Legacy*, edited by Kjersti Ericsson and Eva Simonsen, 115–37. Oxford: Berg.

Richmond, Anthony. 1994. *Global Apartheid: Refugees, Racism, and the New World Order*. Oxford: Oxford University Press.

Ristović, Milan. 2000. *A Long Journey Home: Greek Refugee Children in Yugoslavia, 1948–1960*. Thessaloniki: Institute for Balkan Studies.

Rosenthal, Gabriele. 1995. *Erlebte und Erzählte Lebensgeschichte*. Frankfurt: Campus Verlag.

Rossos, Andrew. 1997. Incompatible Allies: Greek Communism and Macedonian Nationalism in the Civil War in Greece, 1943–1949. *Journal of Modern History* 69 (1):42–76.

Roudometoff, Victor, ed. 2000. *The Macedonian Question: Culture, Historiography, Politics*. New York: Columbia University Press.

———. 2002. *Collective Memory, National Identity, and Ethnic Conflict: Greece, Bulgaria and the Macedonian Question*. London: Praeger.

Royal Greek Embassy, Information Service. 1950. *Iron Curtain Holds Greek Children Captive: A Survey of the Case of the Kidnapped Greek Children*. Washington, DC.

Rushdie, Salman. 1991. *Imaginary Homelands*. New York: Viking.

———. 2002. Step Across This Line. In *Step Across This Line: Collected Nonfiction, 1992–2002*, 347–381. New York: Random House.

Said, Edward. 2000. Reflections on Exile. In *Reflections on Exile and Other Essays*, 173–86. Cambridge, MA: Harvard University Press.

Samuel, Raphael. 1994. *Theatres of Memory*. Vol. 1, *Past and Present in Contemporary Culture*. London: Verso.

Seremetakis, Nadia, ed. 1996. *The Senses Still: Perception and Memory as Material Culture in Modernity*. Chicago: University of Chicago Press.

Sereny, Gitta. 2001. *The Healing Wound: Experiences and Reflections on Germany, 1938–2001*. New York: W. W. Norton.

Servos, Dimitris. 2001. *To paidomazoma kai poioi fovoundai tin alitheia*. Athens: Sinhroni Epohi.

Simovski, Todor. 1998. *Naselenite mesta vo egejska Makedonija*. Skopje: Institut za Nacionalna Istorija.

Skroumbelos, Thanasis. 2005. *Bella Ciao*. Athens: Ellinika Grammata.

Skultans, Vieda. 1998. *The Testimony of Lives: Narrative and Memory in Post-Soviet Latvia*. London: Routledge.

Slyomovics, Susan. 1994. The Memory of Place. *Diaspora* 3 (2):157–183.

———. 1998. *The Object of Memory: Arab and Jew Narrate the Palestinian Village*. Philadelphia: University of Pennsylvania Press.

Stein, Barry N. 1981. The Refugee Experience: Defining the Parameters of a Field of Study. *International Migration Review* 15:320–30.

Stephens, Sharon, ed. 1995. *Children and the Politics of Culture*. Princeton, NJ: Princeton University Press.

Stojanovik-Lafazanovska, Lidija, and Ermis Lafazanovski. 2002. *The Exodus of the Macedonians from Greece: Women's Narratives about WWII and Their Exodus*. Skopje: Eurobalkan Institute.

Sulzberger, C. L. 1948. Abductions by Greek Rebels Spur Vast Child Aid Project. *New York Times*, June 21, 1948, 1.

Sutton, David. 1997. Local Names, Foreign Claims, Family Inheritance and National Heritage on a Greek Island. *American Ethnologist* 24 (2):415–37.

Theoloyis, Thomas. 2006. *Freideriki kai paidopoleis horis fovo kai pathos*. Athens: Pelagos.

Thomson, Alistair. 1994. *Anzac Memories: Living with the Legend*. Melbourne: Oxford University Press.

*Time Magazine*. 1950. Innocents' Day. January 9, 1950.

Todorova, Maria. 1997. *Imagining the Balkans*. Oxford: Oxford University Press.

Troebst, Stefan. 2004. Evacuation to a Cold Country: Child Refugees from the Greek Civil War in the German Democratic Republic, 1949–1989. *Nationalities Papers* 32 (3):675–91.

Tzoukas, Vangelis. 2006. "As mi vrexei pote": Ta Apomnimonevmata ton melon tou Ierou Lohou tou EDES. Presented at the Conference on Memories of Civil Wars, Kastoria, July 6–9.

UNESCO. 1949. *A Child Named Marika . . . The Fate of 340,000 Greek Refugee Children*. Paris: Georges Lang.

UNHCR (United Nations High Commissioner for Refugees). 1994. *Refugee Children: Guidelines on Protection and Care*. Geneva.

———. 2006. *The State of the World's Refugees 2006: Human Displacement in the New Millennium*. Oxford: Oxford University Press.

———. 2008. *2007 Global Trends: Refugees, Asylum-seekers, Returnees, Internally Displaced and Stateless Persons*. Geneva.

United Nations. 1948a. *Report of the United Nations Special Committee on the Balkans*. General Assembly, Official Records: Third Session, Supplement No. 8 (A/574). Lake Success, NY.

———. 1948b. *Supplementary Report of the United Nations Special Committee on the Balkans*. Covering the period from 17 June to 10 September 1948, General Assembly, Official Records: Third Session, Supplement No. 8A (A/644). Paris.

———. 1949. *Report of the United Nations Special Committee on the Balkans*. General Assembly, Official Records: Fourth Session, Supplement No. 8 (A/935). Lake Success, NY.

———. 1950. *Yearbook of the United Nations, 1948–49*. Lake Success, NY.

Urry, John. 1990. *The Tourist Gaze: Leisure and Travel in Contemporary Societies*. London: Sage Publications.

Van Boeschoten, Riki. 1997. *Anapoda hronia: Silloyiki mnimi kai istoria sto Ziaka Grevenon (1900–1950)*. Athens: Plethron.

———. 2000. The Impossible Return: Coping with Separation and the Reconstruction of

Memory in the Wake of the Greek Civil War. In *After the War Was Over: Reconstructing the Family, Nation, and State in Greece, 1943–1960*, edited by Mark Mazower, 122–41. Princeton, NJ: Princeton University Press.

———. 2003a. The Trauma of War Rape: A Comparative View on the Bosnian Conflict and the Greek Civil War. *History and Anthropology* 14 (1):41–54.

———. 2003b. Unity and Brotherhood? Macedonian Political Refugees in Eastern Europe, Jahrbücher für Geschichte und Kultur Südosteuropas. In "Minorities in Greece—historical issues and new perspectives." Special issue, *History and Culture of South Eastern Europe* 5:189–202.

———. 2005. "Little Moscow" and the Greek Civil War: Memories of Violence, Local Identities and Cultural Practices in a Greek Mountain Community. In *Memory and World War II: An Ethnographic Approach*, edited by Francesca Cappelletto, 39–64. Oxford: Berg.

———. 2007. Broken Bonds and Divided Memories: Wartime Massacres Reconsidered in a Comparative Perspective. *Oral History* 35 (1):39–48.

Van Boeschoten, Riki, Eftihia Voutira, Tasoula Vervenioti, Vasilis Dalkavoukis, and Konstandina Bada, eds. 2008. *Mnimi kai lithi tou ellinikou emfiliou polemou*. Thessaloniki: Epikendro.

Varda, Christina. 1993. Opseis tis politikis afomoiosis sti ditiki Makedonia sto mesopolemo. *Ta Istorika* 18 (19):151–70.

Vasiliki Pronoia. 1957. *Apoloyismos dekaetias 1947–57*. Athens.

Verdery, Katherine. 1996. *What Was Socialism and What Comes Next?* Princeton, NJ: Princeton University Press.

Vermeulen, Hans. 1984. Greek Cultural Dominance among the Orthodox Population of Macedonia during the Last Period of Ottoman Rule. In *Cultural Dominance in the Mediterranean Area*, edited by Anton Blok and Henk Driessen, 225–55. Publicatie-serie Vakgroep Culturele Antropologie, 16. Nijmegen: Vakgroep Culturele Antropologie.

Vervenioti, Tasoula. 1999. Saved or Kidnapped? The Children of the Greek Civil War. Paper presented at the international conference, "Domestic and International Aspects of the Greek Civil War." King's College, London, April 18–20.

———. 2001. Saved or Kidnapped? The Children of the Greek Civil War. Unpublished manuscript.

———. 2002. "Charity and Nationalism: The Greek Civil War and the Entrance of Right-Wing Women into Politics." In *Right-Wing Women: From Conservatives to Extremists Around the World*, edited by Paola Bacchetta and Margaret Power, 115–26. London: Routledge.

———. 2005. Peri "paidomazomatos" kai "paidofilagmatos": O logos i ta paidia sti dini tis emfilias diamahis. In *"Ta opla para poda": Oi politikoi prosfiyes tou ellinikou emfiliou polemou stin anatoliki Europi*, edited by Eftihia Voutira et al., 101–23. Thessaloniki: Panepistimio Makedonias.

Vigil, Alicia A., Maria E. N. Marin, and Roger Gonzalez Martell. 1999. *Los niños de la Guerra de España en la Unión Soviética: De la evacuación al retorno (1937–1999)*. Madrid: Fundación Francisco Largo Caballero.

Vlavianos, Haris. 1992. *Greece, 1941–49: From Resistance to Civil War: The Strategy of the Greek Communist Party*. New York: St. Martin's Press.

Voglis, Polymeris. 2002. *Becoming a Subject: Political Prisoners in the Greek Civil War*. Oxford: Berghahn Books.

Volkan, Vamik, and Norman Itzkowitz. 2000. Modern Greek and Turkish Identities and the Psychodynamics of Greek-Turkish Relations. In *Cultures under Siege: Collective Vio-*

*lence and Trauma*, edited by Antonius Robben and Marcelo Suárez-Orozco, 227–47. Cambridge: Cambridge University Press.

Vournas, Tasos. 1981. *Istoria tis sinhronis Elladas: O emfilios*. Athens: Tolidis.

Voutira, Eftihia, and Aigli Brouskou. 2000. "Borrowed Children" in the Greek Civil War. In *Abandoned Children*, edited by Catherine Panter-Brick and Malcolm T. Smith, 92–110. Cambridge: Cambridge University Press.

Voutira, Eftihia, Vasilis Dalkavoukis, Nikos Marandzidis, and Maria Bondila, eds. 2005. *"Ta opla para poda": Oi politikoi prosfiyes tou ellinikou emfiliou polemou stin anatoliki Evropi*. Thessaloniki: Panepistimio Makedonias.

Ward, Michael. 1992. *Greek Assignments: SOE 1943–1948 UNSCOB*. Athens: Lycabettus Press.

Watson, Rubie, ed. 1994. *Memory, History, and Opposition under State Socialism*. Santa Fe, NM: School of American Research Press.

Wertsch, James. 2002. *Voices of Collective Remembering*. Cambridge: Cambridge University Press.

White, Hayden. 1981. The Value of Narrativity in the Representation of Reality. In *On Narrative*, edited by W. J. T. Mitchell, 1–23. Chicago: University of Chicago Press.

Whiteman, Dorit. 1993. *The Uprooted: A Hitler Legacy*. New York: Insight Books.

Winter, Jay. 1995. *Sites of Memory, Sites of Mourning*. Cambridge: Cambridge University Press.

———. 1999. Forms of Kinship and Remembrance in the Aftermath of the Great War. In *War and Remembrance in the Twentieth Century*, edited by Jay Winter and Emmanuel Sivan, 40–60. Cambridge: Cambridge University Press.

———. 2006. *Remembering War: The Great War between Memory and History in the Twentieth Century*. New Haven: Yale University Press.

Winter, Jay, and Emmanuel Sivan, eds. 1999. *War and Remembrance in the Twentieth Century*. Cambridge: Cambridge University Press.

Wittner, Lawrence. 1982. *American Intervention in Greece, 1943–1949*. New York: Columbia University Press.

Wood, Nancy. 1999. *Vectors of Memory: Legacies of Trauma in Postwar Europe*. New York: Berg.

Yavis, Constantine. (1944) 1987. Propaganda in the Greek-American Community. *Journal of the Hellenic Diaspora* 14 (1–2):105–29.

Young, James. 1993. *The Texture of Memory: Holocaust Memorials and Meaning*. New Haven: Yale University Press.

Zelizer, Viviana A. 1985. *Pricing the Priceless Child: The Changing Social Value of Children*. New York: Basic Books.

Zolberg, Aristide R., Astri Suhrke, and Sergio Aguayo. 1989. *Escape from Violence: Conflict and the Refugee Crisis in the Developing World*. Oxford: Oxford University Press.